Between
Capitalism
and
Socialism

Books by Robert L. Heilbroner

The Worldly Philosophers

The Future as History

The Great Ascent

The Making of Economic Society

The Economic Problem

The Limits of American Capitalism

Between Capitalism and Socialism:
Essays in Political Economics

Essays in Political Economics

Between Capitalism and Socialism

by Robert L. Heilbroner

Vintage Books

A Division of Random House   New York

Library of Congress Catalog Card Number: 79–117700

Manufactured in the United States of America
by The Colonial Press, Inc., Clinton, Massachusetts

ACKNOWLEDGMENTS

"Rhetoric and Reality in the Struggle between Business
and the State" was originally delivered at a workshop
at the University of California. It appeared in *Social
Research*, Autumn, 1968, and has been revised for
this book.
"The Eye of the Needle" was delivered as the Vawter
Lecture on Business and Society at Northwestern
University and appeared in *Moral Man and Economic
Enterprise*, Northwestern University, Evanston,
Illinois, 1968.
"Innocence Abroad" appeared in *Commentary*,
February, 1963.
"The Anti-American Revolution" appeared as
"Making a Rational Foreign Policy Now" in *Harper's
Magazine*, September, 1968.
"Reflections on the Future of Socialism"
appeared in *Commentary*, November, 1969.
"Marxism and the Economic Establishment" appeared
in slightly different form as "Putting Marx to Work"
in *The New York Review of Books*, December 5, 1968.
"Marxism Restated and Reviewed" appeared as "Marxism:
For and Against" in *The New York Review of Books*,
June 5, 1969.
"Technological Determinism" appeared as "Do Machines
Make History?" in *Technology and Culture*, July, 1967.
"Is Economic Theory Possible?" appeared in *Social
Research*, Summer, 1966.
"On the Limits of Economic Prediction" appeared in
Diogenes, April, 1970.

"Transcendental Capitalism" appeared as "Capitalism Contained" in *The New York Review of Books*, Vol. I, No. 2, 1963.

"The Industrial State" appeared as "Capitalism Without Tears" in *The New York Review of Books*, June 29, 1967.

"A Marxist America" appeared in *The New York Review of Books*, May 26, 1966.

"The Power Structure" appeared as "Who's Running This Show?" in *The New York Review of Books*, January 4, 1968.

"Futurology" appeared in *The New York Review of Books*, September 26, 1968.

"Ecological Armageddon" appeared in *The New York Review of Books*, April 23, 1970.

for Hans Staudinger

Preface

*T*hese are articles, essays, and reviews written over a period of nearly a decade for a variety of occasions, publications, and audiences. As in all such collections, some things are said more than once, and some parts are considerably different in texture and accessibility from others. This is the curse of all collections, for which I can only apologize.

On the other hand, these defects have their advantages, if not their virtues. The format of a collection enables me to cover a range of topics that might be awkward to encompass within the aesthetic confines of a unified text. More important, the absence of the need to develop a single line of thought permits me to envelop my central subject, viewing it from many angles and vantage points—historical in the first section of the book, technical or methodological in the second, and critical—in the sense of an examination of other persons' work—in the last.

What is the central problem that these essays attack? As my main title indicates, it is the question of *where we are in history*. Readers of my previous books will recognize this as the main focus of all my inquiries into history and economics. The present volume brings together further efforts to shed light on this problem, some verging on journalism, some rather technical, some of a generalized nature, others more specifically concerned with the insights and deficiencies of economics: conventional, Marxian, and political.

A word about the last. In the opinion of the great majority of my professional colleagues, economics is not properly political. By this they mean, first, that it should stay clear of questions that require for their answers a statement of political or moral values; and second, that it should confine itself to those problems of allocation and efficiency for which its established techniques are so well adapted. As a number of essays in this book make clear, I am not so convinced that these techniques are as pertinent as my colleagues believe, but that reservation aside, economics has never interested me primarily as a "kit of tools" for the examination or repair of the existing social mechanism. Perhaps because my first serious work plunged me into the worlds of Adam Smith, David Ricardo, John Stuart Mill, and Karl Marx, I have always found the greatest attraction of economics to lie elsewhere, in the astonishing capabilities of the discipline to elucidate the problem of large-scale historical and social change.

This broad conception of economics is not in much favor today. The idea of using the discipline to describe or predict —or, to use a softer word, foresee—the main trends of social evolution is no longer seriously entertained by the great majority of economists. Nor are their reasons far to seek. The dependable regularities of social and economic behavior on which the great economists from Smith to Marx built their remarkable models of social change now appear as attributes of a bygone age. No less critical, the all-important linkages between economic change and political attitude and action also appear to have lost their erstwhile simplicity, so that the stereotypes of class behavior, so essential to the magnificent dynamics of the classical economists, appear as well to be relics of the past. As a result of these and still other changes in the economic view of things, the very search for a "political" economics—that is, for a theory of social evolution in which a core of economic dynamics would be systematically related to social and political change (which in turn would feed back on the economic process) —has been virtually abandoned.

I regard this abandonment as a great loss for economic thought. By divorcing itself from the need to struggle with the elements of the political and social world, however recalcitrant they may be, conventional economics has ensured its technical virtuosity and its internal consistency, but at the cost of its social relevance. Every freshman who studies economics learns that each concept with which he deals is in reality inextricably enmeshed in political, sociological, and psychological considerations, so that the very discipline of economics itself only comes into being in the first place through the most heroic process of abstraction. Yet by the time he leaves graduate school, the impossible has been accomplished, and the young Ph.D. has come to regard the abstractions of economics as representing so much of "reality" that he now ignores the political and social context from which they were originally derived. The result is a proliferation of economic "models" of society that have neither social nor political antecedents or consequences, and in which "paths" of development are explored that generate neither the friction (nor the heat) of social reality. Such models are useful for some purposes, but they are useless for one great purpose, namely, in helping us locate our position and trajectory in the process of historic change in which we find ourselves.

I would like to go on to say that the contents of this book, which I have boldly subtitled Essays in Political Economics, would now remedy this grave shortcoming. In point of fact, however, my ambition is necessarily much more modest than that. For the hard fact is that there is no easy way of restoring the missing social and political dimensions to economics. The simple behavioral tenets of the older political economy, including those of traditional Marxism, are clearly unusable, for reasons that some of these essays explore. Nor have we been able to supplement the imposing—if treacherous—theoretical edifice of economics with an equally imposing set of "laws" for political science or sociology.

Most basic of all, we are hampered in our search for a genuine political economics by the powerful influence of the ruling conception of what is required of economics as a social "science." Together with nearly all empirical studies, economics has subscribed to the ruling intellectual "paradigm" of our times—a paradigm represented by the theoretical models of physical science. It need hardly be said that this scientific paradigm has proved to be an enormously powerful engine of investigation into the physical world. Yet it must be clear that it has severe limitations *as a model for social inquiry*. For in its elevation of "value-free" inquiry and mathematical equations as the prime constituents of a proper scientific representation of physical reality, the paradigm unwittingly imposes these same considerations on the representation of social reality. As a result, it rules out of court aspects of society that we know to be determinative of much of the course of historic change. The fact that there is no place within the scientific paradigm for the expression of will or belief by the particles of nature, or for intrasystemic "forces" for which no quantitative measurement can be found, excludes from the concerns of economics those elements of social valuation and social interaction that are central and intrinsic to the process of social change itself.

What is needed, then, is a new paradigm that will permit a major enlargement of economics—not one that discards the relationships that economics can often usefully reveal, but one that absorbs them into a much larger and more complex system of social cause and effect. Let me be clear, however, that no such new paradigm yet exists. Hence the "political economics" of my subtitle is very far from announcing a solution to the problems that diminish the scope of contemporary economics. These essays, with their insistent emphasis on the connectedness of economic and noneconomic processes are no more than an effort to mark out some of the boundaries within which I believe the new paradigm must be sought. At most, the essays constitute a set of problems of the kinds to which I think a genuine political economics should address itself, but the answers I give to these problems no doubt suffer from the fact that we do not yet know how to manage the complexities that must be admitted to an enlarged economic vision.

I must add only one last word. All of these essays, at one stage or another of their composition, have been looked at by the person on whom I have come to depend as the last and best court of judgment for nearly everything I write. I refer, of course, to Adolph Lowe, to whom I have paid my tribute before, and to whom I am happy once again to make a smiling bow.

Robert L. Heilbroner

New York City
March, 1970

Contents

Preface   *xi*

From Capitalism to Socialism

1 *Rhetoric and Reality in the Struggle
   between Business and the State*   *3*

2 *The Eye of the Needle*   *33*

3 *Innocence Abroad*   *51*

4 *The Anti-American Revolution*   *57*

5 *Reflections on the Future of Socialism*   *79*

Political Economics

6   *Marxism and the Economic Establishment*   *117*

7   *Marxism Restated and Reviewed*   *127*

8   *Technological Determinism*   *147*

9   *Is Economic Theory Possible?*   *165*

10   *On the Limits of Economic Prediction*   *193*

Alternative Futures

11   *Transcendental Capitalism*   *211*

12   *The Industrial State*   *225*

13   *A Marxist America*   *237*

14   *The Power Structure*   *247*

15   *Futurology*   *259*

16   *Ecological Armageddon*   *269*

Index   *287*

From
Capitalism
to
Socialism

*Rhetoric and Reality
in the Struggle between
Business and the State*

Anyone who examines the political economies of the Western world during the past century and a half is bound to be struck by a broad pattern of change, almost a Toynbean advance-and-retreat, observable in all of them. This is the extraordinary expansion of the realm of business within society for the first hundred or so years of the period, followed during the last fifty-odd years by an equally striking growth of the realm of government. Even at a cursory glance, this pattern is manifest in the changing statistical contours of public and private activities. But the change has permeated the fine structure of society as well. If we can imagine a series of historical x-rays showing us, from generation to generation, the operative influences on daily life, or the relative esteem accorded to men in various pursuits, or simply the content of the national table talk, there is little doubt as to what the sequence of photographs would reveal. During the nineteenth century, a salient feature of nearly every aspect of life was the growing presence of business; in the twentieth century, it is the increasing prominence of the state.

I doubt that there is much disagreement that this phenomenon constitutes a central historical fact of our times. What is curious is how ambiguously and unclearly it is still understood. One would think that by now this central pattern would have been fashioned into an historical narrative whose main themes were perceived and accepted alike by everyone. Instead, we find that the very plot of the drama is still open to the most contradictory explanations. In fact its two leading critics present diametrically opposed versions of its meaning. According to one, the Marxian, the rise of the state must be understood essentially as a defensive reaction of capitalism against its internal disorders, a reaction that utilizes the state—the "executive committee" of its ruling class—to shore up the system against collapse. According to the other, the libertarian, far from being a committee for managing the common affairs of the bourgeoisie, the state is its chief enemy, and the long swing toward state power accordingly portends not the defense but the decay and destruction of capitalism.

This striking clash of views is in one sense a wry commentary on the relation between history and historians, or perhaps a case study for the sociologists of knowledge. But there is more here than an opposition of rhetorics, important as they are. At least in my view, the existence of these two contradictory explanations suggests that neither has succeeded in fully elucidating the problem of the business-state relationship because neither has fully grasped the central reason for the change in that relationship. Taking courage from the example of David, what I wish to attempt in this essay is to suggest what that reason may be.

I

Let us begin by looking briefly at the conflicting interpretations of the problem that emerge from the two rhetorics themselves. It is to be expected, of course, that history would reveal itself very differently, according to whether it was being studied from the vantage point of libertarian thought,[1] essentially as the social expression of ideas, or from the Marxian angle, as the manifestation of class interests, but it is nonetheless enlightening to note how the business-state struggle appears to each side.

The divergence of interpretations begins not with the attempt to explain the rise of the state in the twentieth century but with the preceding rise of business enterprise in the late eighteenth and nineteenth. In the Marxian view, there is little here that needs explication, once one accepts the

---

1. There is something of a problem in defining the core of libertarian thought, since it lacks the authoritative counterpart of the Marx-Engels canon. The nearest one can come to an unimpeachable representation is Herbert Spencer or William Graham Sumner, but few modern libertarians lean any longer on these spokesmen of classic thought. I have mainly relied on three writers whose views, while not wholly alike, seem to me to represent a fair sample of the modern school: Walter Lippmann, *The Good Society* (Boston, 1937), Friedrich Hayek, *The Road to Serfdom* (Chicago, 1944), and Frank H. Knight, essay on "Free Society" in *On the History and Method of Economics* (Chicago, 1963).

premise of the underlying propulsion of the forces of economic history. As a kind of preview of the expected fate of capitalism in the twentieth century, the eighteenth and nineteenth centuries are seen as a time when the relations of production and exchange were uneasily contained within a legal and political integument incompatible with their full expression, and the revolutions of those centuries were, accordingly, the sign that these integuments had been finally burst asunder. What followed thereafter was simply the dazzling trajectory of the hitherto inhibited market forces now operating in the benign environment of a "capitalist" society. In a famous sentence in the *Communist Manifesto,* Marx and Engels have aptly described the period as one in which "the bourgeoisie . . . created more massive and more colossal productive forces than . . . all preceding generations."

The libertarian explanation of this same phenomenon of capitalist growth comes as a sharp contrast. In its interpretation of history the propulsive force making for change is not an economic drive that seeks an appropriate political and social superstructure, but a profound reorientation of political thought—in the words of Frank H. Knight, "the greatest revolution of all time or since the dawn of conscious life." [2] It is this political change that eventually creates a social order in which a new kind of unfettered economic relationship becomes possible. Thus, whereas in Marxian analysis economic forces constitute the independent variable of history and political forces the dependent variable, in libertarian thought it is the other way around. Hayek, for example, describes the emergence of the business world in these terms:

2. Knight, *op. cit.,* p. 289.

During the whole of the modern period of European history the general direction of social development was one of freeing the individual from the ties which had bound him to the customary or prescribed ways in the pursuit of his ordinary activities. The conscious realization that the spontaneous and uncontrolled efforts of individuals were capable of producing a complex order of economic activities could come only *after* this development had made some progress. The subsequent elaboration of a consistent argument in favor of economic freedom was the outgrowth of a free growth of economic activity which had been the undesigned and unforeseen by-product of political freedom.[3]

Starting from such different angles of incidence, it is not surprising that the two rhetorics see the next decisive stage of the drama in opposite perspectives. For the libertarian, the rise of the state represents a reversion—an "astounding counterrevolution," in the words of Frank Knight—from the pursuit of freedom that had given meaning and direction to the nineteenth century; for the Marxians, it represents simply the next stage in the economic unfolding of history.

In detail, each side has a more complex explanation of the trend of events. The libertarians are not content merely to ascribe the rise of the state to a falling away of belief in freedom. Rather, they trace this decline of belief to two still more fundamental developments. One of these, ironically, is generated by the rise of freedom itself—a desire for improvement that races out ahead of capabilities, a rise in impatience unmatched by a necessary rise in public understanding.

The eyes of the people [writes Hayek] became fixed on new demands, the rapid satisfaction of which seemed to be barred by the adherence to the old principles. . . . And, as

3. Hayek, *op. cit.,* p. 15 (emphasis added).

the hope of the new generation came to be centered on something completely new, interest in and understanding of the functioning of the existing society rapidly declined. . . .[4]

Frank Knight makes the same point even more explicitly:

> . . . [I]n essential ways the liberal movement went wrong, partly because of a failure to think out its problems, but essentially because it generated expectations and implied promises incapable of fulfillment.[5]

An impatience with the liberal order was not, however, the whole reason for the decline of the liberal philosophy. At the very time of the trial of liberal society, there also began, Hayek tells us, a significant transfer of intellectual leadership from England to Germany, whence radiated the counterliberal thought of Hegel and Marx, List and Schmoller, Sombart and Mannheim.[6] In a word, freedom was faced with the active competition of another idea whose historic magnetism had begun to rival it—the idea of collectivism. As Walter Lippmann writes:

> It may be said, I believe, that between say, 1848 and 1870, the intellectual climate of the western society began to change. At some time in that period the intellectual ascendance of the collectivist movement began. . . .
> More than seventy-five years passed before the collectivist movement was dominant in actual affairs, but in the middle period of the nineteenth century it established itself in men's thought . . . [F]reedom ceased to be the polestar of the human mind. After 1870 or thereabouts men thought instinctively once more in terms of organization, authority, and collective power.[7]

4. Hayek, *op. cit.*, pp. 19–20.
5. Knight, *op. cit.*, p. 290.
6. Hayek, *op. cit.*, p. 21.
7. Lippmann, *op. cit.*, pp. 46–47.

As might be expected, the Marxian explanation of the rise of the state eschews considerations such as these, and hews to the direct line of economic history, with its main theme of an unfolding process of production confined within a more or less appropriate legal and political framework. The Marxians thus see the twentieth-century rise of the state as a functional change rendered necessary by the "inherent contradictions" of the market process itself. For looking more closely into the origin of various state interventions, the Marxians discover that both the authors and the beneficiaries of state power were, in large part, the business community itself. The point has since been made by numerous non-Marxian historians, for example, E. H. Carr:

> The Federation of British Industries and the National Union of Farmers were more effective forces than the trade unions in determining the course of British economic policy in the great depression. . . . It was thus the capitalists—the industrialists, farmers and financiers—who, unwilling to see the capitalist theory of the elimination of the unfit applied to themselves, begged the state to save them by laying the foundations of an ordered economy.[8]

II

Therewith, in brief, the salient argument of the contradictory rhetorics. Each provides a consistent rationale for the pendulum swing of business and state, and each lays bare, I think, important aspects of the problem. Yet it is equally clear that neither gives us a wholly satisfactory explanation of the underlying phenomenon of change itself, for reasons which we must now review.

8. E. H. Carr, *The New Society* (Boston, 1947, paperback ed.), p. 28.

The strengths and weaknesses of the libertarian position are perhaps easier to deal with than those of the Marxian. To begin with its strengths, there is undoubtedly something to be reckoned with in the liberal contention of a changed point of view—a "spiritual collectivization," in Wilhelm Roepke's phrase[9]—discernible toward the end of the nineteenth century, and increasingly dominant in twentieth-century thought. The problems that are left unsolved are to account for this change in the prevailing direction of ideas and to account for the eagerness with which the new "collectivist" notions were welcomed. In libertarian writing, the change is treated as a kind of inexplicable shift, attributable at best to the rise of a malign "Germanic" influence, and the popular reception accorded it, a result of the unfulfilled aspirations generated by the idea of freedom. At best this seems a partial explanation that overlooks two deeper-lying reasons for the new trend of thought. One of these, which I shall hold in suspense for the moment, would connect the rise of collectivist thought—i.e., the new ideas of *social control*—with other related currents of intellectual activity in Europe and America during the last years of the nineteenth century. The second reason would seek to connect the disillusion of the public with the actual performance of the economy under the reign of laissez faire.

Certainly its failure to draw this second connection exposes libertarian thought to the most serious criticism. For as many nonlibertarians have pointed out, the irony of freedom, at least in its economic expression, is not that it leads to aspirations that outdistance achievements, but that it proposes an economic system that can only function with a

9. *The Social Crisis of Our Time* (Chicago, 1950), p. 13.

network of controls. As one historian of economic development has recently written:

> Free competition, if it is not to degenerate rapidly into imperfect forms of marketing, needs—more than any other form of marketing—to be subject to all-embracing regulations and strict control. The laissez-faire regime does not produce perfect markets, but provides an opportunity for the stronger to liquidate the weaker or reduce them to a subordinate position.[10]

Alone (to my knowledge) among the libertarian thinkers, Frank Knight acknowledges this point:

> As the system has been more fully worked out in the light of criticism and experience, in the generations since Smith's *Wealth of Nations* was published in 1776, more and more implicit assumptions have been brought to light, conditions more or less contrary to fact, that must be fulfilled if the working of the system is to be such as can be ethically approved. Many of these conditions could be established only by social action going far beyond the laissez-faire ideal of policing against force and fraud.[11]

Thus the system poses a paradox. Unregulated, it will lead to results (in particular, as Knight goes on to point out, concentration of industry and instability of output) that are not only "ethically" intolerable, but that require government intervention to assure its continued functional operation. Regulated, the system is—at least, in the eyes of its libertarian theorists—a contradiction in terms.

This intellectual weakness of libertarianism is compounded by its failure to trace the part played by business-

10. Celso Furtado, *Development and Underdevelopment* (Berkeley, 1964), p. 98.
11. Knight, *op. cit.*, p. 292.

men themselves in the erection of the state apparatus that presumably curtailed their freedom. The relationship between business and the state, as we shall have a chance to see in the next section, is a very complex one, but certainly no careful historian can ascribe the rise of the state in economic life as constituting a wholly antibusiness sequence of events. Indeed, according to one recent historian, "The dominant fact of American political life at the beginning of this century was that big business *led* the struggle for the federal regulation of the economy." [12] This may overstate the case, but I think it would be generally admitted that important sections of the business world were always favorably inclined to the use of government power to eliminate the competitive dangers, and to a lesser extent the cyclical risks, of the laissez-faire world. In fact, on one occasion Judge Gary, the very conservative head of United States Steel Corporation, told an astonished Congressional committee:

> I believe we must come to enforce publicity and government control . . . even as to prices, and, so far as I am concerned I would be very glad if we knew exactly where we stand, if we would be freed from danger, trouble, and criticism by the public, and if we had some place where we could go, to a responsible government authority, and say to them, "Here are our facts and figures . . . now you tell us what we have the right to do and what prices we have the right to charge." [13]

In a word, libertarianism fails to explain the rise of the state by failing to ground its prime mover—the change in

12. Gabriel Kolko, *The Triumph of American Conservatism*, New York, 1963, pp. 57–58 (emphasis added). Cf. also his *Railroads and Regulation*, Princeton, 1965.

13. Kolko, *op. cit.*, p. 124.

the climate of ideas—either in the intellectual currents of the era, or in the direct malfunction of the system of economic freedom itself. In its noble, but single-minded and uncritical, fixation on the idea of "freedom" it loses sight not only of the self-destructive properties of an economic system based too casually on uncoordinated economic behavior, but of the independent development of other ideas rooted as securely in the development of their times as libertarianism was in its own.[14]

The Marxian rhetoric is much more difficult to criticize succinctly. Its strengths are obvious, particularly to a generation raised in the tradition of a mild economic determinism. The very weaknesses and hiatuses of libertarian thought are precisely where Marxian analysis is most searching and concentrated. Indeed, as a first approximation of a theoretical explanation of the events of the nineteenth and twentieth centuries, the Marxist approach to the changing characteristics of capitalism seems essentially correct.

At second glance, however, a serious problem emerges.

14. It seems necessary to add a word in passing on the libertarian concept of freedom itself. The notion is originally centered in political and intellectual freedom, but economic freedom—at first only a by-product, as Hayek mentions—is rapidly elevated to a position of equality with, then to one of guardianship over, these primary freedoms. This key point is vehemently asserted, but never demonstrated empirically (cf. Paul Samuelson in *The Business Establishment*, New York, 1964, pp. 225–227). In its most extreme expression we find, "What alone can prevent the civilized nations of Western Europe, America, and Australia from being enslaved by the barbarism of Moscow is open and unrestricted support of laissez-faire capitalism" (Ludwig von Mises, *The Anti-Capitalist Mentality*, Princeton, 1956, p. 112). Even in its milder expressions, the defense of the market system becomes central: "History speaks with a single voice on the relation between political freedom and a free market" (Milton Friedman, *Capitalism and Freedom*, Chicago, 1956, p. 9). As a result, libertarianism tends to end up as a philosophic defense of the status quo. It is also worthy of comment that for all their rhetoric, the libertarians are not notable for their defense of academic or civil liberties.

It lies in the unconvincing description of the relationship between the forces of the economy, whose dysfunction Marxism makes explicit, and the interventionist action of the state, presumably for the purpose of restoring capitalist health. As Strachey has put it:

> The undeniable fact is that the typical American businessman and to some extent his British counterpart also today hates and fears the American and British state. Even under his own Right Wing Eisenhower Administration, the American businessman keeps up a violent propaganda against what he calls "big government," that is to say, against the encroachments and interference of the state in economic activity. . . .
>
> Now how could this attitude of mind have developed in the American and British capitalist class if the state was still *their* state? If the British and American capitalist classes had still a secure and undisputed control over their state machinery, they would certainly not hate and fear it. They might— no doubt they would—restrict its activities very closely. They would prevent it from interfering with their profit-making activities, although they would employ it unhesitatingly to regulate and control the wage-earners. But in any case, they would not regard it as something which could possibly be used against them.[15]

Strachey's statement goes to the core of the Marxian problem. If the rise of the state is to be viewed primarily as a defensive maneuver of capitalism, it is difficult to account for the intense antigovernmental bias of capitalists themselves. This difficulty has, in fact, led to an attempt to redefine the Marxian view of the state in a somewhat more flexible way.[16] Paul Sweezy, for example, qualifies the orthodox view as follows:

15. "Has Capitalism Changed?" in the book by the same name, Shigeto Tsuru, ed. (Tokyo, 1961), p. 81.
16. It is interesting to note, if only in passing, that Marx himself is

The liberal and to a large extent also Social Democratic view that the state is a neutral agency which exists to serve the interests of the whole society is of course false. But this does not mean that it can be replaced by what may be called the vulgar Marxian theory that the state always and everywhere and automatically serves the interests of the ruling class.

The main weaknesses of the latter theory may be formulated as follows:

(a) There are conflicts between the true long-run interests of the ruling class and the short-run interests of particular segments of it.

(b) Because it wears ideological blinkers which distort its view of reality the ruling class does not see clearly what its true long-run interests are and hence acts on a false conception of ruling-class interests.

(c) Under certain circumstances, other classes or segments of classes can force the state to make concessions to their interests. There are naturally limits to all these qualifications, and it is doubtless true that *in general* the state serves the interests of the ruling class. But in any given situation the range of alternatives is wide and the course to be followed is far from mechanically predetermined.[17]

Sweezy's position is far from representative of prevailing Marxian doctrine today,[18] but it does offer an attempt to rescue Marxian thought from the dilemma that Strachey has pointed out. Unfortunately, Sweezy's retreat leaves Marxism

---

not of one opinion about the state. In a number of places he specifically speaks of it as having an existence "above" the class structure (e.g., in the *18th Brumaire*), although this position is retrieved in the end by having the state "represent" the "dominant class interest." For a discussion of this ambiguous state of affairs, see Ralph Milliband, "Marx and the State," in *The Socialist Register,* New York, 1965, p. 283f.

17. Tsuru, *op. cit.,* pp. 87–88.

18. Cf., for example, Bettelheim's essay in the Tsuru book previously cited, or Baran's and Sweezy's view in *Monopoly Capital* (New York, 1966). In this latest book, the view of the state is much more inflexibly stated as an instrument of the ruling class.

with an essentially indeterminate relationship between business and the state. The question-begging introduction of "true" versus "false" class interests, and the admission that there are effective political forces other than those exercised or controlled by the capitalist class itself open up, rather than seal off, the problem at hand. At best we are left with a plausible case for the identity of interests between the business world and its executive committee, the state, in the nineteenth century, when, however, the growth of the state apparatus was *least* conspicuous. But this clear identity of interests breaks down just when we need it most, in the second quarter of the twentieth century.

III

Thus, neither the libertarian nor the Marxian rhetoric provides a very satisfactory account of the central phenomenon of capitalist development—the growing prominence of the state associated with the maturation of capitalism. The libertarian view alerts us to a pervasive change in the climate of ideas without in any way relating that change to the changing realities of the times, and the Marxian view explains the defensive function of state intervention without, however, explaining why this intervention was so bitterly resisted.

Faced with these deficiencies, most liberal (as contrasted with libertarian) thought seeks an eclectic "middle" position today. Eschewing on the one hand the problems associated with the idea of a waning commitment to "freedom," and on the other those of defining the class orientation of the state, it deals with the phenomenon of a growing government presence within capitalism as a fact to be explained in a highly pragmatic way, without rhetorical overtones. For example, in his sophisticated treatment of capitalism in Europe and America, Andrew Schonfield describes the critical changes within modern capitalism as follows:

1. There is the vastly increased influence of the public authorities on the management of the economic system. This operates through different mechanisms in different countries. . . . In all of them the government's expenditure has become enormously enlarged and determines directly a large segment of each nation's economic activities.

2. The preoccupation with social welfare leads to the use of public funds on a rising scale. . . .

3. In the private sector, the violence of the market has been tamed. Competition, although it continues to be active in a number of areas, tends to be increasingly regulated and controlled. . . .

4. It has now come to be taken for granted . . . that each year should bring a noticeable increase in the real income per head of population. . . .

5. The characteristic attitude in large-scale economic management, both inside government and in the private sector, . . . is the pursuit of intellectual coherence. Its most obvious manifestation is long-range national planning.[19]

This essentially matter-of-fact, nonideological point of view is unquestionably the one that commends itself most naturally to American thought, with its traditionally political rather than economic, and pluralist rather than polarized, way of looking at things. The rise of government authority then becomes a purely "functional" development, a matter of attending to the "public interest," without inquir-

19. *Modern Capitalism* (New York, 1966), pp. 66–67.

ing too closely into precisely what functions it serves, or whose interests the "public interest" represents.

This apolitical approach is extremely useful, so long as analysis is confined to problems "within" the system as a whole. Thus when we discuss the nature of the planning that Schonfield describes in Europe and America, the simplest approach is one that treats the government as if it were itself only one of the numerous constituencies contending to shape national policy. In this way, the emergence of government power becomes particularized as the study of the specific conditions that lead now to the regulation of such and such an industry, or again, to the public assumption of responsibility for such and such a problem.

Accustomed as we are to dealing with the problem of government from such a pragmatic, pluralist set of preconceptions, the underlying sense of drama of both libertarian and Marxian rhetorics strikes us as an unnecessary encumbrance, an embarrassment rather than an enlightenment. Yet there is a weakness in the liberal approach—a weakness that is, in the end, no less vitiating than those that impair the usefulness of the rhetorics it seeks to replace. The weakness is a lack of a consistent rationale to explain the secular drift to the facts it investigates one by one. In a word, what the nonideological approach misses is the ingredient that the rhetorical approaches have in surfeit—a sense of overall direction to events. It is significant, for example, that in his treatment of capitalist planning mechanisms, Schonfield has no word as to the long-term structural implications of the tendencies he observes, and that he does not even consider the question central to both rhetorics: whether or not the rise of public authority implies the preservation or the transformation of capitalism itself.

IV

Is it possible to discover such an underlying trend—a rationale that will enable us to see the struggle between business and the state in the light of a long evolutionary swing, while avoiding the excesses of the prevailing rhetorics? I believe it is, and in the final sections of this essay I hope to sketch out what such a secular tendency might be.

It may help set the stage if we take a moment to establish some empirical dimensions to the historic swing we have been discussing. In precisely what ways has the presence of government become manifest? In what areas of life has it entered? These questions may lead us toward the subterranean propulsive force that we seek.

The questions are not easy to answer, for despite general agreement that the public sphere has greatly enlarged during the twentieth century, its appearance varies widely from one country to another. For example, the most unambiguous form of increased public economic activity—the actual nationalization of production—runs a wide gamut among contemporary nations, ranging from perhaps 15 to 25 percent of output in a few countries—mainly France, England, Austria, and Italy—to a negligible fraction in the United States or in the supposedly "collectivist-minded" Scandinavian group.[20]

Moreover, the reasons for the growth of these nationalized sectors are themselves varied. In England, for instance, the nationalization of industry resulted from the deliberate

20. See M. M. Postan, *An Economic History of Western Europe*, London, 1967, p. 220f.

efforts of the Labour Party to take over certain strategic sectors of the private economy that had performed very poorly; in France, by way of contrast, the nationalized sector expanded largely in response to the conservative tradition of *étatisme,* aided by the pure happenstance that the Renault company collaborated with Nazis and was therefore seized by the government after the war. By way of still further contrast, the growth of the Austrian nationalized sector was mainly the result of a transfer to the Austrian government of German assets captured by the Russians, whereas the Italian sector is an outgrowth of Fascist policies and institutions, transformed by the postwar Italian government into a means for the economic development of the country. Thus, if the growth of a government presence is a universal capitalist phenomenon, this phenomenon is certainly not universally manifest in an expansion of public production, or in a common history of the expansion of nationalized industry.

Then in what is it manifest? The answer seems to lie not so much in the actual transfer of production from private to public hands as in the marked expansion of a common range of *activities* in all capitalist nations, regardless of how large or small their nationalized sectors may be.

The first of these activities is obvious from even the most cursory survey of the main economic events of this century. It is the enormous growth of *military expenditure* in all nations of the world, dominated by the vast expansion of the American military sector. Western European nations today spend between 3 and 4 percent of their gross national products on defense activities, and while we do not have comparable statistics for the beginning of the century, there is no doubt that this represents an increase of many times over. In the United States, a more exact comparison can be made.

In 1900 major national security expenditures of the United States amounted to much less than a quarter of one percent of GNP; in 1970 they were equal to 9.2 percent. In this single factor alone we can trace a major cause for the rise of the government's presence in the United States: forty percent of the federal budget and approximately one out of every two federal civilian employees is directly connected with defense activities.[21]

A second activity seems quite different from the first. This is the proliferation within all capitalist nations of a network of *controls and regulations* by which governments intervene into the formerly unhindered operation of their private sectors. From one country to another the extent and effectiveness of these interventory procedures vary, but in all we find some form of supervision over the operation of certain industries, such as transportation, conventional or nuclear power, communication, etc., as well as a range of measures dealing with limitations on the permissible actions of business enterprise. Although the growth of this activity is essentially unquantifiable, I doubt that many would deny either the fact or the importance of government intervention as a major element in the expansion of the public sector.

A third universally discoverable area for expanded public activity lies in yet another field. This is the recent growth of the *educational sector* in all these nations as a response to an increased demand for universal higher education. Thus in the United States the education explosion has resulted in a threefold increase in the percentage of the labor force required to man the educational apparatus since the beginning of the century; and whereas we do not have comparable statistics for Western Europe, we know that the rate of uni-

21. *Statistical Abstract,* 1969, pp. 244, 246.

versity attendance there is rising at a rate of 8.9 percent a year.

Finally, we turn to a fourth area of general governmental growth, again different from the previous areas. This is the striking rise in the provision of *welfare,* meaning not alone family allowances, social security, or direct payments to the poor, but a broad spectrum of social services including public health, urban facilities, recreation, etc. Together, all social welfare expenditures have risen in the United States from about 2.5 percent of gross national product in 1900 to over 13 percent today, and social security benefits in most European nations are double the percentage of gross national product that they are in the United States.

Thus the main evidences of the growing public presence are incorporated in the expansion of a group of seemingly unrelated activities—military expenditure, industrial regulation, the expansion of education, and the provision of social welfare. But now let us push our inquiry further by asking *why* public activity has risen in each of these fields. The answer that comes immediately to mind with regard to military expenditures is simple: military techniques and equipment are vastly more complex and expensive than they were in 1900. So too, when we inquire into the reason for the growth of industrial regulation, the obvious reply is that industrial processes are much more complicated than they used to be, and that the entire economy is somehow more tightly interconnected than was once the case. As for the rise in education and welfare expenditures, the most apparent answer is that modern life necessitates a higher degree of training than was formerly the case, and that the prevailing urban character of life has made necessary the provision of some kind of security to individuals who may lose their place on the national assembly line.

It is by no means necessary to claim that any of these reasons entirely explains the growth of the public presence in its area. Rather, what is important is that each of these rationales, which are surely integrally connected with the phenomenon in question, contains a more or less obvious common element. *This is the presence within all of them of the most powerful and disruptive force of the twentieth century—the force of science and scientific technology that is the true revolutionary agency of modern times.*

V

I shall not waste words to establish the fact of the extraordinary development of science and its related technological capabilities during the past six or seven decades. Rather, what is necessary for our purpose is to review the impact that the cumulative entrance of science and technology has had on the capitalist mechanism, and in particular on the role of the government within that mechanism. And here I suggest that the main effects of this new force have been these:

1. *The creation of socially dangerous processes or products.*

Examples abound, of which the most apparent are the terrible machines of war. But the automobile, the new medical drugs, high-speed machinery, even the radio and the television set are also to be counted in this class. These and similar inventions increase the scope and reach of public intervention because their inherent physical dangers must be curbed or organized (the regulation of air transportation on the one hand; the creation of a strategic air command on the other), or because the increased capability of individuals to injure or interfere with one another must be monitored (giving us traffic control, or the control over television).

2. *The disarrangement of social relationships.*

Science and technology not only inject new physical artifacts into society, but they also reshape the relationship between man and man. This in turn creates situations in which the power of the public sector is increased. In part this may be the direct effect of scientific discoveries, such as the medical advances that create a growing stratum of older people who require public support; in larger part it is the consequence of the profound changes resulting from the separation of families from the land and their concentration in the city. Technology is the prime cause for the enormous urbanization of modern times, and it is to urbanization that we must look for the rise of both social welfare and administrative expenditures.

3. *An impetus toward organizational growth.*

The scientific-technological force further encourages the growth of government because of the impetus it gives to the growth of large-scale organizations. In the economic field, this impetus derives from the economies of large-scale production brought by technology; in the noneconomic sphere (and in the economic as well), technology speeds the growth of large units through the technical means of information dispersal and retrieval—the telephone, the TV circuit, the computer—without which the effective management of large organizations would be impossible. From this increase in organizational size the public presence is again encouraged to grow, in part as government units themselves utilize the new techniques for organization, partly as the emergence of powerful private organizations creates a need for a public counterforce or regulatory body.

4. *A threat to economic stability.*

Finally, the growth in organizational size brings with it another cause for the expansion of public power. This is the need to create public means of assuring against the economic damage that might result if a substantial number of these units were to perform very badly. The extreme dependence of the American economy on the rate of investment of perhaps 100 corporations, or its vulnerability to the rate of sales of two or three automobile producers, are instances in point. Hence we find, in all technologically advanced societies, the presence of fiscal and monetary controls as a first line of defense against instability, and the gradual development of planning techniques as a further insurance against the risk of serious reversals.

In singling out these effects of the entrance of science and technology, I do not wish to exclude other factors that have contributed to the growth of the government's presence. Behind the emergence of the enormous military sector lies not alone the refinement of the scientific technology of war, but the climate of ideological hostility of our politically polarized times. So, too, behind the appearance of a complicated web of government regulatory and protective agencies lies not just the need to buffer the effects of technology or to intervene into a social and economic process that technology has rendered more difficult and dangerous, but also the independent growth of ideas as to the possibility of using the government as a vehicle for social betterment and guidance. In the same way, again, when we look to the rise of education and welfare activities, behind the influence of technology in creating a society that requires technical schooling and that is saddled with the problems of urban helplessness, we can also discern other causes: affluence, for example, is certainly a causal factor in the growth of both education and social welfare (although affluence itself rests on a very important technological base).

Thus it is neither necessary nor wise to load everything on the single force of technological change. And yet, if we are looking for the deepest root of the central phenomenon of the business-state shift, I feel it is absolutely necessary, even if by no means sufficient, to put the major emphasis on the eruption of science and its technological effects. To put the case as strongly as I can, I would contend that had the advance of science and technology come to a halt at the end of the nineteenth century, it is very likely that the growth of government would have proceeded at a greatly diminished pace. It is in this sense that I would call the scientific-technological revolution the ultimate cause of the change in the public and private spheres that is so central to our century.

VI

There remains to be investigated one further attribute of this disruptive force. It is that the emergence of science and technology as a prime mover in history represents the appearance of a powerful new historic current whose importance—indeed, whose very existence—is overlooked both by the libertarian and the Marxian rhetorics, as well as by the pragmatic liberals.

We are so accustomed to thinking of the scientific-technological wave as "part" of capitalism that we forget that it arose within capitalism considerably *after* that system had established itself on the footing of a nonscientific technology. Arkwright, Stephenson, the iron masters and mill-owners and enterprisers who were the tutelary spirits of capitalism throughout the Industrial Revolution and well into the third quarter of the nineteenth century, had virtually no dependence on nor connection with the rise of the independent scientific establishment.[22] The latter, represented by the tradition of Newton, the Royal Academy, Darwin, Maxwell, Rutherford, Mendel, Freud, etc., did not join hands with the forces of production until the last quarter of the nineteenth century or even the beginning of the twentieth century. Research and development as such may begin with Menlo Park in the 1870's, but the first industrial laboratory was not built until 1900 by the General Electric Company. The enormous economic propulsion of science and technology is essentially a *new* historical element, which has its genesis largely independent of capitalism, and which joins fully with it only in the fairly recent past.[23]

Thus I believe the swing toward the state in the twentieth century should be seen, at least in part, as the expression of a new directive force within history—a force comparable to the impact of trade in the Middle Ages or to the development of a market framework and a laissez-faire legal system in the eighteenth century. For technology guided by science not only represents a new stage of technology itself, but it also expresses a social view different from that of capitalism. Essentially, this view mirrors the scientific commitment to the conscious direction over and control of the environment, including the social environment—a commitment that stands

22. James Watt did work closely with the chemist Joseph Black, but the contribution of "science" to the development of the steam engine was small. See Charles Singer, et al. (eds.), *A History of Technology* (Oxford, 1958), Vol. IV, p. 673f.
23. H. Neisser, *Sociology of Knowledge*, New York, 1966, Ch. 4; and my *The Limits of American Capitalism,* New York, 1966, Ch. 2.

directly opposed to the philosophy of capitalism which yields control over the environment to the uncoordinated and undirected influences of individual entrepreneurs and consumers.

It is here, I hazard, that one must look for the true core of that "spiritual collectivization" that the libertarians discover diffusing through the intellectual world beginning in the last quarter of the nineteenth century. Here too, in the gradual infusion of an aim of social control ultimately alien to capitalism, although still used in its behalf, does one find a clue to the contradictions of business attitude that have so bedeviled Marxian doctrine. And not least, here is the current of thought needed to give to the nonideological researches of liberalism a sense of historic destination.

VII

It remains only to extend these reflections into the future, and that I shall do very briefly.

I am aware that we have today reached a point of relative balance between state and business, when the relevance of the traditional rhetorics seems to have faded almost to the vanishing point. Yet if the preceding analysis is valid, it would be premature to consider the present division as between public and private prerogatives a stable one. On the contrary, it is clear that the propulsive forces that seem to have induced the rise of state power are far from spent, and as a consequence it is difficult to avoid the conclusion that the distribution of power between business and the state will alter substantially over the future in favor of the state and to the detriment of business.

I suspect there will be little dissent from the proposition that the threat of war is not likely to diminish during the foreseeable future, or that the technology of war will present smaller demands on the national economy. On the contrary, it would seem that the coming two or three decades will be those during which the demand for both nuclear and non-nuclear defense equipment will be very large, to which must be added the semimilitary activity of space exploration. To that extent the future promises a retention, if not expansion, of the present proportions of the public sector.

The same conclusion is certainly indicated in a second main area in which we find direct public economic activity —education and welfare. The proportion of high school entrants going on to college is rising, but by 1975 will still be only one-half of high school students. The proportion of the nation living in urban areas is also growing, and by 1975 will comprise three-quarters of the population. These facts augur a continued growth of government activity at the state and local level, and very probably at the federal level as well.

Meanwhile the entrance of new products and processes, with their direct and indirect disruptive effects, bids fair to rise. At any rate, the curve of research and development expenditures points upward and the time lag between discovery and application diminishes. We need not suggest that the technological outcome of this process will be more "control-inducing" than in the past, but merely as much so, to imply the likelihood of new regulatory devices designed to buffer the physical, social, and economic effects of technical change. In addition, we must now take into account the potentially vast regulatory requirements imposed by the ecological problem.

To these factors we can add the "collectivization of thought," now tentatively identified as the social expression of the growing scientific orientation of society. I believe that this collectivization of thought—that is, the matter-of-fact acceptance of conscious social control in more and more areas of life—will be a marked feature of society in the future, within the business community as well as among the emerging elites of the technical, scientific, administrative, and professional world. Indeed, the very diminution of political controversy over the business-state issue implies that the ideological battle is already won and that big business is slowly making its peace with big government. The acceptance of planning by businessmen in Western Europe indicates, I would suggest, the direction of business thought in America tomorrow.

The Marxian rhetoric tells us that this steady growth of state power will be used to maintain the viability of the present social order. I would suggest, rather, that insofar as the movement toward state power resides in the independent rise of the scientific view as a ruling idea in history, the use of state power as a bulwark for capitalism is only a transitional stage of events. At the moment, it must be remembered, the protagonists of the scientific movement, whether in physics or economics, have no social or political goal that differs from that of business. Indeed, by and large, the social vision of "science" is deliberately made to conform with that of business, except insofar as a modest penchant for ad hoc planning infuses the social science community more than that of business.

But the comparison here, as I have suggested elsewhere, is best made to the merchants who huddled around the walls of thirteenth-century castles, wholly subservient to the prevailing order, and oblivious to the thought that some day it might be *their* interests and ideas, and not those of the feudal seigneurs, that would establish the laws of motion of the social universe. In like manner, the technicians, scientists, planners, etc., who constitute the vanguard of the society of the future, today have no independently formulated conceptions of society and are happy to lend themselves to the ends specified by their capitalist masters. But the divergence of their long-term train of thought from that of the businessman is plain enough. In the long run the ascendant elites within capitalism are not themselves capitalist in mentality or outlook, and will slowly incline society toward that deliberate application of intelligence to social problems that is characteristic of their professional commitment. As they do so, the role of the state will rise and that of business shrink. Like all such great processes, the course of events cannot be tidily predicted. The change may require several decades, perhaps even generations, before becoming crystal-clear. But I suggest that the direction of change is already established beyond peradventure of doubt.

CHAPTER 2

The Eye of the Needle

I have taken as my title a phrase that expresses a certain skepticism as to the rich man's chances of entering heaven, and while I do not propose to settle the theological merits of that argument, the Eye of the Needle serves me in good stead as a point of reference. For I wish to discuss a well-known and yet little-discussed problem—a problem with which we are all familiar and which is yet somehow embarrassing to vent in public. It is the problem of the ambivalence of our feelings about wealth—the mixture of envy and disdain, admiration and disrepute with which riches have always been surrounded.

I do not know if I need to document this curious ambivalence, but a few shorthand references to the critique of wealth may serve to highlight the problem. We all know the age-old Biblical injunctions against wealth. "Woe unto you that are rich," says the Sermon on the Mount, "for ye have received your reward." All through the Bible from Deuteronomy to the New Testament runs the theme of a theological suspicion and rejection of wealth, for reasons that we will examine shortly. But the disdain for riches is not just a theological concern, dismissible as mere pietism. We hear a similar charge levied by nontheological writers whom we might call professional "students of human nature"—meaning by that phrase not alone the psychologists and psychiatrists of our generation, but the novelists, dramatists, and essayists of all generations. One has only to think of Shylock, or Père Grandet, or of Dickens' gallery of characters, or to turn to the pages of clinical journals to recognize a secular version of the theological warning that the pursuit of wealth, when carried too far, can warp the person and even destroy life.

All of us are familiar with and, as I have said, made faintly uncomfortable by such warnings. But there is a second and even more penetrating critique. This one also has its churchly setting, although its rationale is no longer theological but social. It is eloquently stated by Ambrose, the magnificent fourth-century bishop of Milan, who thundered: "Think you that you commit no injustice by keeping to yourself alone what would be the means of life to many? It is the bread of the hungry you cling to; it is the clothing of the naked you lock up; the money you bury is the redemption of the poor."

I need hardly dwell on the secular extension of this argument. Beginning with the earliest communistic experiments of the Church Fathers themselves, it bursts forth in the nineteenth and twentieth centuries as the central theme of socialism. For whatever the other purposes of socialism, the inner core of the socialist critique has always been simple. It has attacked the institutions of a society that has permitted the accumulation of private wealth, because it has identified wealth—as did Ambrose—with injustice.

Yet even this example does not yet fully underscore my initial point. Just as we can shrug off the theological indictment of wealth-seeking because it is, after all, "only" religious; so we can discount the socialist critique of the pursuit of wealth because it is socialist. But there is a last argument that gives us no such easy out. It lies, curiously, in the very discipline to which we resort when we come to the intellectual defense of wealth—economics. Economics is, of course, very polite in the face of the theological and socialist criticisms of acquisitiveness and the system that encourages it, but it has an answer we all know very well. "If you want a society to increase its output," says the economist, "then you must give the acquisitive drive its head. The profit motive may not represent man at his noblest, but it nonetheless serves society better than any other motive force."

We shall have to look into this defense more carefully, both as to its strengths and weaknesses. But at the start there is something to note that attests, from this unimpeachable source, as to the curiously mixed regard in which the accumulation of wealth is held. Having given their full blessing to the motivation of acquisitiveness, the economists now cunningly design an economic system that places every possible obstacle in the way of realizing that motivation in fact. For at least in the ideal economy envisioned in their textbooks, the economists proceed to hamper the accumulation of private wealth by insisting that the acquisitive drive be exercised only in an environment of pure competition, the purpose of which is to prevent "monopoly gains," and to temper the licit "competitive profits" to a point at which economists have to use a theoretical microscope to find them at all. Thus even the economic sanction of wealth-seeking turns out to be an implicit condemnation of wealth-getting. Indeed, in the extraordinary frustrations that it imposes, the economist's endorsement of acquisitiveness is like some eugenic enthusiast's plan for improving the race by the encouragement of uninhibited sexuality— a plan that was to be realized by such an arduous program of physical fitness that the successful participants would be much too exhausted to put their prowess to the test.

All this by way of introduction. The ambivalence of our regard for wealth, the ambiguity of our sanctions for wealth-gathering are evidently deeper-rooted than we like to admit. What is to be asked now is what we can say about the substance of the charges that have been brought. What do we know about the relation of wealth and personality? Of wealth and injustice?

Surprisingly little has been written about the complex phenomenon of the drive to amass wealth.[1] Yet it is clear that the activity of wealth-seeking has more than one root. At its base it would seem that men seek wealth because they must eat and clothe themselves and shelter their bodies from

1. The single most comprehensive article is still, to my knowledge, Otto Fenichel, "The Drive to Amass Wealth," *Psychoanalytic Quarterly,* VI (January, 1938).

the elements, so that reduced to its fundamentals the drive for wealth becomes nothing but the social expression of the drive for self-preservation.

Yet, although it may be true as far as it goes, this is clearly an inadequate answer. For one of the commonest observations of social anthropologists is that people in poorer countries do not show the insatiable desire to improve their standards of living characteristic of people in so-called "advanced" countries. Homeostasis, not maximization, is the descriptive word for the attitude of the peasants of the world. The peasant may be avaricious, stingy, greedy; but in the sense in which it refers to a drive to enjoy an ever-larger income, he is not acquisitive.

No doubt it will be rejoined that he is not acquisitive because he cannot be. Precisely. The point is that the drive to amass wealth is a *social* manifestation, whatever its psychological basis. There are, of course, acquisitive types even in the poorest nations. But to find the acquisitive orientation as the normal mode of *behavior* we have to turn to the developed economies, and particularly to those with highly developed market systems.

Why do men behave acquisitively in market systems? In part, because they have to. At every level of society we are taught and trained to try to "make money"—and the environment reinforces these lessons with severe punishments if we ignore or forget that we live in a world where each man is for himself and devil take the hindmost.

Yet here we come full circle. There is certainly an element of self-preservation that motivates the actors in a market system, but it does not explain their actions fully. For just as the peasants of the world fail to display much of an acquisitive behavior pattern, so the normal participant

in the developed economies goes far beyond the requirements imposed by sheer need. Indeed, it is a typical observation that the more we have, the more we want—that the
more successful we are at making money, the more whetted,
not satiated, becomes our appetite.

Thus, if there is an inextricable social element in acquisitiveness, there is also an indissoluble psychological element as well. What do we know about it? No one has described it better than William James in his *Principles of
Psychology* in 1890:

> It is clear that between what a man calls me and what he
> simply calls *mine,* the line is very difficult to draw. We feel
> and act about certain things that are ours very much as we
> feel and act about ourselves. . . . In its widest possible
> sense, a man's Self is the sum total of all that he can call
> his, not only his body and his psychic powers, but his clothes
> and his house, his wife and his children, his ancestors and
> his friends, his reputation and his works, his land and horses
> and yacht and bank account. If they wax and prosper, he
> feels triumphant, if they dwindle and die away, he feels cast
> down—not necessarily in the same degree for each thing, but
> in much the same way for all.[2]

There is more than psychology that is interesting in
James's statement, as we shall see later. But James has made
very clear the basic psychological mechanism at work in
all acquisitive processes. Acquisitiveness is a means of for-
tifying and enlarging the Self by projecting it into objects
that will expand in social value. In a peasant's world this
may be his children, which are all he has. In a market world
it is apt to be money.

2. William James, *Principles of Psychology* (New York: Henry Holt,
1890), pp. 291–292.

There is no doubt that students of human nature have known about this projective capability long before James's time; Plato wrote about "the makers of fortunes [who] have a second love of money as a creation of their own, resembling the love of authors for their own poems, or of parents for their children." Contemporary psychoanalysis brings some additional enlightenment to the problem, however. It has discovered for us the persistence of the child encapsulated in the adult, and has taught us to look for infantile meanings and origins and symbols in acts that we would otherwise judge solely in adult terms. Thus, modern psychology emphasizes the ease with which the accumulation of wealth becomes the vehicle for the expression of childhood needs and longings, whether for love or security or for other primitive satisfactions. Behind the voracious acquisitor we now see not a wicked adult, but a hungry and importunate child.

This symbolic aspect of acquisitiveness helps explain more fully the dangers that the theologian and the student of human nature have both sensed in the wealth-oriented individual. The typical obsessive-compulsive attributes of the money-oriented character, with its social blindness and its self-destructiveness, can now be seen, not in moralistic terms, but as symptoms of a personality that has not overcome its infantile demands and which therefore pursues external goals with a childish selfishness or with a near-autistic intensity. In the same way, psychoanalytic insight helps explain our own ambivalent feelings toward acquisitiveness. It is not only the rich man's money that we envy, but the uncurbed expression of his infantile megalomania, the memory of which can be roused in everyone. And it is not only the moral meaning of his acquisitive acts that we reject, but his right to unleash an infantile trait that we have painfully mastered.

There is, I suspect, not too much objection to this psychiatric commentary on an ancient antipathy. Certainly the contemporary businessman looks with as much distaste as any churchman on the more pathological expressions of the acquisitive drive. He is even prepared to admit that an ordinary degree of acquisitiveness exacts its psychological price—that the drive to make money, even when it does not reach grotesque limits, brings out an unlovely side of human nature.

Yet this general line of criticism against the quest for wealth does not deeply trouble him. More and more, he would maintain, businessmen are interested in the creative or administrative aspects of business rather than in sheer money-making—indeed, the waning of the very competitive discipline that the economists prescribe has permitted a much more relaxed and unacquisitive style of business. And then, perhaps even more important, the businessman is prepared to defend the psychological cost of acquisitiveness as a lesser burden for society than the costs of some alternative driving motivation. Although it may seem like the Devil quoting Scripture, the businessman could call on John Maynard Keynes to confirm his view:

> Dangerous human proclivities can be canalised into comparatively harmless channels by the existence of opportunities for money-making and private wealth, which, if they cannot be satisfied in this way, may find their outlet in cruelty, the reckless pursuit of personal power and authority, and other forms of self-aggrandizement. It is better that a man should

tyrannise over his bank balance than over his fellow-citizen; and whilst the former is sometimes denounced as but a means to the latter, sometimes at least it is an alternative.[3]

Finally the defender of the acquisitive motivation sets a last string to his bow. He points out that neither clergyman nor social critic nor economist objects to the effort to gain wealth when it is exercised by the poor. The "honest workingman" seeking a rise in pay, the underdeveloped country trying to increase its gross national product, do not incur the opprobrium of the critics of the acquisitive drive. It is only after some indefinitely located middle ground has been crossed that the criticism begins. But this leads to hypocritical results, says the businessman. Why is an attitude that is encouraged in the poor man or the poor nation to be condemned in the rich? Is not the critic of the quest for wealth logically bound to urge an asceticism on poor as well as rich, or else to recommend acquisitiveness for the rich as well as for the poor?

The defense is well taken. There *have* been those who have urged a universal abnegation of riches—Christ was one —and there are those who have taken the opposite tack and glorified acquisitiveness as the universal standard—I think of Ayn Rand. But I think it is fair to state that neither view, however logically consistent, has commanded much general respect. Whether it is psychologically in their best interests or not, we *do* commend the effort to gain wealth on the part of the poor; and whether it is morally or logically consistent or not, we *do* look with reservations on the same drive on the part of the rich.

How can this be? The very illogicality of the psychological

3. John Maynard Keynes, *The General Theory of Employment, Interest, and Money* (New York: Harcourt, Brace, 1936), p. 374.

argument gives us the key. It is that we see the acquisitive drive not only as a personal activity to be judged by its inner consequences, but as an activity inextricably mixed into the social world where it is to be judged as part of the whole scheme of social relationships. And here the ambivalence of our view about the same drive in the rich and the poor reveals a feeling that is deeply imbedded within us. It is the reverberatory echo of Bishop Ambrose's accusation, the lingering conviction that the juxtaposition of rich and poor, whether men or nations, is a condition that is fundamentally unjust. From there it follows that every step that widens the gap between rich and poor—that is, every act of the rich to grow richer—worsens a condition that is already profoundly wrong.

There is no accusation that so deeply offends the businessman as this one. He will accept the charge that he may be ruining his character by running after money, just as we all accept the risk that we may be ruining our health by smoking. But tell the businessman that in pursuing wealth he is undertaking an activity that is in itself unjust and he will rise up in righteous indignation.

Furthermore, he makes a very plausible case for his anger. Far from grinding the faces of the poor, he insists, the wealth-seeker is releasing the force that will ultimately free the poor from their poverty. For if the great escape from poverty is to be made, it will surely require the massive accumulation of capital, and the most effective way of amassing that capital, he will tell you, is through the activities of individual private accumulators, each striving for his own enrichment.

Moreover, says the businessman, the process of amassing private wealth in a dynamic economy is basically differ-

ent from that in a static one, such as that described in the
Bible. In the latter situation, one man's riches were very
likely squeezed from another's poverty, through consumption loans or onerous rents. Indeed, the businessman will
gladly admit that poverty is the other side of riches in any
society where the sum total of the social product remains
the same. But once the terrible stasis of underdevelopment
is broken and a process of economic increase is inaugu-
rated, we leave behind the situation of "I win—you lose."
In the expanding economy of the wealth-driven society it is
possible for rich and poor to gain together, and indeed for
the poor to gain more rapidly than the rich.

Finally the defense goes further still. Not only is the
drive for wealth justifiable as the necessary means to the
abolition of poverty, but the system that promotes the individual search for wealth also provides an invaluable framework for the achievement of other no less desired goals,
high among them social mobility and political liberty. The
market system, in other words, not only gives us economic
efficiency, but by virtue of its self-regulating, unsupervised
operation, it sets the stage for other kinds of freedoms.
Indeed, these freedoms can be asserted to depend not only
on a market system but on the careful restriction of firms
to the single goal of money-making and on their exclusion
from noneconomic activities. As one staunch defender of
the acquisitive society has written, "Few trends would so
thoroughly undermine the very foundations of our free society as the acceptance by corporate officials of a social
responsibility other than to make as much money for their
stockholders as they possibly can." [4]

4. Milton Friedman, *Capitalism and Freedom* (Chicago: University
of Chicago Press, 1962), p. 133.

Like the tempered defense of the acquisitive drive, the worldly defense of the acquisitive society is impressive. I think a valid case *can* be made for the usefulness of the money-making system as an instrument for social accumulation, at least in certain stages of history and in certain social settings. Unquestionably it did the trick for the West. I think as well that the acquisitive drive in an expanding economy does lead to results different from those in a static, zero-sum world, and that in the capitalist market systems the poor have grown richer, together with and faster than the rich, predictions of Karl Marx to the contrary notwithstanding. And whereas I believe that the equation of economic freedom and political freedom is a vast oversimplification of a very complex problem, I am even prepared to concede that there is a certain protective value for personal freedom in the refuge provided by a market system for those who do not wish to join the approved institutions of society in order to make their livings.

Yet however reasonable, indeed however true, these counterarguments, I do not think they quite come to grips with the problem that wealth and wealth-seeking stubbornly impose. After all the doubts associated with the pursuit of wealth have been smoothed away, the canker of unease remains. There is something about the acquisitive drive, and perhaps even more important, something about the nature of the system erected on the foundation of that drive, that continues to trouble us. In the remainder of this essay, let me try to voice what these lingering and recalcitrant problems are.

One problem is relatively simple to diagnose. It is a peculiar moral opacity that afflicts a society that is dependent on the continuous exercise of the acquisitive propensity as the very precondition for its economic cohesion.

It is certainly not difficult to find examples of this opacity at work. The Market System, as every student of economics knows, is essentially a rationing mechanism, an institution for the efficient distribution of scarce resources among claimants. By virtue of its self-enforcing dynamics, its speed and clarity of operation, its usefulness in solving the difficult tasks of production and distribution, it has proved indispensable for complex industrial economic systems. Nonetheless, *the market mechanism solves its tasks efficiently just because it applies to the varied and tangled needs of a human community one and only one criterion— the criterion of wealth*. Those who have the requisite wealth may, if they wish, exercise their claims on the resources to be divided. Those who do not, may not.

I have already admitted that the market mechanism, operating under the crude but efficient calculus of wealth, brings many advantages in its wake. Nonetheless, with each cut of its blade, it imposes a rule of allocation that is utterly without considerations of a noneconomic kind. Wants, needs, just deserts or ill-gotten gains play no part in the market's distribution of goods. Thus the acquisitive society is one that caters to every whim of the rich but that ignores the elemental requirements of the poor.

But the issue posed by this enthronement of the market principle is not that it calls its particular solution to the rationing problem "just." It is that it submerges *all* considera-

tions of justice under the cloak of an economic calculus. I
have often remarked on this in connection with the reconstruction of Park Avenue in New York City. In the twenty-
five years since the war, a row of apartment houses from
46th Street to 59th Street, formerly the undistinguished-
looking buildings in which the rich lived, have been torn
down and replaced by the very distinguished-looking buildings in which the rich work. There has been considerable
comment on the architectural achievements and failures of
this multi-hundred-million-dollar transformation. Yet, so far
as I know, not a single voice has pointed out a grotesque
failure, an unbelievable misallocation, that occurred here.
The buildings were built in the wrong place. As every citizen
of New York knows, the crying need for the steel and glass,
concrete and brick, that went into Park Avenue from 46th to
59th streets was fifty blocks up that avenue where Harlem
begins in all its overcrowded misery.

Now, had the Gosplanners in Russia committed a similar
mistake—had they squandered the scarce resources of steel
and concrete on fancy offices for themselves while the majority of Moscow slept four to a room—one can picture
the satisfaction with which we would have pointed out the
moral turpitude of the Soviets. But in our own case, the
exact self-same misallocation was removed entirely from the
realm of moral considerations by the overriding calculus
of the market.

Or take another case, that of advertising. There is much
hue and cry as to the aesthetics of advertising. But the fuss
over the raucous quality of commercials misses the moral
point. It is that advertising represents an effort on the part
of some individuals to persuade other individuals—quite
without any knowledge of their circumstances, desires, or

problems—to take certain actions in life, i.e., to acquire certain possessions or to expend their wealth in certain ways. Were this outrageous intrusion into private life taken for any other purpose, it would be regarded as intolerable. But under the obscuring shadow of the economic calculus we do not consider what violations we perform on the human being when we reduce him to the unidimensionality of a "consumer."

I do not think I need labor the point. The injustice of a market society is not that of the rich abusing the poor or snatching bread from their mouths. It is rather the peculiar screening effect that economic considerations cast over life, causing us to act in ways or acquiesce in actions that, were they not justified by the money-making principle, would be judged out of hand as wrong.

This is one source, I believe, of the uneasiness that afflicts an acquisitive society. But there is another, also passed over silently in the usual cogent defenses of the usefulness of the acquisitive drive. It concerns the historic relevance of the social system that emerges as a result of that drive.

Here again I refer to William James's explication of the possessive Self. What James fails to note—and his failure is itself revealing of the preconceptions of an acquisitive society—are the different meanings in the word "his" with which he illustrates a man's projective propensities. When James speaks of the relationship between a person and "his" body, or "his" wife, or "his" land and horses, yacht and bank account, he is confusing physical, social, and legal meanings of the possessive pronoun. No doubt there is a certain universality in the projection of our psyches into the physical and familiar world. But as we have already noted, its projection into *economic property* is not a psychological but a social phenomenon. The ability or the permission to accumulate material wealth (in which one may therefore vest one's psyche) is not found in all societies. The acquisitive society is not therefore the inevitable embodiment of an imperious psychological drive, but a historical social structure in which that drive is allowed or encouraged to vent itself in the accumulation of economic goods and resources.

Thus the acquisitive manifestation cannot be considered without reference to the entire social structure that has been built upon it and around it—a structure that entails not alone the freedom of acquisitive action on the marketplace, but the extension of acquisitive action to the personal "ownership" of vast assemblages of productive assets. In a word, we cannot appraise the acquisitive drive unless we take into account the entire system of private ownership of the means of production that we call capitalism.

To render a judgment on capitalism is far too complex a task to be attempted here. But I think all would agree where its strengths lie. Indeed, we have already enumerated them. Above all, capitalism is justified by the enormous powers of production that it generates. There are of course other strengths, including the economic freedom it permits, and there are as well flaws—some of them having to do with the moral opacity I have just discussed; others, of perhaps greater functional seriousness, related to the dangers of fortresses of private economic power, or of property-oriented ideologies. Yet, to the extent that these flaws are excused or excusable, it is always by reference to the overriding consideration of capitalism as an unsurpassed engine of production. *As economists and social philosophers from Marx to*

*the most conservative have always agreed, the historic task
of capitalism is to produce.*

But what if production is no longer the central historic
requirement? What if the technological virtuosity of the
capitalist nations has now reached the point at which satiety
and superfluity rather than scarcity are the impending
problems? Let us bear in mind the trajectory of our present economic growth. It has been calculated that if the rate
of real output per capita continues to increase by two percent a year, as it has since the mid-nineteenth century, our
average family income (in terms of today's purchasing
power) by the end of the century will be almost $15,000.
Twenty-five years later it will have grown to over $30,000.
A century ahead—say, at the time when our great-grand-
children go to work—it will have reached a level of well
over $100,000 per family.

I do not offer these mechanical calculations as indicating
anything more than the general orders of magnitude as to
what is technologically possible. But it is important to consider what such a prospect offers by way of affecting the historic relevance of an acquisitive society. If there is one thing
that is unmistakably implicit in the vista of impending
affluence, it is the increasing pointlessness of an economic
system whose main claim to historic worth has been its
ability to produce.

To be sure, the world may still be poor a century hence,
so that our huge productive powers could be put to good
use. The question then is whether an equitable and efficient
distribution of wealth from rich nations to poorer ones will
be made under the aegis of a society that still abides by the
calculus of wealth, or whether it will not require the emer-

gence of new pillars of social belief and new directions of social motivation more closely attuned to the problems of an age of the administration, rather than the acquisition, of wealth.

The attainment of that age lies still in the future, although not so far as to be merely a vision at the horizon. Already the first embarrassments of an age of partial abundance are upon us, and already its arrival challenges the paraphernalia of capitalism to the very core. The economic agencies, the class privileges, the social conceptions of a society whose main purpose has been the accumulation of wealth are put to the test in an age that begins to seek the private realizations and the public attainments that are only possible in— but that go counter to the grain of—a society of wealth.*

Beyond that, the social usefulness of the underlying drive itself begins to wane in a society in which the advance and mastery of a gigantic technology will clearly be the first order of business. Acquisitiveness, not as a psychological propensity but as a social form of activity, thus begins to display its historic irrelevancy, just as the new drives of scientific and technical discovery and administration begin to assert their historic paramountcy. If the rich man—or better yet, the rich society—finally wins admission to heaven, I suspect it will be not because capitalists have pure hearts, but because scientists will have succeeded in breeding exceptionally thin and agile camels, and because technology has succeeded in making needles with very large and very wide eyes.

---

* Since writing this essay, the ecological crisis has challenged the acquisitive drive of capitalism from another quarter. See the final chapter of this book for an elaboration of that argument.

CHAPTER 3

Innocence Abroad

> As we rode into Magdala not a soul was visible. But the ring of the horses' hoofs roused the stupid population, and they all came trooping out—old men and old women, boys and girls, the blind, the crazy, and the crippled, all in a ragged, soiled, and scanty raiment, and all abject beggars by nature, instinct, and education. How the vermin-tortured vagabonds did swarm! How they showed their scars and sores, and piteously pointed to their maimed and crooked limbs, and begged with their pleading eyes for charity! . . .
>
> *The Innocents Abroad*

*I*t is the voice of Mark Twain which mocks the beggars of the Near East. He has previously had his fun with the cripples of Constantinople: the three-legged woman, the faceless dwarf, etc. But perhaps we should not be too shocked. After all, Mark Twain was writing almost a hundred years ago, when to many American eyes Asian poverty appeared as a kind of gigantic circus side show, an amusing grotesquerie. We no longer read *The Innocents Abroad* to learn about the state of the world in 1869; we read it to learn about the state of the American mind.

It seems a very far cry from the innocent eye of the nineteenth-century tourist to the knowing glance of the twentieth-century development expert. "Walk down the main street of Kasai village in the Congo," writes Paul Hoffman. "Look at the gaunt frames of the men and women—the swollen bellies of the children. This is hunger—with starvation just a yard away. Look at their eyes. As they meet yours, a glimmer of hope springs up. They cannot believe that you can see their plight and do nothing about it."

What has changed since Mark Twain's day are not so much the real conditions: these are all too depressingly the same. What is different are the subjective conditions, and specifically the American frame of mind. Where a Mark Twain chuckles, a Hoffman or a Galbraith draws in breath. Where Mark Twain looks for the outstanding "sights," they look for the hidden structures. Where he wants only to divert his readers, they want to instruct, alert, even alarm them. And not least, whereas Mark Twain never gave a thought as to what the "beggars by nature, instinct, and education" might think of his words, both Hoffman and Galbraith write with one eye cocked in the direction of the underdeveloped countries themselves.[1]

What they see and what they say is not fundamentally different: the American view of development is not signally affected whether one is an ex-Harvard professor serving as ambassador to India or an ex-businessman serving as Director of the United Nations Special Fund. Common themes, common stresses run through both books. The backward nations are in the throes of a desperate struggle to escape

1. *World Without Want* by Paul G. Hoffman and *Economic Development in Perspective* by John Kenneth Galbraith.

from the hopeless past. The richer nations must help. But help is not merely a matter of transferring money, as we once thought. Before the massive transfer of capital must come a period of intensive preparation. Education is no less a part of development than steel, and must precede or at least pace industrialization. Good government must be cultivated as assiduously as good land. Rigid preconceptions about the programming of development are apt to miscarry: countries differ in their needs, and at different stages in its development the *same* country differs in its needs. Development is impossible without planning, but planning is unlikely to make much headway without a considerable degree of autonomy for the productive units. Excellent suggestions, cogent warnings abound. The tone is mild but firm. The outlook is cautious but hopeful.

And yet, and yet—what is the note that reminds us of the past? It is not, of course, the brashness, the heartlessness, the uninterest of Mark Twain. Is it not, rather, an innocence which pervades the books of the twentieth century no less than those of a century ago—an innocence identifiable not so much by what is seen in each era as by what is not? Mark Twain, writing in the flush of the American spirit of the mid-1800's, cannot see the mountainous fact of underdevelopment looming over his landscape of beggars. Hoffman and Galbraith, writing in the flush of the American spirit of the mid-1900's, cannot see the mountainous fact of social revolution looming over their landscape of economic development.

Their innocence, in other words, is a failure to recognize that the central, inescapable, and indispensable precondition for "economic" development is political and social change on a wrenching and tearing scale. Economic development is not, alas, a mere matter of tactics to be decided among men of good will and then put into effect with all possible dispatch. It is, anterior to that, a contest among social classes. It is a process of institutional birth and institutional death. It is a time when power shifts, often violently and abruptly, a time when old regimes go under and new ones rise in their places. And these are not just the unpleasant side effects of development. They are part and parcel of the process, the very driving force of change itself.

But this is not the view of development that strikes the American eye today. So it is that Mr. Hoffman can write a primer on economic development and mention only in passing the words *land reform* and deal nowhere at all with the idea of political struggle, or that Mr. Galbraith can write a series of sophisticated essays on various aspects of the development process but leave unexamined the central question of who is to do the developing or of how is the enormous sacrifice and commitment necessary for development to be adduced and sustained. These are, of course, *political* questions, and as such they do not naturally fall within the view of the American expert on *economic* development. But that is just the point.

To be sure, there are mitigating circumstances. Ambassador Galbraith has here reproduced no more than the text of a few speeches he made in India, and he could scarcely be expected, in his official position, to dwell on such delicate and disruptive matters. So too there are reasons behind Mr. Hoffman's reticence. Like Galbraith, he is not only writing about development but he is striving at first hand to help it to take place, and what is more, he is doing so admirably and persistently in the face of endless discouragements. Hence we cannot expect him to go sounding off on revolutionary notes. He must confine himself to matters of description and prescription within a smaller focus, and this he does very well.

Nonetheless, even if certain distressing matters must be eschewed, what should be the general expectation in regard to economic development given us by so knowledgeable a man? "By 1970," writes Hoffman—in 1963—"perhaps twenty nations will have achieved self-sustaining economies. . . . By the year 2000, we can be living in a world that has overcome poverty—a world without want."

Are these valid goals to hold out to the readers of the industrially advanced—or the industrially backward—world, even assuming as Hoffman does that the rich nations will fully support the advance of the poor? Can the United States, with its core of military expenditures, be counted, in 1970, as among those twenty nations launched into "self-sustained" growth? Will the American Negro be freed from poverty by the year 2000? I would like to suggest these two goals, so infinitely much easier to engineer, so enormously much less tangled in social frictions and political bitterness, as proper bench marks by which to measure the feasibility of the global Great Ascent which Mr. Hoffman so blandly projects before us.

"We often had occasion to pity Americans whom we found traveling drearily among strangers with no friends to exchange pains and pleasures with," writes Mark Twain at the end of his happy voyage. "Whenever we were coming back from a land journey, our eyes sought one thing in the distance first—the ship—and when we saw it riding at anchor with the flag apeak, we felt as a returning wanderer feels when he sees his home. When we stepped on board, our cares vanished, our troubles were at an end . . . we always had the same familiar old stateroom to go to, and feel safe and at peace and comfortable again."

Thus the innocent tourist in 1869. Today the expert retires not to the haven of a ship but to the comfortable stateroom of his preconceptions. Looking out from his veranda, he has seen the banners of a distant parade about which he makes thoughtful observations, but his sheltered vantage point has saved him from the sight of the great juggernaut itself, carrying along its millions, crushing other millions, as it lurches majestically and dangerously down the road of history.

CHAPTER 4

The Anti-American Revolution

*T*he great lesson of the Vietnam war is now clear. It is that the mightiest nation in the world has not been able to defeat the forces of revolutionary nationalism in one of the smallest nations in the world. We may even yet work out the kind of settlement that will enable us to proclaim at least some kind of victory in the struggle against "aggression," but it is quite plain that the United States has lost the war. For the ultimate purpose of our intervention in Vietnam was not to beat a *national enemy*—no one ever accused North Vietnam of threatening our territorial integrity. It was to beat a *revolutionary force,* to demonstrate beyond a doubt that "wars of national liberation" would end in disaster for the revolutionaries.

Now, by a supreme irony, we have shown just the opposite. For what the Vietnam war has revealed above all else is the extreme difficulty of defeating a determined national revolutionary group. Inevitably this must both encourage the rise of such groups elsewhere and discourage our own future willingness to meet their force with counterforce. Thus if the Philippines explodes in an outraged revolt, as seems very probable in a nation where half the customs receipts disappear between the dock and the Treasury; or if guerrilla warfare on a large scale breaks out again in Guatemala, as seems entirely possible in view of the increased revolutionary activity there; or if India dissolves into linguistic parts, and these parts are taken over by revolutionary parties, as would certainly be the case in some areas; or if the muted civil war in Venezuela or Colombia or Bolivia or Northeast Brazil again assumes major proportions, it will not be so easy for the United States to intervene on the side of the existing governments. For the first rule of American politics in the next years will be: *No more Vietnams!*

But will revolutionary activity break out in these nations? For reasons that I shall spell out in this essay, I think it extremely likely, although it is easier to indicate the broad areas where revolution impends rather than the individual countries. I would think that by the year 2000 and possibly much sooner, we would find revolutionary governments installed, or formidable revolutionary armies fighting, in most of Asia, in at least a half-dozen Latin-American countries, and probably in a fair number of nations in West and Central Africa, and the Near East.

The prospect, in other words, is one of worldwide upheaval in which, retrospectively, the Vietnam war will have been only the first successful campaign. If this prospect comes about, it will present the United States with the gravest challenge of its national existence. It would entail nothing less than the risk of becoming embroiled in Vietnam-like situations in many countries at once. If it has proved almost unbearably costly to wage war against revolutionary nationalism in a nation of fifteen million, what will it be like trying to quell the forces of revolution that can call on the human resources of three continents?

There is no more pressing requirement for the American people than to consider what policies their nation can pursue to pass safely through this unprecedentedly dangerous era. But it is little use seeking to articulate policies until we have a clear idea of what it is that we are up against. And here there is a fundamental lesson that has yet to be learned about the origins of the revolution that threatens us.

We have been taught that the ultimate cause of the world-wide threat of revolution is the subversive and conspiratorial activities of communism. Now, although these activities have often been grossly exaggerated, they certainly exist, and there is no doubt that communist maneuvering can be discovered near the center of nearly every revolutionary situation. Yet to blame the danger of these explosive situations themselves on the presence of Communists is like blaming the inherent danger in a huge mass of exposed combustible materials on the possible presence of arsonists. The revolutions we must come to terms with would break out even if communism as an idea and as a political force disappeared from the face of the world tomorrow. For the harsh facts we have yet to acknowledge are these: (1) *in many countries of the underdeveloped world only revolutionary activity will rescue the populace from its unending misery, and* (2) *the United States has consistently opposed the kinds of revolutionary action that might begin such a rescue operation.* Thus the real tragedy of the coming decades is not that revolutionary action will be necessary, but that it is likely to have a bitter anti-American flavor because of our unwillingness to allow the forces of economic development to take their essential course.

This is an assertion that seems to fly in the face of the facts. No government among wealthy nations has tried harder to promote economic development than the United States. Our foreign-aid program may not be very large in relation to our capabilities, but it towers over the efforts of other Western nations, not to mention those of the Soviet Union. Moreover the struggle for economic development has captured the natural sympathies of the vast majority of Americans; indeed, the very slogan that we ourselves have coined for development—"the revolution of rising expectations"—conveys in itself our good will for the peoples struggling to escape from poverty.

All this is true. But the problem is that few Americans understand what the process of "economic development" entails, or what the "revolution of rising expectations" really means. To most of us, development is merely a matter of money with which we assume economic advancement is bought. Unfortunately, money is the last, if not the least, step in the development sequence. For the long climb out of backwardness is not merely a matter of getting "richer." It is first and foremost a matter of changing an entire society in ways that must go to the roots of its ordinary life and that are bound to shake or topple its basic structure of power and prestige.

Actually, we have had a glimpse of the difficulties and dangers in trying to initiate "economic development" in the problems we have encountered at home in Harlem or Watts. We have learned, for example, that an enormous gulf must be bridged between the people who have to "develop" and those to whom the guidance of development is entrusted. The business and government leaders of Caracas or Rio de Janeiro or Calcutta have little or no contact with the dirty, ignorant, primitive people of the urban and rural slums of their countries—in which live, however, not 10 or 20 percent, but 70 or 80 percent of the population. In turn, the inhabitants of the villages and urban slums regard the upper classes as representatives of a class whose only relation with themselves has been arrogant, exploitative, patronizing, or indifferent.

Second, both the slum and the underdeveloped areas smart under the constraints of absentee domination. We know of the resentment of the "radical" Negro against white-owned stores. Far greater is the resentment of the radical Asian, African, or Latin American against the foreign ownership of the main instruments of production in his country —the utilities, the manufacturing plants, railroads, plantations, or oil fields. To be sure, one can answer that the supply of native entrepreneurship is small and that these foreign companies introduce capital and expertise that would otherwise be lacking. But they introduce as well a steady drain of earnings out of the country, and a basic orientation of business interest that is geared at least as much to the needs of the corporate home office as to the requirements of its host nation.

Last, we find another similarity between ghetto and backward land that may help us visualize the problems of economic development. This is the population problem that cuts away at both milieus. At home the rolls of relief mount steadily as the city poor produce more children than can be easily absorbed into society. Abroad, this disproportion between the rate of production of impoverished human beings and their social absorption takes on horrendous dimensions. Each year we have watched Asia, the Near East, much of Africa and Latin America in a race between survival and starvation—a race that has already produced a devastating famine in India in 1967. By the year 2000 we shall have to run this race with twice as many human beings, and even with the brightest hopes for agricultural improvement, no one can face that prospect without flinching. Ex-President Ayub of Pakistan put the threat succinctly: "In ten years' time, human beings will eat human beings in Pakistan."

These are some of the obstacles to economic development—obstacles that are obscured behind the bright slogan of "the revolution of rising expectations." They make it clear that much more is needed to bring improvement to the backward areas than money, just as much more is needed in our slums. At home, moreover, we are dealing with a minority that is in some kind of touch with a prevailing culture into which most of its members would, if they could, gladly enter. Abroad we are dealing with an ingrown, suspicious peasantry that has little or no understanding or acceptance of the modern ways that produce "loose" women and "disrespectful" children and a snubbing disregard of the wisdom of the village elders. So, too, at home we have an upper class that, however insulated from the slums, does not find its social position fundamentally incompatible with slum clearance. Abroad the clearance of the vast rural slums requires that its beneficiaries—the landed ruling class—give up their power and position to another ruling group. And finally, whereas the population problem at home exacerbates the problem of bringing economic improvement to the slum, abroad it renders this problem unmanageable.

Thus although Harlem and Watts give us some insights into India and Brazil, the problems of the latter are a thousandfold larger and more intractable than those at home. That is why the changes needed to bring development to the backward areas are so far-reaching that they are hard to describe as "reforms." Take, for example, the question of land reform—the breakup of the vast semifeudal land holdings that everyone, including our government, recognizes as incompatible with development. In Latin America, according to Oscar Delgado, an official in the Inter-American Committee on Agricultural Development in Washington, "There are families who own more land than is occupied by a number of sovereign states. . . . Statistically speaking, Latin America has the highest index of concentrated rural property in the world."

To urge land "reform" on such a society is tantamount to a visitor from Mars urging stock "reform" on us—telling us that great social benefits would accrue from breaking up the concentration of two-thirds to three-fourths of all privately owned corporate stock that lies in the hands of the top two percent of American families. With how much enthusiasm would such a proposal be received in the United States and with how much carried out? Precisely the same response has greeted other proposals for land reform in Latin America.

But the trouble is not wholly that of upper classes who are unwilling to change the social system on which their power and prestige are based. There are other nations in the world—India is of course the prime example—where the terrible and persisting absence of necessary social change comes from the inability of mild men of goodwill to translate good intentions into effective deeds. Somehow a squabbling Congress, a nepotistic bureaucracy, and an overpowering atmosphere of futility have smothered every impetus to change, so that despite the intelligence and humane aspirations of the national leadership, we look with horror at the spectacle of the rotting poor who somehow cannot be housed or fed or put to work; at the world's largest collection of cattle, roaming through the country as an untouchable symbol of holiness and active agent of famine; at tens of thousands of still isolated villages where tens of millions of women remain in ignorance or fear of birth control.

It would be cruelly wrong to suggest that no progress has been made in the underdeveloped world. Compared with the past, giant strides have been taken. In Asia and Africa, millions of persons who, had you asked them to identify themselves a generation ago, would have answered that they were so and so of such and such village, now answer that they are Pakistani, or Algerian, or whatever: the dangerous but necessary infection of self-conscious nationalism has become virtually pandemic. So, too, stirrings of modernization have made their way into the remote hamlets of Asia and Latin America alike: radios bring news of events in the capital city and the outer world; the cinema stirs imaginations; visitors from the cities bring new seeds which, cautiously tried, often bring better crops; there is talk of a school; a road is improved; an irrigation dam is built.

These changes are important and cumulative, but they must not be magnified out of proportion. First, were there no such changes, the Malthusian dilemma would by now have pushed even more millions below the starvation line (as it is, an estimated 10,000 people a day die of malnutrition in the underdeveloped areas). Second, the sum total of all these changes has not been enough to accelerate the rate of economic growth. In Latin America as a whole, gross national product has grown by a *smaller* percentage in each successive five-year period between 1950 and 1965. Virtually nowhere in Southeast Asia or the Near East or Africa does output per capita show a strong steady upward trend.[1] And last and most important of all, there is no evidence that the people themselves have been roused from their torpor, no release of energies from the great stagnant reservoir of humanity that *is* the basic repository of backwardness itself.

Instead what we see in virtually every corner of the underdeveloped world is a terrible changelessness that it seems impossible to affect. What we call "economic development" is in truth little more than a holding action that has succeeded only in building up the dikes just enough to keep the

---

1. But what about the fabulous new agricultural techniques, such as the new seeds that yield up to twice the weight of output of present varieties? Our eager endorsement of technology as the cure for underdevelopment reveals all too clearly our failure to understand the social environment in which the process of change takes place. For the new seeds (in India and South America) are first used by the richer peasants. The poorer ones cannot afford to experiment for fear of starvation if the seed fails, or simply because, being poor, they are least "ready" for change. As a result the disparity in income between the upper stratum of peasants and the lowest widens. There is more food—but there is also more social discontent.

mounting population from washing away everything, not a movement that has invested life with a new quality. Change, insofar as it is being introduced, comes at a pace that is discouraging even to the most dedicated enthusiast. Thus we no longer hear the trumpets sound for the Alliance for Progress or the U.N. Development Decade. The outlook is for a continuation, no doubt with some small improvements, of the prevailing misery, filth, ill-health, and hunger for as long ahead as we can see.

This is not a "pessimistic" estimate. To be pessimistic would be to suggest a *worsening* of current trends—a cut in foreign aid, a petering out of the few birth-control programs that have begun, a collapse of foreign or domestic investment in the underdeveloped world because of growing unrest there, a deterioration rather than an improvement in the caliber of governments. An optimistic appraisal would assume the contrary of these things. A realistic appraisal, I think, assumes that matters will go on much as they have gone on—a forecast that offers little room for rising expectations on our part.

To this general outlook for a continuation of the prevailing hopelessness of the backward world we must now add one final, all-important exception. It is that the sapping inertia of the underlying populace *has* been overcome within the last half-century in a very few nations.

One of these is of course Russia, whose leap into modernity has been the most extraordinarily rapid social transformation in history. Another, still more striking, is China. Even more hopeless, corrupt, and miserable than Russia, China was the source of endless horror stories of peasants eating mud when the crops failed, of the sale of daughters into prostitution to ward off starvation, of the subhuman degradation of the "coolie," the ricksha boy, the city home-less. China, in a word, was like India. But that too has changed. In China, we no longer find the homeless on the street, or forced prostitution, or children deliberately mu-tilated to become appealing beggars, although we still find all of these things in India. Nor do we find corruption in government, or an inability to distribute food supplies in bad times so as to provide a fair ration for all. More sig-nificant, we see an all-important redirection of Chinese life away from the endlessly static past to a new future—a re-direction nowhere more dramatically expressed than in the spectacle of the youthful Red Guards indulging in the here-tofore unthinkable action of defying their elders. To be sure, as the Red Guard also symbolizes, China is a nation in a paroxysm of change that has brought much that is ugly, cruel, and mean. And yet, before we condemn it for its very obvious evils, let every reader ask himself into which society he would take his chances as an anonymous human being today—India or China?

Last, there is the case of Cuba, never so impoverished as the other two, but also afflicted with the curses of under-development in an uneducated rural proletariat and a cor-rupt city one. Every report from Cuba emphasizes that a tremendous effort is being made to eradicate these ills. Gambling and prostitution have disappeared in Havana. A great effort is being made in the countryside to bring education and agricultural reform. And if we may believe the testimony of articles both in *Look* magazine and in *The New York Times,* a new and genuine spirit of idealism and endeavor is to be found among the young.

I do not wish to rhapsodize over these countries in which life is still hard and harsh, and if one is an intellectual, often impossibly demeaning. Nor should one slight the important fact that China has not tackled its population problem and that Cuba has not yet built a well-functioning economy. Both nations may fail to bring about economic growth. Yet I would insist on one central achievement whose importance it is impossible to overstate. It is that these nations *have* succeeded in touching and bringing to life the deadened humanity that is the despair of the underdeveloped world. Even if they fail now, they have opened the way for a future assault that can succeed. One may fault the communist nations on many grounds, not least that of morality—and on that score I will have more to say later—but one must also admit that they have brought hope, enthusiasm, and effort to the common people of their lands. *Of how many other backward nations can this be said?*

Does this imply that only a communist government can bring about the revolution of rising expectations that is indeed the foundation on which development must rest?

This is not the conclusion I wish to urge. There is no reason why noncommunist revolutionary movements could not carry out a program of mass awakening, as happened to a limited extent in the Mexican and Turkish revolutions. Thus it is not communism, either as a system of philosophy or as a particular party, that makes the crucial difference, but a political movement that has the courage, conviction, and ruthless energy to carry through a program of modernization from top to bottom.

What is the galvanic force of such a movement? It lies first in the overthrow of an existing regime that is unable or unwilling to change the social order on which it rests. But that is only the initial stage in a developmental revolution, as contrasted with a purely political one. Next, such a movement must move with the full power of an authoritarian will to impose a program of change—often unwanted change—upon the very people in whose name the revolution has been waged—the underlying peasantry. Finally, it must bring to bear whatever economic compulsion is needed to mount the massive redeployments and concentrations of labor that will be needed to move the economy off dead center.

In this painful process, the spread and degree of development that can be accomplished depend very largely on the willingness and ability of the revolutionary group to press relentlessly for change. It is for this reason that democracy and capitalism are not instruments of the revolutionary impulse, for there are certain changes that neither one permits even when they are essential for modernization. For instance, our own national goal of racial equality—a change that might be regarded as part of our own modernization—has been seriously impeded by the democratic process of consulting the will of the majority. How fast can one bring equality when large numbers—perhaps even majorities—do not wish to have it brought? So, too, our ability to raze and rebuild the slums is crippled by our insistence on relying on a market mechanism and on deferring to prerogatives of private property, with the result that urban renewal has come to a virtual halt. It is not surprising, then, that revolutionary parties, facing emergencies of far greater seriousness than anything we must deal with at home, utilize authority and command, and do not brook democratic dissent or rely on market incentives.

Thus revolution, authoritarianism, and collectivism are often the *only* instruments by which essential social changes can be made. But having stated this as a generalization, let us now modify and soften the case as it applies to many individual nations. One need hardly say, for instance, that the prognosis for revolutionary change does not apply to Europe, where communism is an agent not at all for modernization but rather for political retrogression. But even in the backward world it would be wrong to deny the possibility of a more gradual and less traumatic evolution in some instances. In Africa, for example, many new nations are now undergoing the first trials of nationhood, including above all that of creating national consciousness and loyalties where only tribal affiliations existed before. These countries may experience their share of coups and turmoil, but it is unlikely that they will constitute fertile ground for mass revolutionary activity until a genuine national community has been forged. And perhaps by that time a workable "African socialism" will permit the rigors of a revolutionary movement to be by-passed.

In Latin America the situation is much more revolution-prone, but even here some important nations may carry out their internal transformations without wholesale revolution. Argentina, with its relatively high standard of living and its low rate of population growth, may be one such; Chile— provided that the reforms of President Eduardo Frei are not blocked by the landholding and foreign interests—is another. As we have already said, Mexico, with a bloody revolution of national identity and foreign expropriation behind it, should be a third. In Asia, the long-run outlook is perhaps least propitious of all, and yet even here a few nations may bring development to pass without resort to violent upheavals. Moreover, even in these most labile areas, it is unlikely that revolution impends immediately. The incumbent governments in Latin America have strong military forces at their disposal (and are using them); the peasants in Asia are as yet largely unorganized and apathetic. Hence the outlook is not for uprisings everywhere, but for a gradually mounting pressure, a growing instability, as the combination of weak and inept governments and cancerous population growth works its fatal results.

Finally, taking the world as a whole there is always the possibility that a heroic effort to bring birth control to the masses, especially through the use of the plastic intrauterine device, might slow down the Malthusian timetable sufficiently to allow slower processes of change to work their way. Yet realism tells us that such a program will take decades to carry out; less than 5 percent of the world's women use the pill or the plastic insert.

Last, when revolution comes, the leadership may spring from many sources other than Communist party membership. Angry and disillusioned army officers, idealistic middle-class intellectuals, even peasant guerrilla leaders, may provide the nuclei that seed the clouds of potential disaffection. A movement that begins as a mere palace coup may find itself carried on its own momentum into a revolutionary trajectory. Thus revolution and communism are by no means synonymous, although it is undeniably true that Communists are working for and eager to lead a revolutionary thrust.

Whatever the leadership, however, it is clear that some sort of authoritarian nationalist socialism will be the vehicle of change. Whether or not this socialism will become communist—that is, whether it will accept the dogmas and doctrines of Marxism and Maoism or seek active alliance with Russia and China—depends on many events internal and external to the nation in question (including our own actions). The nationalism that is so powerful a motive force in revolutions tends to drive the leadership away from communism because of its danger of vassalage to a great state; the need for moral support and technical advice may drive it toward accepting or concocting some version of the communist catechism.

But it is important to realize that we should not expect the attitude of a noncommunist revolutionary regime toward the United States to be very different from that of a communist one. For it is the unhappy fact that the United States in recent years has thrown its support against *all* revolutions and provided its backing for *all* groups that have opposed revolutions, regardless of the merits of the one or the demerits of the other—the scandal of our Dominican invasion, our Guatemalan "success," and our Cuban "failure," our backing of the militarist Castelo Branco in Brazil, and now our intervention in Vietnam all being instances in point. In the essential process of social surgery that must be performed if many backward nations are to be brought to life, it is the United States—for good reasons or bad—that delays the necessary stroke of the blade. That is why the revolution of economic development must become an anti-American revolution unless the United States changes its ways.

But how to change our ways? How to cope with the force of economic development? To date we have lived with it in a curiously schizophrenic way. On the one hand we have been the leading agent of international assistance through the Agency for International Development (AID), the Peace Corps, Food for Peace, etc. On the other hand we have been the leader of the antirevolutionary forces of the world.

We have not, of course, meant to be schizophrenic. The possible connection between revolution and development has never been pointed out to us, particularly since the modernizing efforts of communism have been obscured by our steady emphasis on its repressive elements. Nor have we meant to oppose development in backing right-wing or center governments of Latin America or Asia. We continue to believe that development can take place gradually and peaceably, preferably with governments that "understand" the needs of the American business community. Hence our schizophrenia has ultimately been the price of self-deception —of unwillingness to confront the demanding process of development fearlessly or to acknowledge the inadequacies of our client governments to initiate deep and rapid social change. But now, if my prognosis is correct, this self-deception will be increasingly difficult to practice. As the pressures of revolutionary change build up, partly as a result of the bankruptcy of American policy in Vietnam, we shall have to face more squarely the harsh calculus of the developmental process. Indeed, the rise of the development revolution will force us to choose among one of three courses for the future.

The first of these is a continuation of our present policy. This will commit us to determined antirevolutionary activity, both political and military, wherever radical elements threaten to overthrow existing governments. I will not argue the consequences of this policy except to point out again that it presents the likelihood of a succession of Vietnam wars for the indefinite future.

An imaginable alternative is a volte-face in policy that would turn us away from all contact with the underdeveloped world. This would entail the creation of a fortress America, without diplomatic or economic—or direct military—contact with any revolutionary nations, defensively turned away from the inimical changes taking place in the underdeveloped continents. In the end this may be a policy to which we are forced to retreat, but it presents obvious dangers to the United States. An isolationist America, at bay in a revolutionary world, would bring forth the worst tendencies in this country, encouraging every superpatriot, fanning the fires of suspicion and fancied subversion, and submerging the humanitarian impulses that are the best side of the American national character.

The third policy is by far the most difficult to pursue, but is ultimately the only constructive course to follow. It is a policy of neutrality toward the revolutionary movement— a neutrality that ceases to oppose all revolutions as such, although not ceasing to differentiate between revolutionary regimes that we can actively support and those that we cannot. Such a policy does not ask us to endorse regimes that are bitterly anti-American in utterance or intolerable in behavior, nor does it prevent the political and military support of conservative government regimes threatened by subversion or submersion from neighboring states, *provided that these governments have the support of their people as a whole*.

But it would force us to change our present attitudes and actions in several regards. First, it would call for an immediate halt to military aid to reactionary regimes and for a cessation of clandestine activity against revolutionary movements. Second, it would require an acceptance of some form of revolutionary nationalist socialism as the political and economic order most suited to guide many developing nations in their desperately hard initial stages of change. Third, it would permit the continuation of humanitarian programs of food and medical aid, as well as technical assistance of a nonmilitary kind, for all governments, revolutionary or not, provided that reasonable standards of international behavior were met.

I need not point out the problems of steering such a course —of determining which revolutionary governments were acceptable and which governments under pressure warranted our support. But these problems would certainly be less than those encountered under a policy that recognized no revolutionary governments and that supported all antirevolutionary ones. Indeed, if such a pragmatic and noninterventionist policy could be pursued in the future, a kind of victory could yet be snatched from the otherwise pointless and hideous sacrifices of the Vietnam war. For then it could be said some day that this war was for American foreign policy what the Great Depression was for domestic policy.

However difficult to carry out abroad, the real difficulties of such a policy of neutrality are apt to be encountered at home. For in changing our stance from one of belligerent opposition to one of neutrality, recognition, and selective aid, we would be sure to hear two frightening accusations from many groups in America.

The first of these would be that we were aiding and abetting an international aggressive movement whose rise would eventually engulf us. Frightening though it is, this accusation could be answered with some degree of assurance. For one thing, the alternative—military action abroad —has been revealed by the Vietnam war to be a policy that can bleed us white. For another, it is increasingly evident that communism is no more of a unified world force than capitalism ever was, and that the rise of many intensely nationalistic revolutionary states is much more apt to result in internecine warfare among themselves than in military action against us. Let us recall the tensions between the Soviet Union and its satellites, between the Soviet Union and China, and between both nations and Cuba when the cry of a communist "bloc" is raised. And last, there is simply the enormous disparity in industrial and military strength between America and Europe (and perhaps the Soviet Union on our side as well), and the populous but impoverished masses of the revolutionary world. A revolutionary world will assuredly be an extraordinarily dangerous, thin-skinned, and rhetorically aggressive environment in which to make our way; but the specter of concerted military action of its impoverished governments against the rich nations an ocean's distance away is a fantasy that should not be difficult to destroy.

Not so easy to allay is another alarm that would accompany a policy of neutralism. It is that in acquiescing in the rise of communist (or even noncommunist) regimes, we were condoning evil for expediency's sake.

This is not an accusation that can be readily countered by an appeal to reason. There is a strain of fundamentalism among sections of the American people that regards communism as the ultimate evil with which no compromise is imaginable and toward which no attitude but fear and loathing is possible.

It is true enough that communism has been a perpetrator

of evil and it is all too likely that more evil will be committed in its name (or in whatever name is inscribed on the banners the revolutionists of development will carry). Yet if one cannot and should not seek to minimize the weight on that side of the scale of human suffering, one should also have the courage to pile up whatever weights belong on the other side.

This is not an operation we have carried out honestly. We tend to count carefully each corpse attributable to the terrorists, guerrillas, or avowed soldiers of revolutionary action, but to ignore the bodies of those who perish because of the actions of our own side, military or not. To whom, for example, should be charged the permanent and irreversible mental and physical stunting of Latin America's children that follows from an inability to alter the established social order? To whom shall we debit the grisly corpses, living and dead, in the streets of Bombay? In what account shall we enter the hunger of those who live within sight of the expensive restaurants of New Delhi or Lima or Hong Kong?

One does not know which way the scales of history would tilt if all the evils attributable to both sides were piled on their respective balances. But there is the uncomfortable suspicion that ours might not necessarily be the lighter side of the scale. What exists in most of the world beyond our borders is a condition of human indignity and degradation that verges on the unspeakable. If we are to set ourselves against a movement, however violent or cruel, that has demonstrated its ability to lead such men out of their misery for at least the first critical stage of the journey, we must at least offer something as good in its place. At this juncture it is the shameful fact that we have nothing as good, and worse than that, have ranged ourselves against nearly every movement that might have led men toward a better life, on the grounds of our opposition to communism. Now the question is whether America will take its ultimate stand on the side of humanitarianism or moralism, self-reliance or fear, open-mindedness or dogma. The challenge goes to the very core of this nation—its structure of power and economic interest, its capacity for reasoned discussion, its ultimate inarticulate values. It is not alone the life and death of anonymous multitudes that is weighed in the balance, but that of the American conscience, as well.

CHAPTER 5

Reflections on the Future of Socialism

I

Some years ago, writing on the prospects for American capitalism, I began by asserting that the capitalist system, whatever the strains and stresses to which it would be subject, bade fair to remain the dominant system in America and Western Europe during our lifetimes, and that any serious attempt to project large-scale social trends should begin from that premise.[1] Now I should like to undertake a similar speculative examination of the prospects for socialism, for I also take it as a datum that some form of socialism will be the predominant economic system in most of the rest of the

1. See *The Limits of American Capitalism*, Ch. 1, pp. 3–4.

world during our lifetimes, and that even in Europe and America it will constitute the image of a society against which capitalism will be measured by its critics.

But no sooner do we raise the question of the prospect for socialism than we encounter a difficult problem. It is the problem of deciding what we mean by socialism. How is one to speak of the prospects of a "system" that presumably embraces Norway as well as Soviet Russia, or that is expressed by the ideas of Bernard Shaw as well as of Mao Tse-tung? If there is a single identificatory mark of socialism, it is certainly not immediately visible on the surface.

Yet, at second look, perhaps we can find a way of penetrating the surface variety of socialist institutions and thought to reach a common core. For it is not socialism alone that presents us with a confusing heterogeneity of systems, but capitalism as well; and yet we feel perfectly assured in applying the common term "capitalist" to worlds as far apart as those depicted by Sinclair Lewis and Thomas Mann, or Faulkner and Proust. And there is a very good reason for our generalizing approach to the societies of capitalism. This is the presence within all of them of a common set of institutions and ideas—the institution of the basically uncontrolled market system and the ideas of the legitimacy of the private ownership of the means of production. In a word, we find a *business system* at the core of all capitalist societies, no matter how diverse their other characteristics. Whatever their incompatibilities in culture or lifestyles, Buddenbrooks and Babbitt were both businessmen, and as such they understood and shared important common activities and values and goals.

Hence the obvious question is whether there is not, within the variety of socialist nations, a similar core of institutions and ideas that might play the same identificatory role as does business within the many forms of capitalism. The question has an obvious answer: one element of the socialist system must certainly be the structural element that we find in all socialist societies, corresponding to the market system in capitalism. This is the predominance of some form of *planning*.

But this structural element is by no means enough in itself to provide an infallible identification for socialism— after all, one can find some degree of planning in all capitalist nations and some evidences of the market in all socialist societies. Hence we must add a critical second attribute by which socialism can be identified. This is the common presence of a guiding socialist *ideology*, corresponding to the business ideology in capitalism.

What is the content of this socialist ideology? It will help if we begin by differentiating it from that of capitalism. I think it is fair to say that the beliefs of the business system mainly concern themselves with the justification of the prevailing economic order, especially the institution of private property and of the relatively free market. To put it differently, no capitalist nation or philosopher or economist has any grand designs for the fundamental reshaping of society through capitalism. Certainly capitalism aims at the material well-being of its constituents, but equally certainly it entertains no thought that the pursuit of well-being will alter the basic class character of the system or modify the competitive or acquisitive drives from which the system derives its momentum. That is what it means to say that capitalist thought is essentially conservative.

By way of contrast, socialist thought is primarily concerned with bringing into existence a social order very different from that which it finds in the world. Thus its use of planning—or, for that matter, of the market mechanism—is guided by purposes wholly at variance with those of capitalism. Capitalism uses the market or planning to service and support a social system in which the prosperity of the capital-owning class is a central aim of economic policy. Socialism not only denies the legitimacy of this underlying conception, but it intends the instrumentalities of plan and market to create an egalitarian society in which no class may gain the strategic position conferred by the ownership of society's productive assets. Further, far from ignoring the effects of economic progress on classes and motives, as does capitalism, socialism intends progress to lead to the creation of a wholly new kind of society, free of invidious striving and built on motives of cooperation and confraternity.

It need hardly be said that there is a long step between socialist declaration and socialist reality. In addition, let us reiterate the point with which we began—that the variation among socialist nations is very great. Clearly, the mere presence of similar institutions and ideologies no more produces a common existential quality under socialism than it does under capitalism—indeed, life in "socialist" Yugoslavia may well resemble life in "capitalist" Italy more than it does that in "socialist" China.

What, then, is the usefulness of emphasizing the common features of planning and ideology? The answer is that these features make it possible to talk about the future of socialism. For the central presence of planning and its ideology has as important a consequence for socialism as the presence of the business system for capitalism. It is that within each type of society *these common elements give rise to common kinds of problems.*

Thus in reflecting on the prospects for, say, capitalism in Japan and America, it is necessary to bear in mind that for all the dissimilarity of their social and cultural environments, both are societies that must contend with the peculiar problems of a business structure and a business ideology. And in the same way, when we attempt to reason prospectively with regard to the outlook for the socialist nations, we must recognize that underlying their varied internal and external challenges, all of them must cope with problems characteristic of the institution of planning and endemic to the ideological goal in whose service the activity of planning is carried on.

II

Our aim, in the following pages, will be mainly to explore the nature of these problems of socialism. But we must begin by bringing to the fore an aspect of the problem of socialism that complicates any discussion of its future trajectory. It is that socialism in our day must be considered with reference to two very different kinds of societies in two very different settings. On the one hand, socialism appears as a powerful force for change in the most backward and under-developed countries in the world; on the other hand, as an agency or as an ideal for social change in the most advanced and wealthy nations.

It is hardly surprising that the problems associated with planning or with the realization of the socialist vision are not at all alike in these two radically contrasting environments; the analogy is with the striking contrast between the problems of primitive capitalism, with its grim struggle between the classes, and those of advanced capitalism, with its vast middle class obedient to an advertising culture. The difference, however, is that whereas the problems associated with nascent capitalism are now largely relegated to the history books, those of "early" socialism exist side by side with those of "late" socialism. Thus we cannot discuss the problems of socialism without distinguishing between the form these problems take in each of its two contemporary manifestations.

Of the two, it is easier to describe the problems of socialism in the underdeveloped nations. I have written previously on this, so here I shall be very brief. The situation in most of the backward nations today can only be described as desperate. Present standards of living exceed subsistence requirements by so little that the least misfortune threatens catastrophe on a giant scale. Strongholds of foreign capital inhibit the redirection of the energies of the people. Incompetent or indifferent regimes seem unable or unwilling to galvanize their stagnant societies. And above this nightmarish landscape in which everything moves in slow motion towers an oncoming tidal wave of population advancing with horrendous speed: within the next ten years the number of women in the most fertile age brackets will double.

In these circumstances, the task of those socialist governments that have come to power, or of those that will, is clearly marked. It is to place their nations on a war footing against existing conditions, to mobilize whole populations for production, to attack the psychological as well as the physical handicaps of the backward areas with all the zeal and ardor of a military campaign.

Moreover, there is little doubt that revolutionary socialism, utilizing all-out planning, can accomplish these objectives. The prodigies of the Russian advance, the extraordinary achievements in the modernization of China, the remarkable arousal of the Cuban people, all testify beyond possibility of doubt that "war planning" can realize its giant, but essentially simple, aims.[2] That this kind of massive planning is likely to be accompanied by enormously costly errors, or that it may, from time to time, imperil the success of the whole development effort through an excess of mindless zeal, is also to be expected. Yet the most serious and deeply rooted problems of planning in the backward world are not likely to be these perhaps inevitable mistakes of planning. Rather, as the examples of Russia and China and Cuba all show, *the endemic problem of planning in the underdeveloped nations resides in the noneconomic measures required to bring about the economic changes that revolutionary socialism so imperatively seeks.*

For the objectives of economic development do not lie, like a military citadel, exposed to the thrust of a single daring campaign. On the contrary, the development assault is better likened to a long grueling march through a hostile hinterland. The real resistance to development comes not from the old regimes, which can be quickly overcome, but from the masses of the population who must be wrenched from their established ways, pushed, prodded, cajoled, or threatened into heroic efforts, and then systematically denied an increase in well-being so that capital can be amassed for future growth. This painful reorientation of a whole culture,

2. Let me cite the three most objective sources I know to buttress these assertions. On Russian growth, Richard Moorsteen and Raymond Powell, *The Soviet Capital Stock, 1929–1962* (also Charles K. Wilber, *The Soviet Model and the Underdeveloped Countries*); on Chinese modernization, Barry Richman, *Industrial Society in Communist China;* on the Cuban effort, Wassily Leontieff, *New York Review of Books,* August 21, 1969.

judging by past experience, will be difficult or impossible to
attain without measures of severity; and when we add the
need to maintain a fervor of participation long beyond the
first flush of spontaneous enthusiasm, the necessity for
stringent limitations on political opposition and for forcible
means of assuring economic cooperation seems virtually
unavoidable.

To be sure, one must not overgeneralize as to this grim
prospect. As with the not unrelated distortions of life imposed under the aegis of early capitalism, the extent of the
deforming pressures of early socialism will vary from one
milieu or regime to another. Some nations, unfortunate in
their resource endowments or in their political connections
with the industrialized nations, may be forced to undergo a
more or less thoroughgoing totalitarian transition. Others,
better endowed or better connected, may pass through the
thirty or fifty years of the modernizing transformation with
a minimum of repression.

In general, however, when we seek to project the problems of socialism in the underdeveloped areas, we cannot
sidestep the probability that intellectual stiflement, political
repression, and enforced social conformity will figure prom-
inently among them. Let me be quite explicit that when the
alternatives of such a disciplined existence are degradation,
misery, and premature death, the exercise of sternness and
indoctrination appears in a very different light from that of
an arbitrary and capricious tyranny. Nonetheless, the exercise of these measures, however necessary to assure the
success of the development effort, is likely to affect the
future of the nations who must suffer them no less severely
than the hated influence of imperialism affected their past.
When we look to that future and inquire as to the outlook

for socialism in the backward lands, it is necessary to recognize that it is likely to emerge both as the salvation of its otherwise doomed people, and also as the source of a moral and intellectual infection from which it may take generations to recover.

III

However uncertain its outcome, it is at least clear what the general objectives of revolutionary socialist planning must be in the underdeveloped areas. But the matter gets much more complicated when we now begin to look into the problems of socialist planning at the other end of the spectrum—in the advanced nations where the modernization process is already complete.

Here it may help if we quickly review the history of the problem before examining its present-day characteristics. It is interesting to note that the very identification of planning as an intrinsic aspect of socialism is a relatively modern development. Before the Russian Revolution, the main concern of the leaders and theoreticians of socialism was largely historical—namely, how a new social order would emerge from the conflicts within an old one. Not until an actual socialist society had come into existence did the question of planning, only glancingly referred to by Marx and airily dismissed by Lenin, assume the central position of importance that it occupies today.[3] And not surprisingly,

3. In a famous passage in *State and Revolution* (Ch. 5, p. 4) Lenin described the activities of administering a socialist state as having been "*simplified* by capitalism to the utmost, till they have become the extraordinarily simple operations of watching, recording and issuing receipts, within the reach of anybody who can read and write and knows the first four rules of arithmetic."

shortly thereafter came an attack on planning as the Achilles' heel of a socialist system. Indeed, the most intellectually respectable criticism of socialism in the mid-1930's was the effort of Ludwig von Mises and Friedrich Hayek to destroy the credibility of socialism as a desirable social order, not by inveighing against its ideals or its excesses, but by demonstrating that the economic system on which it was based would not work.

In brief, their criticism was based on the contention that socialism was intrinsically unable to achieve a *rational* economic order—that is, a system in which all the factors of production were employed as efficiently as possible—because it lacked one critical mechanism: a market in which capital could be valued by the free offers of owners of capital and by the free bids of would-be hirers of capital. Since by definition there could be no private ownership of capital, no free market price for it could ever be ascertained. As a result, the only way of deciding which enterprises were to have capital, and which were not, was perforce the essentially arbitrary decision of some Central Planning Board. Such a system, it was presumed, could not long endure.

This line of attack against socialism did not fare very well. In the mid-1930's it was effectively demolished by Oscar Lange, the brilliant Polish economist then at Harvard. Lange demonstrated in two incisive articles that Mises had failed to see that a Central Planning Board could indeed plan rationally for the simple reason that it would receive exactly the same information from a socialized economic system as did entrepreneurs under a market system.[4] The only difference was that the Board would not learn about

4. *Review of Economic Studies,* October, 1936 and February, 1937, subsequently published in *On the Economic Theory of Socialism,* 1938.

the condition of relative scarcity or plenty of capital goods or other commodities by price changes, as under capitalism, but by the building-up or running-down of inventories. That is, when a good was underpriced, instead of its price going up, as in a free market, the planners would discover that supplies of the good were being depleted faster than they were being replaced. All the Board would then have to do was to raise the price until the level of inventories was again constant. As a result, it could allocate its resources quite as efficiently as any capitalist system. In fact, the allocation of capital (or other factors) arrived at in this way by a socialist state would not only be rational, but would be in many ways the *same* as that of a market system. The main differences would lie in the ability of the Board to supply articles of public consumption (such as education or parks or welfare services) on a more generous scale than in a laissez-faire system, and in its ability to set a higher rate of saving-and-investment than might be forthcoming under an uncontrolled system. But since a major criticism against laissez faire was precisely its failure to provide adequate public services or to generate a sufficiently high rate of growth, these departures from the market idea seemed certain to enhance rather than to diminish social well-being.

Indeed, Lange quickly shifted from the defensive to the offensive. Not only would a planned economy meet the criteria for rationality, but its superior performance would soon reveal the outmoded inadequacy of a free enterprise economy. *"[T]he real issue,"* Lange wrote in italics, *"is whether the further maintenance of the capitalist system is compatible with economic progress."* [5] Or as Benjamin Lippincott wrote in 1938 in the introduction to the little

5. *Ibid.,* p. 110.

book in which Lange's articles appeared, "Where many under a capitalist economy must choose between a coat and a pair of shoes, under a socialist, many could choose between a radio and a telephone." [6]

More than a generation has now elapsed since the Lange articles appeared, and it should be possible to pass some sort of judgment on the debate. And the first judgment seems to be the irrelevance of the problem itself.[7] It is true, of course, that the absence of a market for capital can distort planning efforts—the Soviet predilection for huge and uneconomical dams and factories during their first Five Year Plans reflected their failure for many years to include a charge for capital in their projected industrial enterprises. But the obvious irrationality of this neglect of capital was eventually recognized, and a charge for capital was thereafter instituted.

But the whole question has an air of unreality. For what is the value of "rationality" as a criterion of economic performance? Are we to judge the Russian planning effort irrational because it has sacrificed present consumption for future growth to a far greater degree than the sacrificing generation might have voted for, had it been given the oppor-

---

6. *Ibid.*, p. 32.

7. It is interesting to note that in an article written toward the end of his life, Lange declared that were he to compose his famous articles on the possibility of rational planning again, he would give the problem much shorter shrift. For the computer, Lange believed, would give the Planning Board even *better* information than the market was capable of, especially with regard to long-term planning. "The market process with its cumbersome *tâtonnements* appears old-fashioned. Indeed, it may be considered as a computing device of the pre-electronic age" ("The Computer and the Market," in *Socialism, Capitalism and Economic Growth*, ed. C. H. Feinstein, p. 158).

tunity, but not, in all likelihood, to a greater degree than future generations would have voted for, if they could have? Per contra, are we to deem the American economy rational because it obediently provides its consumer markets with often trivial goods while it starves its housing market, or its central cities?

Clearly the trouble with rationality is that it has two meanings. On the one hand, it implies "reasonableness"—an attribute that is often glaringly absent under the market disposition of things as well as under a planned disposition. On the other hand, rationality also means that we will conserve the scarce resources of society by applying them where the need is greatest. That might seem to be a definition identical with "reasonableness," except for one thing: in a market society, "need" is determined by the existing distribution of income and wealth. An economy that produces lavishly for the rich and meanly for the poor is therefore "rational" in the sense that it is devoting its resources to those uses for which the greatest market demand exists, but it is hardly rational in the sense of being reasonable or just.[8]

Lange himself sensed that the basic problem was not really that of rationality at all. *"The real danger of socialism,"* he wrote (again in italics), *"is that of a bureaucratization of economic life."* [9] It is true that he raised the problem almost to dismiss it—bureaucratization would happen in any event, he thought, and there would actually be a better chance of controlling it under socialism because "officials subject to democratic control seem preferable to private corporation executives who are practically responsible to

8. Economists will recognize as well that whereas it is easy to specify what a rational distribution means in a static economy, it is impossible to do so when we deal with an economy growing over time.

9. Lange, *On the Economic Theory of Socialism, op. cit.,* p. 109.

nobody" [10]—but at least he saw that the test of socialist planning would be provided by criteria very different from those of a textbook on microeconomic perfection.

It need hardly be said that the experience of socialist planning, especially in the Soviet Union and Eastern Europe, has amply confirmed Lange's fears. For decades Lange's plan for a market-based socialism was ignored or dismissed as heresy, while socialist bureaucracies proved themselves increasingly incapable of handling their enormous ministries. Retrospectively, it is now far from clear whether corporation executives "who are practically responsible to nobody" do not find themselves under greater necessity to combat the stagnation of bureaucracy than socialist factory managers who find themselves personally responsible to a bureaucrat. The lesson of the postwar socialist experience is that the mechanism of planning is much more effective in laying in the foundations for an industrial society than in administering such a society after it has been brought into being. The more tightly linked the industrial activities of an economy, the more numerous its nodes of interdependence, the more problems does the planning apparatus encounter—not necessarily in the strictly economic form of irrational allocations of goods, but in the guise of low morale and productivity, frequent bottlenecks and partial breakdowns, faulty delivery schedules, poor quality of output, etc. As Paul Sweezy has commented with regard to the Soviet sphere in 1968, "Mass apathy, faltering productivity, economic stagnation—these and other symptoms of impending crisis were visible throughout the region." [11]

Thus the debate on socialist planning has come to a curi-

10. *Ibid.*, p. 110.
11. *Monthly Review*, October, 1968, p. 11.

ous conclusion. If the theoretical dispute has been settled in favor of socialism, the practical question seems to have gone the other way. On balance, the giant corporations of capitalism seem to have outperformed the lumbering ministries of production. This does not mean, however, that socialism has met an impassable barrier in the form of an inherent limit imposed by its planning capabilities. On the contrary, it has only brought about a belated move in every advanced socialist nation in the direction urged by Lange— away from centralized toward decentralized planning, and in particular away from the directives of a monolithic Central Planning Board toward the autonomy and flexibility of a market-based system. In the Soviet Union we have the much-publicized reforms of Liberman, in Czechoslovakia those of Ota Šik (at least until the Russian invasion), in Yugoslavia the adoption of a virtual "laissez-faire" market system in which the individual firm is run as a profit-making enterprise that vanishes via bankruptcy if it fails to meet the test of market viability, and in which the reach of central planning has been steadily reduced in scope.

Thus, ironically enough, socialist planning has been able to survive the difficulties inherent in the supervision of a complex industrial state only by reverting to the very market system whose shortcomings it was originally intended to redress. And yet, socialism has passed one test only to face another. The use of the market mechanism has unquestionably rescued socialism from a severe functional crisis. The question must now be faced as to whether it has done so by ceasing to be socialist.

IV

Why should the market mechanism constitute a threat to socialism? The answer takes us back to the purposes for which planning exists under socialism. And among those purposes, it will be remembered, was the goal of equality, the ideal of a society in which men were no longer unfairly dealt their chances in life by virtue of their unequal access to the prerogatives of property.

Is the market intrinsically tied to this condition of inequality? The question is not an easy one to answer. On the one hand, there seems no more reason why the market cannot be used for socialist ends under a socialist state than why planning cannot be used for capitalist ends under a capitalist state. On the other hand, just as the mere presence of planning poses a sharp challenge, both structurally and ideologically, to capitalism, so the introduction of the market poses its inescapable problems for socialism.

Essentially the difficulty lies in the fact that in a market-run society, as we have seen, it is the distribution of purchasing power that sets the effective demands to which social effort will cater. But this raises a deep-seated problem for a socialist order. For if dollar votes are to shape the purposes for which social activity is carried on, it is important that these votes be distributed in accord with some principle of socialist equity. Nor is it difficult to discern what that principle should be. By every tenet of socialist belief in the inherent equality of men as human beings, there is a strong inherent bias toward a distribution of dollar voting power that will minimize the difference between one man's power

to influence the outcome of the economic process and another's. To put it differently, there is a deep socialist belief
in the propriety of income equality, perhaps tempered by
social allowances for age, family size, etc.[12]

But the trouble with this solution is that incomes serve
another purpose, even in a socialist society, beside that of
constituting the source of the demand for goods and services. Incomes also constitute the rewards for labor; and
insofar as labor has different degrees of difficulty, danger
or unpleasantness, skill and so on, it must be expected to
command different rewards. Were this not the case, it would
be exceedingly difficult for any economy that depended on
the market to organize its production effectively. If skilled
labor were paid no more than common labor, there would
neither be any incentive for factory managers to economize
on the former, nor much incentive for workers to undertake
training that would ordinarily lead to a higher income.

Hence there are powerful reasons why a market society,
socialist or other, must use a hierarchy of remunerations.
But whereas this solves the problem of efficiency, it raises
awkward questions of ideology. Is a society that permits or
deliberately encourages differentials in income truly "socialist"? Is not the moral basis of socialism impaired when one
man, who happens to be more adept or intelligent, is allowed
to enjoy a higher standard of living than one who is not,
although the latter may be more loving, or loyal, or more
dedicated to the ideals of socialism?

If these questions should be brushed aside as smacking of
impractical idealism, there is another reason to fear the
inequality of rewards—to wit, that in allowing income differences to exist, a socialist society will be reintroducing,

12. See A. P. Lerner, *The Economics of Control,* Ch. 3.

wittingly or otherwise, the very institution of class privilege against which it presumably struggles. At least in the eyes of some socialist critics, the emergence of a genuinely autonomous market sector (as in Yugoslavia) signals nothing less than a "peaceful transition from socialism to capitalism." The fear of these theoreticians is that the recrudescence of the profit motive as the driving force of society will lead inexorably to the reconstitution of the factory manager as capitalist and to the reenslavement of the worker to the wage system.[13] And beyond these particular institutional threats lurks the still more profound fear that the very existence of market relationships constitutes in itself a source of "corruption" for a socialist society. "[M]arket relationships," writes Paul Sweezy, a leading socialist critic of market socialism, "are *inevitable* under socialism for a long time, but they constitute a standing danger to the system and unless strictly hedged in and controlled will lead to degeneration and retrogression."[14]

To these charges not all socialists would agree. The Yugoslavs, for example, point out that in their system the factory manager is legally subservient to Workers' Councils elected from the factory floor and empowered with full directors' rights over the manager, including the right to fix his salary or to fire him. Other socialists would argue that a certain amount of economic inequality is compatible with socialism,

13. Not the least interesting aspect of this controversy is the abandonment of the traditional Marxist belief that the movement from capitalism to socialism was a "one-way street." The admission that the trend toward socialism is reversible, even if only for a while, constitutes a profound challenge to the classical Marxian analysis of historical evolution.

14. *Monthly Review,* March, 1969, p. 12 (author's italics). See also "Peaceful Transition from Socialism to Capitalism?" *Monthly Review,* March, 1964, and the exchange between Bettelheim and Sweezy, *ibid.,* March, 1969. Also Ernest Mandel, *Marxist Economic Theory,* p. 655.

provided that it does not bring with it political or social inequality. As for the matter of corruption, that is a question
we shall look into ourselves later on.

Thus it is difficult, perhaps impossible, to decide the
merits of this controversy now. On the one hand it is clear
that socialism is being steadily forced to retreat from the
centralized planning that was its original ideal: "It is plain
at the present day," writes the English sociologist and socialist T. B. Bottomore, "that the public ownership of industry
is not by itself sufficient to establish a socialist society, and
that it may in fact produce conditions which are directly
inimical to the creation or functioning of such a society." [15]
At the same time there seems as well to be a rise of a "capitalist" spirit in Yugoslavia, and the probable consequences
of Russian decentralization in giving new power to the class
of Soviet industrial managers have been frequently commented on.[16]

All this suggests that socialism has yet to make its peace
either with the market system or with centralized control.
Perhaps one had better use the Marxian terminology and
point out that there are "contradictions" as deeply rooted in
the institutions and ideology of socialist planning as those
lodged in the operations of a capitalist market system—contradictions that will not be resolved as long as socialism must
be concerned both with the workaday problems of production and distribution in a world of scarcity on the one hand,
and with its pursuit of the ideals of human equality and
confraternity on the other.

15. "Industry, Work and Socialism," in *Socialist Humanism,* ed. Erich
Fromm, p. 362.
16. See, for example, the essays in *Planning and the Market in the
U.S.S.R. in the 1960s* by Balinky, Bergson, Hazard, and Wiles.

V

But will not this contradiction be resolved by the "abolition" of scarcity? It has become only a commonplace to point out that science and technology constitute the truly revolutionary force of our day. Is not the *social* aspect of that revolution the impending end of the age of scarcity through the immense abundance that a completely technologized society will enjoy? [17]

That scientific technology has the capability of vastly raising the level of productivity and thereby ushering in an era of material abundance is beyond doubt. But just as this very abundance, with its scientific and technological preconditions, poses deep-seated challenges for the maintenance of the traditional structure of capitalism,[18] so I also believe that it holds equally profound difficulties for the prevailing realities or conceptions of socialism.

The challenges to socialism as well as to capitalism are of two kinds: psychological and organizational. With capitalism, the psychological problem lies in the likelihood that affluence will weaken the condition of economic dependency on which the market system is tacitly based, opening the prospect that normal differentials of income payments will no longer suffice to attract men where they are needed, and thereby requiring that capitalism resort more and more to planning and coercion. Much the same motivational prob-

17. For a recent (pre-invasion) Czech statement of this prospect see Radovan Richta, *Civilization at the Crossroads, Social and Human Implications of the Scientific and Technological Revolution*, Prague, 1969. Cf. also Mandel, *op. cit.*, Chs. 16–17.
18. See *The Limits of American Capitalism*, Part II.

lem is likely also to affect the operation of a socialist market economy, pushing it, however unwillingly, in the direction of coercive planning, with all the difficulties of efficiency and morale that such measures must bring.

These psychological problems are apt to be less important, however, than the organizational necessities imposed on socialism by the domination of science and technology. There is a romantic tendency on the part of some socialists to picture the age of science as inherently favorable to the egalitarian aims of the socialist ideology. But this is not in fact what the hegemony of science promises. For both the production and the maintenance of the scientific mastery of the New Society will require the presence of a highly trained research elite supported by a large technical service staff. This necessary organizational core, with its collective expertise so essential for the maintenance of the general society, has all the attributes of a potential ruling class. "There is nothing to be gained," writes Radovan Richta, head of a Czech interdisciplinary team for research into the social implications of the scientific revolution, "by shutting our eyes to the fact that an acute problem of our age will be to close the profound cleavage in industrial society which, as Einstein realized with such alarm, places the fate of the defenseless mass in the hands of an educated elite, who wield the power of science and technology. Possibly this will be among the most complex undertakings facing socialism." [19]

Is elitism inherent in a society dominated by scientific technology? Certainly the underlying conditions for a highly stratified social system are implicit in the pyramidal educational requirements and the vastly differing social powers of the technologized society in which many will tend automated

19. Richta, *op. cit.,* p. 250.

machines and a few will carry on the critical activity of discovery. "Ultimately," writes Richta, "the only solution will be to make professionals of us all"—a solution that reminds us of pious suggestions in our society that everyone should become a capitalist.

But even if the tendency toward elitism is successfully curbed, there remains one final challenge for socialism posed by technology. It is that the hastening race of technical change has begun to pose a wholly new problem for all mankind—the problem of maintaining the ecological balance, the very viability, of the earth itself.

For the other side of the coin of affluence has been a steady deterioration in the quality of the environment—a deterioration brought about by enormously enhanced demands for resources, by gigantic scales of physical and chemical transformation of materials, and by the need to dispose of gargantuan quantities of end products, including the peculiarly lethal ones of radioactive wastes. Meanwhile, as the proliferation of production spoils the environment, it also makes possible the support of larger and larger concentrations of humanity, which in turn exacerbates the pollution process.

This spectacle of a steadily worsening environment coupled with an unsustainable rate of population increase gives rise to the uncomfortable feeling that the technological process is "running wild." And so it is. For at bottom, the ecological disequilibrium only reflects a still more profound unbalance between the technological and scientific capabilities of society and its social and self-governing capacities. The problem is that the first are cumulative and the second are not: each generation of scientists and technicians stands on the shoulders of preceding generations, bringing to the control over nature successively larger powers, whereas each generation of statesmen or administrators begins, for all intents and purposes, from scratch, in no way enhanced by the activities of its predecessors in understanding or controlling social processes. In its paradigm, of course, we have the spectacle of the unbelievable magnification of the capabilities of mass weaponry which is placed in the charge of men who are in no way whatsoever enlarged in their capability to govern, or even to understand, the world.

In this unequal race, which is visible in the socialist nations quite as much as in the capitalist ones, inevitably the technical capacities of a society come to exceed by an enormous margin its capabilities for exercising effective social control. The result is a technology that continuously escapes confinement, that develops in unforeseen directions, and that disturbs social systems by exerting its influences in unanticipated and unwelcome ways, such as the poisoning of the environment. It is quite probable that socialism will cope with this looming problem more effectively than capitalism, for assuredly planning lies at the very center of an effort to reestablish a workable balance between man and nature. The point is, however, that the technological imperative will present socialist planning with a range of problems requiring extensive and penetrative social intervention, rather than with a condition of general affluence in which a "liberated" community will spontaneously establish itself.

It is difficult at this juncture to foresee exactly what programs of control will be required to bring about a balanced ecology. All that can be said is that stringent limitations will have to be imposed, not alone on the productive apparatus of society, but very possibly on its consumptive patterns and certainly on its reproductive freedom. This will pose enormous problems for all social systems, but in the case of socialism the problem takes on a moral as well as a technical significance. For the fact is that the known techniques of social planning do not today enable us to assert a mastery over the behavior of large communities—at least not if this mastery is to be made compatible with a high degree of civil liberty. Nor, for that matter, can we as yet even design a reliable program for the limitation of the side effects of technological advance. The upshot is that socialism has not been able to formulate a blueprint for the guidance of the advanced countries that carries the compelling logic of its program for the underdeveloped countries. The sobering conclusion is that socialism will find its task made not easier but more difficult by the demands and consequences of the technological revolution on which it pins so many of its hopes.

VI

We have dealt at some length with the particular problems that seem likely to trouble the future of socialism by virtue of the inherent "contradictions" of socialist planning. Now we must examine a second group of problems more closely associated with the content and limitations of the socialist ideology.

Here it will be useful if we once again begin with a comparison of socialism and capitalism. We have already noted at the very beginning of this essay the essentially conservative purpose of the ideology of capitalism. By defining and articulating a consensus of business beliefs, a capitalist ideology serves to mark out the boundaries of "what can be done" within a system whose fundamental commitment is to leaving things alone. The result is twofold. On the one hand, the business ideology acts to limit the interventory reach of the state as an agency for social change. On the other, by buttressing the nature of things as they are, it leaves society without any strong feeling of forward motion, of collective purpose, of high destination. The capitalist ideology is a practical, not an inspirational, one.

A totally different quality strikes us when we examine the ideology of the socialist world. Here the commitment to equality and to fraternal solidarity serves not to inhibit but to encourage the exercise of social intervention. And beyond that, the socialist vision of a transcendent society has shown itself to be second only to religion (if indeed second it be) as a source of inspiration, solace, and conviction.

Moreover, the nature of that extraordinary power of socialist ideas is not difficult to discover. Again in sharp contrast with the indifference of capitalist thought with regard to the matter, socialism has always affirmed its unshakable faith in the perfectibility of man. That is, socialism has always maintained that man is the product of his environment, so that the ugliness of society today or yesterday becomes an indictment, not of mankind, but of its past or prevailing institutions. Furthermore—and this is the crux of the charismatic power of socialist thought—it follows that in a society in which the deforming institutions of the past and present had been removed, man would be "shaped" or "released" to discover his long-delayed fulfillment.

Thus, whereas capitalist thought has little to say with respect to the future, other than to promise a general affluence, socialist thought envisages the transformation, indeed, the liberation, of man:

By abolishing commodity production and opening the age of plenty, socialist society will give the signal for an extraordinary flowering of the human personality. Among hundreds of millions of individuals who today are indistinguishable in one grey mass, this personality will awaken, develop and flower in a thousand different directions, as yet unknown and unsuspected. Released from the wretched servitude of having to struggle for daily bread, human energy will be concentrated in art and science, in education and in physical and mental well-being. The place of competition between individuals for material existence will be taken by emulation in the pursuit of aims of research, of beauty and truth. Aggressiveness will be sublimated into creative purposes.[20]

That such a vision should have the power to motivate mankind is understandable enough. Yet, however moving —indeed, however plausible, for the very long run—we can see at the same time the problems inherent in such a view. One of them, which we have already examined, is a failure to confront with unflinching honesty the social constraints and organizational requirements of the society of abundance. The second, to which we now turn, is the failure to examine with equal fearlessness how men would actually behave in their "liberated" state, at least for the foreseeable future.

There is no doubt as to how socialists would like him to behave. "What exactly is to be considered by *liberated man?*" asks one socialist writer. She describes him as follows:

One might say that the liberated man is the generous and disinterested man; he is also a creative man, who can express his personality and talents in a creative action without constraint, whether in manual, intellectual, or artistic work,

20. Mandel, *op. cit.,* p. 672.

or in his relations and friendship with other men. The free
man is one who feels himself at the same time fully himself
and in accord with other men. He is an individual without
idols, dogmas, prejudices or a priori ideas. He is tolerant,
inspired by a profound sense of justice and equality, and
aware of himself as being at the same time an *individual*
and a *universal* man.[21]

The difficulty with such a description is obvious enough. As
the critics of socialism have maintained since the days of
the Utopian Socialists, this vision of man, however appealing, lacks a sense of toughness, of realism. In the language
of the nineteenth century it was faulted because it was based
on an inadequate appreciation of "human nature," and
whereas we are more chary of such phrases nowadays, we
also sense a certain wishfulness in this delineation of what
man could be. The point, let me emphasize, is not to counter
the socialist vision with mutterings that man is vile. It is
rather to insist that the deepest weakness of that vision has
been its failure to formulate a conception of human behavior
in all its historical, sociological, sexual, and ideational complexity, a conception that would present "man" as being at
once biologic as well as social, tragic as well as heroic,
limited as well as plastic.

To this criticism, socialism has always returned two rejoinders. The first is that it is unfair to expect it to rest its
philosophy on such a "theory" of human behavior without
requiring at least as much of other social systems of belief.
But this answer misses the point. In the first place, capitalism actually has such a theory, for it believes implicitly in
the ubiquitous acquisitive and competitive nature of man.
Second, capitalism does not require such a theory, for as

21. Mathilde Niel, "The Phenomenon of Technology," Fromm, *op.
cit.*, p. 306.

with all social systems that rest content with the status quo, it takes "human nature" as it is—which is to say, it accepts the manifestations of the culture in which it finds itself, adapting its institutions to the prevailing character traits and behavioral characteristics of men rather than attempting to design a set of institutions that will nurture the essence of Man out of his imperfect prevailing self. And finally, in encouraging or acquiescing in these existing traits, capitalism does not claim that it is being more than expedient. "While minds are coarse they require coarse stimuli and let them have them," wrote Mill in his *Principles of Political Economy*. Only socialism, by virtue of its belief in the possibility of creating a liberating environment, requires an understanding of the ultimate nature of the human being whose innate capabilities must now be allowed to unfold.

To this critique, the socialist will offer his second rejoinder. It is that socialism does not try to discover or to nurture a "given," although heretofore stunted, germ of human character. Rather, it is a prime belief of socialism that man makes himself. Thus socialism can dispense with the need to formulate a conception of "human nature" by concentrating instead on the institutions by which that nature will be formed. In a word, human nature will be in the end what we want it to be.

But this rejoinder too misses the mark. For it ignores the very thing we wish to find out—that is, the extent to which man *can* make himself. So far as I know, only Herbert Marcuse has squarely faced the question of the ultimate limits of adaptability of man's psychobiologic makeup. In *Eros and Civilization* he has boldly argued that man's instinctual nature is capable of dramatic change in an environment of genuine abundance. In such a setting, Marcuse claims, where the historic pressures of material scarcity were finally lifted, the social need for the repression of man's narcissistic and erotic nature would no longer prevail, and Eros and the Nirvana Principle could at long last take their places as the organizing elements of both the individual and the society.

Such a statement is indeed a theory of human nature, and if verified would place socialist ideology on a wholly new and much firmer footing. But I do not believe that there is any evidence, either theoretical or empirical, to support Marcuse's view of the instincts as creatures of the environment. As Sidney Axelrad has commented in the *Journal of the American Psychoanalytic Association:* "[I]nstincts are for Marcuse forces capable of being influenced by consciousness, rather than borderline somapsyche phenomena which are always unconscious and which can never lose their homeostatic functions and tendencies. [Marcuse's] prescription for a utopia of the future is not within the confines of psychoanalytic theory. It is a hope, an illusion. . . ." [22]

VII

The absence of a satisfactory foundation of knowledge beneath the socialist conception of human nature is important, not only because it blurs the long-term goals of socialism, but also because it carries short-term practical consequences of considerable importance.

The first of these is the failure of socialism to frame a coherent and cogent attitude toward the problem of motiva-

22. *Supra cit.,* January, 1960, pp. 182, 184.

tion. Inherent in the distinction between "socialism" and "communism," for example—that is to say, between the society that a socialist government might inherit and one that it might make—is the deep-seated Marxist belief that man at a low level of culture and well-being will still require the motivation of invidious striving for monetary rewards, whereas once the high plateaus of a truly affluent society have been reached, it will be possible to discard these "bourgeois" traits and to move people by the famous principle of "from each according to his ability, to each according to his needs."

Yet in actuality we perceive exactly the opposite state of affairs. In the poorest and lowliest of societies—China, Cuba, Russia in the first years after the Revolution—we find the power of nonmaterial, noninvidious incentives to be greatest, whereas in the richer and more advanced socialist societies—Yugoslavia, Czechoslovakia, the present-day Soviet Union—we discover an increasing need to rely on incentives of monetary inequality, managerial preferment, and competitive vying.

Much of this inability to form a reliable theory of motivation hearkens back to an ancient ambivalence toward wealth and its effect on the human personality that socialism has inherited from Western religious and philosophic thought. Socialism continually talks of affluence for society, but it recoils at the contagions that affluence will bring to the individual. An instance in point is the justification of the expropriation of 55,000 small businesses in Cuba in March, 1968. As the Havana newspaper *Granma* explained, this action was needed to remove "nests of parasites, hotbeds of corruption, illegal trading and counterrevolutionary conspiracy":

To get a good idea of the degree of corruption spawned by these activities, we need only cite the results of the investigation made by the Party of private businesses in Metropolitan Havana. According to this report, twenty-seven percent of the proprietors were workers before setting themselves up in business (and the great majority of these sprang up after the triumph of the Revolution). . . . It is intolerable that a worker, whose labor may benefit the whole people, should become a potential bourgeois, a self-centered money-grubber and exploiter of his countrymen.[23]

Such sentiments speak volumes as to the consequences of the psychological views which socialism expounds. If the rise of a worker to the precarious status of a small shopkeeper is enough to endanger the sentiments and institutions on which socialism is based, then socialism must constantly live in fear of betrayal from the secret corruptibility of the people. The parallel with the paranoid purity of extreme religious sects is all too apparent, and in one case as in the other, the vehemence with which evidences of corruption are denounced leads to the suspicion that both movements fear these "corruptions" are deeply embedded in the human psyche.

No less important as a consequence of the uncertain socialist conception of human behavior is its failure to examine the nature and consequences of alternative motivations to those of material incentives. If socialism seeks to perfect man in an environment in which the cash nexus will no longer provide the cohesive force for social organization, it must offer other motivations that will secure the necessary cooperation of the population in the administration and operation of a complex society. Such nonmaterial incentives

23. Paul Sweezy and Leo Huberman, *Socialism in Cuba*, p. 137.

certainly exist—monastic orders, for instance, maintain
their internal discipline by relying on wholly different
motives of personal enlistment from those of a money-oriented society, as do military establishments or some kinds
of professional groups.

What remains unasked, however, is whether a society knit
together by such ties—a society in which a strict internaliza-
tion of discipline has supplanted the external sanctions of
the marketplace—would constitute a favorable environment
for the perfection of man. In this regard, the famous quotation of John Stuart Mill bears repetition:

> The question is whether there would be any asylum left for
> individuality of character; whether public opinion would
> not be a tyrannical yoke; whether the absolute dependence
> of each on all, and the surveillance of each by all, would
> not grind all down into a tame uniformity of thoughts, feeling,
> and actions.[24]

In a word, socialist thought, in its avoidance of a study
of human behavior, has not directly faced the problem of
how the individual is to be integrated into the community,
or the degree to which individual behavior must be governed by social norms, or the appropriate boundaries between social and private spheres of existence. A fervent
commitment to "participatory democracy" is today much
voiced among Western socialist writers, but little or no consideration has been given to the means by which this participation can avoid what one commentator has called "the
merciless masochism of community-minded and self-regulating men and women." [25] (Oscar Wilde once remarked that

24. *Principles of Political Economy* Book II, Ch. 3.
25. The phrase is Melvin Tumin's, quoted in "A Day in the Life of a
Socialist Citizen," by Michael Walzer, in *Dissent,* May/June, 1968. The
remark by Wilde is quoted in the same article.

socialism would take too many evenings, and the quip deserves to be taken seriously.)

Finally, the inadequacy of the socialist grasp of behavior reveals itself in the ferocious impatience with which socialism demands that "human nature" must change. The relinquishment of market incentives, for example, is not regarded as a goal to be achieved over several generations but one that must be sought within a single decade or two; motives of socialist cooperation are not viewed as behavioral patterns to be patiently inculcated over the long run, but attitudes that must be evidenced almost overnight. What lacks so fatally in this view is any appreciation of the depth of behavioral characteristics formed by social experience and of the power of family cultures to transmit these learned patterns of attitude and behavior despite the counterinfluences of organized social pressure. Hence the repeatedly demonstrated unpreparedness of socialist thought before such behavioral realities as the persistence of "Russian" traits of government or "Chinese" xenophobia.

Here the dangers are twofold. On the one hand, the forces of nationalism—surely the single most powerful molding influence on social behavior in our time—are ignored, or worse, incorporated into socialist thought: as Paul Henri Spaak observed, "The thing that socialists have learned to nationalize best is socialism." [26] On the other, there is the grave risk that the innocent inertia of ordinary behavior will be interpreted as a deliberate betrayal of socialist ideals. The Cuban incident above is a case in point.

26. Quoted in "Humanistic Socialism and the Future," by Norman Thomas, in Fromm, *op. cit.*, p. 327.

VIII

These reflections must now be placed in some final perspective. That socialism faces inherent problems springing from the difficulties of planning and from both the reach and the limitations of its ideology is, I think, undeniable. What is necessary is to confront these problems without a sense of either defeat or satisfaction. To examine the future of socialism, in the underdeveloped areas or in the advanced nations, without taking into account these, or perhaps other, challenges it must face is simply not to take socialism seriously—that is, as a political movement which must struggle with the intransigent realities of history and which, like all such movements, is likely to be bested by some of them.

In this struggle, two main resistances can be discerned. One of these is the rampant force of technology, with its new networks of interdependence, its new frontiers of physical and chemical potentiality, its new dangers. In our day, at least, technology will not make its peace with socialism; socialism will have to make its peace with technology. The other is the stubborn inertia of the social personality, no doubt capable of great change, but only slowly and painfully, exerting meanwhile a continuous counterpressure against the radical alterations in actions and attitudes that socialism seeks to bring.

As we have suggested, it is likely that these resistances will establish the "limits" of socialism over the foreseeable future, much as similar forces set the boundaries of possible capitalist adaptation. But it would be wrong to end this essay on such a note. For unlike capitalism, which exists largely for its own sake in the present, socialism exists largely for the sake of the future. Inherent in the indistinct but bright vision of perfectible man is the source of an evolutionary momentum that carries a precious freight of human aspiration. Thus, unlike capitalism, socialism contains a core of belief that should be capable of maintaining its power to move human beings despite the obstacles that will hamper its performance.

Socialism is, at its root, the effort to find a remedy in social terms for the affront to reason and morality in the status quo. As such it is not limited to any particular place or time in history, but adapts its programs and its objectives to the indignities against which it fights. If socialism today in the United States derives its impetus from the spectacle of concentrated wealth, the commercial manipulation of human beings, or the indifference of the established power structure to the plight of the poor or the Negro, in the Soviet Union a genuinely socialist movement would (and some day will) take its organizing impulse from the concentration of political power and from the imprisonment of mind and spirit by communist authorities and doctrines alike. In each and every nation the presence of power and privilege thus establishes the fortresses against which socialism presses its attack.

It may well be that each attack succeeds only to fail; that new walls of power and privilege are built as rapidly as old ones are torn down; that the ultimate goal of a transformed —indeed, transfigured—man is only a chimera. Yet the vitality of socialism seems unlikely to be daunted by that possibility. For taking socialism seriously means more than acknowledging its difficulties as a political movement. It means understanding as well that socialism is the expression of a collective hope for mankind, its idealization of what it conceives itself to be capable of. When the fires of socialism no longer burn, it will mean that mankind has extinguished that hope and abandoned that ideal.

Political
Economics

CHAPTER 6

Marxism and the Economic Establishment

*"I*s society a branch of physics?" asked the Abbé Mably, a minor nineteenth-century pamphleteer and *philosophe*. The absurd question serves very well to introduce a discussion of what modern economics is about and whether Karl Marx still has something to contribute to economic thought. For, essentially, economics has always answered "Yes" to the Abbé's query. That is, it has always proceeded on the belief that there were enough regularities in the social process to enable a skilled observer to discover "laws" that described its movements, just as other laws described the motion of the planets in their orbits.

To be sure, economists have always recognized that there was a vast gulf between the unknowing planets and sentient human beings, and therefore they have never intended the laws to be as strict in the second case as in the first. Yet the gulf was not so wide as to destroy all similarity between the orderliness of the natural world and that of the social. For underneath the seeming disorder of the social universe, two processes could be discerned that imposed a degree of law-like regularity on the events of economic society. One of these was the process of production itself—the actual technical sequences by which wheat became bread and grapes wine and iron ore steel. Although these sequences differed one from another, and although they changed over time with technological advance, nonetheless there seemed to be sufficient regularity, at least in the short run, so that we could talk of "laws" of production, such as diminishing returns or economies of scale or "coefficients of production" or "marginal elasticities of substitution"—all terms that describe the dependability of the productive element within the social universe.

The other order-bestowing element in the economic process concerned its human side, which is to say the behavior of workers and consumers and entrepreneurs. Clearly, this aspect of the underlying social orderliness could not be expected to demonstrate the same degree of invariance that is found in the physical world. Yet in the behavior of buyers and sellers there seemed to be a sufficient degree of repetitiveness so that we could talk of the "law" of supply and demand; and in the responses of consumers to changes in their incomes or of businessmen to changes in the interest rate other lawlike patterns emerged.

Thus from the very beginning, economists have striven

for a picture of society in which the interaction of laws of production and behavior—production and behavior *functions* is the modern term—would describe the major economic events of the social system much as if it were a branch of physics. Moreover, by reducing the complexity of the real world to the simplicity of a "model" dominated by these two great functions, economists, like physicists, have sought to predict the path of motion of their system.

How successful has been this audacious intellectual effort? On the face of it, the achievement has been astonishing. Models of the economy are now so complex that they require the facilities of a computer and the techniques of difference equations, matrix algebra, Lagrangian multipliers, and the like. Sophistication, elegance, rigor—the criteria by which mathematics has traditionally been judged—are now the standards of economic theorizing. Not least, the success of modern economics can be read in the flattery of imitation paid to it by its sister disciplines of sociology and political science which now seek to build models similar to those of the economist. Certainly, when the intellectual history of our times is finally written, the creation of the edifice of modern "neoclassical" economics will occupy a central chapter in it.

The only question is, what will that chapter say about the usefulness and relevance of this extraordinary enterprise? Here I suspect the appraisal of the future will not be uncritically admiring. The theory of economics, magnificent to behold, is considerably less impressive to use. It is true that it has given us a rough picture of how the market system works, both in allocating its resources and in determining the level of overall output. But beyond this conception, which can be taught with ease to a college freshman, the ramifications of economics have produced singularly little. A rococo branch called welfare theory, for example, has not, to my knowledge, yet resulted in a single substantive proposal that has added significantly to the welfare of mankind. The beautifully finished portion called price theory fails to explain the pricing operations of the great corporations. International trade theory does not adequately account for the most important single fact about international trade —to wit, the failure of an international division of labor to shed its benefits on poor countries and rich countries alike. The theory of economic development does not tell underdeveloped countries how to grow.

Even the central achievement of twentieth-century economics—the elucidation of the forces that determine prosperity and recession—fails when we seek to foretell the fortunes of the economy a few months hence. No doubt economists reading these words will deem them vastly exaggerated, which perhaps they are. Yet it is surely an opinion not wholly at variance with mine that must have moved Kenneth Arrow, a well-known economist, to sum up the collected papers of Paul Samuelson, the most brilliant theorist of our generation, with these words: "A careful examination of the papers both on theory and on policy yields only the most oblique suggestion that neoclassical price theory is descriptive of the real world. Of course, there is no denial, but Samuelson's attitude is clearly guarded and agnostic." [1]

1. *Journal of Political Economy,* October, 1967.

Why is it that modern economic theory presents the spectacle of superb intellectual achievement without much social relevance? To my mind there are two reasons. One lies in the difficulties of reducing the real world—both in its technical and in its behavioral aspects—to reliable patterns with which we can then construct dependable models. It is one thing to ascribe an underlying "lawlike" character to the processes of production and to the responses of the economic actors, and quite another to reduce these activities to mathematical functions. In the case of production, for example, we encounter enormous difficulties in devising mathematical functions that will accurately account for the constantly changing nature of technology. And this difficulty is compounded by the even more intractable problem of finding functional representations of human behavior. No doubt, for instance, men tend to buy less when prices rise and to buy more when prices fall. Yet, on occasion, they will do just the opposite, as when they expect a price rise or price fall to *continue*—in which case their self-interest bids them to buy more in a hurry in the first case, and to hold off in the second.

Hence the inherent complexities of the production process and the vagaries of human behavior may well set limits to the predictive possibilities of economic theorizing, and these limits may account for much of the gap that exists between economic theory and economic reality. Yet, however much these difficulties explain the inaccuracy of economic theorizing, they do not account for its irrelevance. I have already mentioned the failure of price theory to explain the behavior of the large corporation and the gap between the theory and the reality of international trade. Now I must point out other areas of economic life over which modern economic theory passes in virtual silence. The distribution of wealth, for example, is a central economic fact about which it is mute. The effects on the distribution of income attributable to the process of growth is another, so that economics gives us no hint of the disturbances and frictions produced by long-run economic advance. The effect of a constantly improving technology on the level of employment is similarly ignored, so that today the theory of technological unemployment is in much the same shape as was the theory of mass unemployment in the days before Keynes. The nature of class interests in a capitalist system is not mentioned in any textbook, so that nothing in the nature of political or social constraints confines the free movement of the economic model.

In all of this, it will be noted, there is a common denominator. This is the systematic exclusion of matters that might connect the functional model with the pressures and resistances of the political world. This exclusion, which accounts for so much of the irrelevance of economics, is by no means accidental. Rather, it results from a fundamental failure of vision on the part of the modern model-builders, *who do not see that the social universe that they are attempting to reproduce in a set of equations is not and cannot be adequately described by functional relationships alone, but must also and simultaneously be described as a system of privilege.* In other words, if a model of economic reality is to be relevant, it must portray both the functional relationships peculiar to the provisioning process and those stemming from the clash of interests generated by this very functional process itself.

Is it possible to construct a system that is at one and the same time a portrayal of functional relationships and of privilege? There is one such system, Marxian economics—that vast *terra incognita* over which the average economics student flies while en route to the oral examination (where it may be mentioned as part of the History of Economic Doctrines) and at which he never again casts a glance. For what is unique about the Marxian system is that the categories, both of production and of behavior, into which it disaggregates the world are considerably different from those of the neoclassical system. On the production side, for example, Marxism lays great stress on the necessity for a "fit" between the output of the capital goods sector and that of the consumer goods sector, a relationship that is unnoticed in neoclassical economics where the aggregate output of *all* sectors is stressed rather than the relationship between them. Similarly, on the behavioral side, Marx approaches the problem of describing the great "human" functions by building up a picture of the actions of producers—that is, workers and capitalists—rather than by analyzing the activities of buyers, i.e., of consumers and investors. In different words, the Marxian analysis breaks down the total flow of economic activity into layers of costs, wages, and profits rather than into the slices of consumption and investment characteristic of the Keynesian approach.

The result of the special categories of abstraction imposed by the Marxian view is to bring into the foreground a number of matters that fail to appear in neoclassical analysis, in particular the instability of the economy stem-

ming from a failure of its productive components to inter-
lock, and the changing division of the social product among
the classes—profit receivers and wage earners—that com-
pete for it. Now it should be said immediately that the
manner in which classical Marxian analysis performs its task
of constructing a model of society is very awkward and
occasionally downright wrong. The "laws of motion" that it
discerns within the capitalist system depend on rigid assumptions about the way in which technology permits labor to be
combined with capital and loses sight of the central effect
of productivity in changing the real shares of wage earners
in the final product. Worse yet, as a means of explaining the
price mechanism by which the system is coordinated, Marxian economics is hopelessly clumsy: if one examines the
efforts of the more liberal Soviet or Czech economists to
create a rational pricing system using Marxian concepts, and
compares these efforts with the results obtained by non-
Marxian price theory, the contrast is like that between a
dull cleaver and a sharp scalpel.

Why then bother with Marxian economics when, as virtually every economist will tell you, it is "wrong"? The
reason is that, unlike neoclassical analysis, which is "right,"
the Marxian model has in surfeit the quality of social relevance that is so egregiously lacking in the other. The neoclassical model has rigor, but, alas, also mortis. The Marxian
model has relevance, but, alas, also mistakes. The answer,
then, is clear. Marxian insights must be married to neoclassical techniques to produce an economic theory that is
both elegant and consistent as a model and freighted with
meaning as a theory of society.

Here and there in this country—I am glad to say, with
increasing frequency—one can see efforts being made to

bring off such a marriage. I would say that the future of the entire intellectual effort called economics depends on whether in fact such a genuinely political economics can be achieved. It is just because society is *not* a branch of physics that we must ask of economics a very special kind of prediction called foresight. I do not myself believe that Marxian economics has very accurate foresight, but I am convinced that neoclassical analysis has none at all. The hope is that in combining the Marxian angle of vision, with its emphasis on class structure and privilege, with the fierce insistence of neoclassical techniques on consistency and clarity, we might have the beginnings of a new and fruitful chapter in the effort to comprehend the social universe.

CHAPTER **7**

Marxism Restated
and Reviewed

I suppose it should not be surprising that Marxian economic theory is little studied in the United States; I understand that the works of Paul Samuelson are largely ignored in the Soviet Union. Yet there is a reason for the lack of attention paid to Marxian economics in our universities, beyond their heretical nature. It is because so much of the work of Marx is either impossibly difficult to understand or —to mention the unmentionable—terribly boring to study.

Of course there are parts of the Marxian canon to which these words could never apply: the *Communist Manifesto*, the brilliant historical essays, the best parts of *Capital*—

above all, the unforgettable picture of the Working Day, the passionate chapter on Primitive Accumulation, and the apocalyptic climax to Volume I, where the integument bursts asunder and the expropriators are expropriated. But for the student who wants to master the *system* of Marxian economics, the task of reading the 2,000 pages of *Capital* is enough to daunt all but a very few. Much of the argument is tediously drawn out and, in critical places, obscure or incorrect, such as the famous transition from value to prices. There is no discernible orderly progression within the work, which seems continuously to double back on itself. And the empirical material, however interesting as historical illustration, is hopelessly out of touch with the realities of modern-day capitalism.

As a result, those few intrepid students who set out to discover what Marxian economics is all about are usually forced to revert to a secondary source, of which the best for many years has been Paul Sweezy's *The Theory of Capitalist Development*. The trouble with such books, however, is that essentially they are efforts to unscramble and clarify the Master, rather than efforts to restate, *de novo,* and on the basis of fresh evidence, the theoretical explanation of capitalism inherent in Marx's approach. Hence the belated appearance of Ernest Mandel's book[1] is an event of great importance. For the purpose of this carefully organized, lucidly written, and strongly argued book is, in Mandel's italicized words, *"to start from the empirical data of the science of today to examine whether or not the essence of Marx's economic propositions remains valid."*

1. *Marxist Economic Theory,* first published in France in 1962.

Mandel is a well-known Marxist writer and critic, the editor of the Belgian paper *La Gauche,* and clearly a person of great erudition. Thirty-six pages of bibliographic references testify to the breadth of research that has gone into this work. What is more noticeable about the list of citations, however, is the relatively small percentage of standard Marxist works it contains. An inexpressibly refreshing sense of release from the intellectual straitjacket of past Marxology is announced in the Introduction, where Mandel writes:

> The reader who expects to find numerous quotations from Marx and Engels or their chief disciples will close this book disappointed. Unlike all the writers of Marxist economic textbooks, we have *strictly abstained* (with very few exceptions) from quoting the sacred texts or interpreting these quotations. As against that, we quote abundantly from the chief economists, economic historians, ethnologists, anthropologists, sociologists and psychologists of our times, in so far as they express opinions on phenomena relating to the economic activity, past, present, or future, of human societies. What we seek to show is that it is possible, on the basis of the scientific data of contemporary science, to reconstitute the whole economic system of Karl Marx. Furthermore, we seek to show that only Marx's economic teaching makes possible this synthesis of the totality of human knowledge, and above all a synthesis of economic history and economic theory, just as it alone makes possible a harmonious integration of micro-economic and macro-economic analysis.

Has Mandel succeeded in this ambitious task? Before passing judgment, let me review the main line of his argument by contrasting the view of economic theory as it appears from a Marxian perspective with that of economics as we ordinarily learn it in the "neoclassical" version that is our standard fare in college.

The critical difference emerges at the very outset. "Economics," writes Paul Samuelson in his famous text (7th ed., p. 5),

> . . . is the study of how men and society [*sic*] *choose*, with or without the use of money, to employ *scarce* productive resources, which could have alternative uses, to produce various commodities over time and distribute them for consumption, now and in the future, among various people and groups in society.

The impression is conveyed of a town meeting in which men and "society" deliberate how they shall make the best use of their limited capabilities. Perhaps this is the way things will some day be ordered under some other social system, but I find it a very strained description of the way things are ordered under ours. For the definition smothers the explicit recognition that "society" and, indeed, "men" are not timeless abstractions, but constitute in themselves the very first object for a critical and analytic "economic" scrutiny. We begin, in other words, by taking for granted the conditions under which, and the historical institutions by which, "choice" will be made—whereupon neoclassical economics proceeds to apply its formal techniques to such questions as why "society" has fluctuations in output, wide variations in individual incomes, etc.

Marxian analysis (as I shall paraphrase Mandel's version of it) starts elsewhere, in the anthropological and physical characteristics of primitive societies as we dimly perceive their outlines in prehistory, and then inquires, as the first problem of economics, into the social and material relationships of these elemental social systems. Did primitive man "choose" how to employ his productive resources among alternative uses? Not so far as we can read the anthropological record. In the unremitting struggle against famine that absorbed the overwhelming portion of human energies in the first million years of human existence, only those modes of social and technical organization that met the test of survival were maintained and passed along; those that did not brought extinction.

In this primeval state of mankind, "economics" is inseparable from sociology, technology, and culture in general. Only with the eventual appearance of a social *surplus*—a quantum of food production over and above that needed for survival—did there arise the possibility of an economic mechanism involving choice, in the sense of alternative dispositions of inputs and outputs. Thus the study of economics, in the Marxian view, coincides with and brings its initial inquiry to bear on the rise and disposition of a surplus of production over the essential requirements of consumption.

With the appearance of a surplus—an appearance probably traceable to the very gradual improvement of skills, material artifacts, and social organization—comes as well the appearance of a "class" division within the society. For the appearance of a material surplus, in nearly all social groups, is accompanied by an unequal appropriation of this surplus among the members of the community. Precisely how this economic stratification of society appears we do not know. Perhaps the capture of prisoners of war, or the armed subjugation of one part of the community by another, provides the original means by which the surplus goods (mainly food) produced by some men are claimed by others. Perhaps the initial uneven distribution follows an older stratification along religious or other lines. All that we do know, as Mandel writes, is that "something which is at first voluntary or intermittent later becomes obligatory and regular. By the application of force, that is to say, by the organization of the state, a social order is established which is founded on the surrender by the peasants of their surplus of foodstuffs to the new masters."

But the division of early society into surplus-producing and surplus-appropriating groups still does not give us the lineaments of the commodity-producing society that is the "given" of neoclassical economics. That is, the seizure of a portion of a primitive tiller's output by an armed lord, or the forced labor of a slave whose surplus output is taken by his owner, does not constitute a relationship of *exchange*. Even trade, as we know it, does not exist in primitive societies where exchanges, as Mandel stresses, begin with fearful contacts among groups, often consummated as "silent barter," and only gradually develop into collective, tribal interchanges of more or less specialized products. From here it is still a long evolutionary process until we meet the widespread existence of individuals *within* communities who will be able to live by specializing their labor, confident that the existence of commonly shared "values" will enable them to exchange what they have made for what they need.

What is this essential common denominator of values that enables exchange to become generalized among men? As a Marxist, Mandel argues that only one such universal calculus exists. This is the expenditure of labor time, the indispensable, and (at an early stage of society) overwhelmingly most important, input. In the language of modern economics, labor time is by far the greatest opportunity cost of primitive production, and thus labor time becomes the "coin," so to speak, by which primitive production is measured.

I shall return later to the question of whether such a labor theory of value serves equally well as a basic measuring rod in more advanced stages of society. What is essential is to see that Marxian analysis plunges us directly into questions that are obscured from view in an economics that is no longer aware of a surplus transferred from one group to another, but only of the production of a mass of commodities from the "cooperation" of land, labor, and capital. Indeed, from the Marxian view, the main task of economic theory now becomes the elucidation of this very metamorphosis—that is, how a surplus-generating and surplus-seizing society gives way to a commodity-generating and commodity-sharing one.

In particular, Marxian analysis calls to our attention the tremendous period of innovation centered in the late Middle Ages when the mode of surplus-appropriation changes from one of more or less overt force to the much more covert dispositions of the marketplace. For as monetary relationships come to be diffused throughout late feudalism (Marx's famous "cash nexus") and as commercial and proto-industrial structures emerge in the agricultural setting of life, a profound alteration takes place in the method of transferring the surplus from one group to another. Explicit acts of forcible seizure, such as the *corvée* performed by the serf for his feudal lord, now begin to disappear from sight. In their place appears a new institution of wage bargains be-

tween three equally "free" legal persons: the worker, the
capitalist, and the landlord. In this new form of social interaction, laborers and proprietors meet with one another in
the marketplace for an exchange of values, during which a
portion of the product of society "naturally" gravitates into
the hands of the owners of society's resources.

How is this done? The answer is that land, and more
especially capital, have taken on a new guise. Not only do
they exist (as they always have and always will) as the
physical resources or the stored efforts of the past, serving
as such enormously to enhance the productive capability
of effort expended in the present, but they now also appear
as legal "personages," claiming (in the name of their owners) their "rightful" share of the increment in productivity
attributable to them.

The full bloom of this society is called *capitalism*—the
very same society that we study under a different perspective in our neoclassical textbooks. But the Marxian approach does more than shift the angle of incidence from
which we observe the system; it also brings into focus
specific problems within the system of capitalism which
arise as a consequence of its special mode of surplus disposition.

The first of these is the famous tendency to a falling rate
of profit. At the heart of the Marxian view of capitalism
lies the conflict between the claims of the surplus-appro-
priators and of the surplus-generators—a conflict that takes
the form of a struggle between capital and labor, between
the shares of profits and wages. Capitalists, seeking to secure
and expand their profits, are driven to use their surplus for
additional investment—in ordinary language, they seek to
expand their businesses in order to make more money. The

trouble is, however, that in so doing they create an added demand for labor, with the result that wages rise at the expense of profits. To counteract this threat to profits, capitalists introduce labor-saving machinery into the process of production. But since machines by themselves are not, in the Marxian view, instruments for the production of new surplus, this substitution of capital for labor tends to depress the profit rate and thus to undermine the vitality of the system itself.[2]

A second source of instability is even more cunningly concealed in the mechanics of the capitalist system. It lies in a hidden "balance of payments" problem in capitalism —not with respect to the rest of the world, but in the relationships of one part of the system to another. For as Marx pointed out, the activities of capitalist production (or for that matter, of the production of any highly specialized industrial society) can be grouped into two "departments" or sectors. One of these sectors produces consumer goods, the other capital goods. Each of these sectors produces more of its own kind of goods than it can use itself: the capital goods department not only turns out machines that will be needed to replace (or expand) its own stock of equipment, but also machines that will be needed for the same purposes in the consumer goods sector; while the consumer goods industries turn out not only the various products that will be demanded by those who earn their livelihood in that sector, but also consumer goods that must be sold to the

2. Why aren't machines capable of producing a surplus? The answer is that workers, who *must* find employment, come to terms with their employers at a wage that is less than the value of their expended labor power, whereas capitalists (who sell machinery) do not have to settle for a price less than the full value to be derived from the use of their artifacts. In the Marxian model of "pure" capitalism all profit arises from the surplus value to be had from employing labor, none from the use of land or equipment.

workers and capitalists of the capital goods sector. Thus there must be a flow of "trade" between the two sectors, with the capital goods industries exporting machines and importing consumer items, the consumer goods industries exporting consumer goods and buying machines.

Clearly, unless these flows of trade balance, one sector or the other will be producing more than it can sell, and its capitalists, accordingly, will not be able to "realize" their surplus. But will the trade flows balance? The Marxian answer is that they will not. In Mandel's words, the "supreme contradiction" of the system lies in the conflict between the increasing need for rationalization, planning, and control, and the continuing absence of any system of social coordination that would not contravene the principles of the capitalist social order. The result is an economic system which is not only "unbalanced" morally—that is, whose production bears too little relation to the priorities of human needs —but which is also unbalanced structurally, in that it is continually threatened with a disproportion between the rates of output of its two main sectors.

> The private form of appropriation [writes Mandel] makes profit the only aim and driving force of production. It causes the development of the productive forces to be uneven and spasmodic. Production develops by leaps and bounds, not in the sectors where the most urgent real needs are to be found, but rather in those where the highest profits can be achieved. The production of alcoholic drinks, of "comic books," and of drugs takes precedence over the struggle against air pollution, the preservation of natural resources, and even the building of schools and hospitals. . . . Underproduction in one branch regularly coincides with overproduction in another. . . . The distribution of human labor between the different branches of production never corresponds exactly to the distribution of purchasing power for the products of

these branches. When this disproportion becomes too extreme, it is resolved by a crisis, which leads to a new equilibrium, itself temporary and ephemeral.

I have thus far paraphrased only a quarter of Mandel's two-volume work, and my précis has given no indication of the wealth of historical and empirical material that is the most interesting part of the argument. Now, before I turn to a critique, I must quickly indicate the remaining sweep of the book. For Mandel has built up his detailed analysis of capitalism not to examine the system as a museum piece, but to understand its operation in the present. What does his Marxian perspective reveal about the outlook for capitalism in our time?

One thing strikes us immediately. It is the absence of that clash of cymbals that provides the climax to Marx's historical symphony. In Mandel's book the expropriators are no longer expropriated in a moment of convulsive justice; it is "long-term stagnation" that impends rather than breakdown and revolution.

This change reflects Mandel's awareness of the existence of means of staving off crisis that did not exist in Marx's time, especially the conscious intervention of the state. As Mandel writes, "the development of new industries; 'aid to underdeveloped countries'; extension of state expenditure both military and nonmilitary; growth of 'distribution costs' and of the tertiary sector, all play the same role of safety valves for capitalism in decline. By offering fresh fields of investment to capital they temporarily offset the tendency to long-term stagnation and the plethora of capital without paying investment."

These safety valves rescue the system from its classic Marxian doom. Instead Mandel sees capitalism moving toward an amalgamation of fascism (militarized, oppressive capitalism) and the welfare state ("more or less real, more or less demagogic, depending on the comparative wealth of the capitalist country involved"). How long this unstable combination can last, Mandel does not say. There are ominous previsions ("The increasing economic role of the state means at the same time the violent compression of social and international contradictions, and so intensifies the advance of capitalism toward explosive outbreaks of war and revolution"), but neither the mechanics nor the timetable of the transformation is clearly given. The implication is that capitalism, however moribund, may last a considerable while.

Finally, socialism. Unlike Marx, Mandel examines in some detail the problems and possibilities of a social order in which commodity production—that is, the production of goods for exchange on a market—will have been largely superseded by a free distribution of most basic goods and services, and in which the surplus produced by labor, working with natural and man-made resources, will be consciously distributed by "men and society" in much the fashion envisaged by Paul Samuelson. Is such a society possible? With the enormous productive potential of industrialism, and on the assumption that this potential was freed from the deformations and misuses presumably stemming from capitalism, certainly the economic basis for such a social order is imaginable. As to what sort of society it would be, it is more difficult to say. Mandel claims it would be less bored, alienated, primitive than ours. A picture emerges of a community populated by men cast in the image of the socialist hero of our day—not the proletarian, but the intellectual.

"[T]hese 'most gifted persons' of today, in so far as they have succeeded in devoting their lives to a creative activity which basically corresponds to their inner needs, come closest to what the socialist man of tomorrow would be. . . ."

It must be apparent that I find Mandel's book not only interesting but, in its broad historical outlines, persuasive. Perhaps this is only testimony to the fact that all persons interested in historical evolution are "Marxists" these days, if by this we mean, not the promulgation of those dreadful catechisms that have passed for Marxism in the hands of the Russians and the Chinese, but an attempt to relate the surface phenomena of history to deep-seated and often hidden causes, especially causes involving technological processes and economic interests. As a fresh and wide-ranging effort along these lines, Mandel's work can only command attention and admiration. Yet it is precisely in reading so free a work as Mandel's that the limitations of Marxism and Marxian economics also stand forth, at least in my eyes—limitations that make it impossible for me to be a formal Marxist, however much I may admire and use certain aspects of Marxian analysis.

The first of these limitations has to do with a certain theological strain that continues to pervade Marxian thought. The basic assumption underlying Marxism is that there is a set of unique "laws" and insights which, once discovered, can be applied to all of human history—how else can one speak, as Mandel does, of a "synthesis of the totality of human knowledge"? Primary among these laws is the presumed "dialectical" nature of historical change, the inherent tension in social relationships that is both the source and the governing agent of that change. And first among these tensions is that of the class struggle over the surplus itself—a class struggle that underlies all human history and that will not be ultimately resolved until classes themselves have been dissolved by an affluent socialist setting.

But is the class struggle the clue to all history? To ignore it is clearly to miss the key to certain epochs, such as the development of Europe during the eighteenth and nineteenth centuries. But to insist upon it seems to me to place large stretches of historical experience on a Procrustean bed of analysis. It is possible also to view many chapters of history through different lenses—those that stress religious divisions or sheer dynastic rivalries, for example—and thereby to discover motives and causal sequences of prime importance that are invisible in an exclusively Marxian approach.

In a word, Marxism as *the* philosophy of historical change is powerful but also parochial. Moreover, its use can at times lead to serious practical problems stemming from a reluctance to drop certain sacred doctrines, even when (as with Mandel) the sacred texts are allowed to rest unconsulted. The labor theory of value, for example, may be immensely useful in elucidating the mode of transfer of surplus as an historical problem, but it is scarcely useful when it comes to the analysis of the operational problems of a modern state, capitalist or socialist.

Indeed, no small part of the problems of the Soviet Union in devising a smooth-functioning system of prices has been its refusal (until very recently) to assign an interest cost to capital, although a glance at Samuelson's text would have made it clear that without such a cost there was no way for the planners accurately to assess the relative advantages of various alternatives. But because interest, in the perspective of the labor theory of value, was associated with the specific mode of surplus transfer of capitalism, the assignment of such a cost was ruled out on grounds of ideological heresy—with disastrous consequences for Soviet economic efficiency.

We can explain such rigidity in the case of the Soviets by making allowances for their lack of experience and uncritical socialist ardor. But why, even in Mandel's book, do we find the clumsy techniques of orthodox Marxian economics retained in lieu of the much more flexible ones of neoclassical analysis? On a larger scale, why do we find even so liberated a mind as Mandel's failing to incorporate into his analysis of the ills of capitalism and the prospects of socialism the profound insights of Max Weber or Freud? The answer, I believe, lies in a certain theological cast of mind that makes Marxism not a philosophy that truly seeks to embrace and synthesize the totality of human knowledge, but an aprioristic system from which dissonant views must be excluded.

My second point may be related to this theological strain, for it has to do with an element of wishful thinking observable in Marxian analysis. Here I do not refer to the Utopia toward which Marxism faces—actually, I find Mandel quite plausible when he discusses the distant shape of things to come. Rather, I refer to the unwillingness of Marxism, particularly in the hands of a humane man like Mandel, to face squarely the problems of transition from the world as it now exists to socialism.

Here two problems strike me as most important. The first has to do with the means by which socialism may be imposed on the underdeveloped societies in which it now seems most likely to appear. Mandel writes: "No socialization (whether *de facto* or *de jure*) of enterprises is justifiable unless the technical conditions make possible a higher output this way than private enterprise can get; and no socialization is justifiable unless the small proprietors agree to it, either from conviction or from material interest, or (what is, of course, the ideal situation) from both motives at once."

As a declaration of democratic socialist intent, this is admirable, but as a guide for policy I suspect it is delusive. Mandel here elevates considerations of economics over those of politics, whereas in revolutionary fact, experience has shown that the political problem always takes precedence over the economic. Some degree of coercion, expropriation, forced nationalization, or collectivization seems an inescapable course for a newly constituted socialism in a backward society—a course that will inevitably affect the tone and character of the regime's subsequent political and economic career. This is a moral dilemma to which no Marxist that I know of has yet fully addressed himself.

The same wishful thinking appears when Mandel discusses the advent of socialism within the affluent world. "Present-day technique," he writes, "has . . . found a 'final' answer to the oldest of objections to a socialist society: 'Who, under socialism, will do the hard, unpleasant, and unhealthy types of work?' Today the answer is clear: machines will perform all these tasks by themselves."

But the answer is not clear. The simple fact is that we have not invented machines that can do most of the tasks that society finds hard, unpleasant, or unhealthy. Furthermore, to do so will not only be exceedingly difficult from an engineering point of view, but will be a staggering task of capital accumulation. To provide robots to do all the "dirty" work would very likely require the full efforts of two or three generations, if we forgot all about the need for capital of the underdeveloped world. During this long period of preparation, what means of coordination, inducement, or sanction will drive the socialist economy?

There is, in fact, one mechanism which, adroitly used, might do the trick—the mechanism of the market (suitably hedged about to avert its worst characteristics). But like many Marxist theoreticians, Mandel turns his back on this mechanism because he fears the "corrupting influence of money" (p. 655) or the incompatibility of the market with socialist objectives. This leaves us, unfortunately, with the necessity of applying some other means of recruiting and allocating the labor of society to the tasks of the transition period, and those other means, once the inducements of the market are ruled out, are either outright coercion or indoctrination. It is curious that many theoreticians of "pure" socialism like Mandel are so obsessed with the corrupting influence of material incentives and money exchange that they never stop to consider the corruption inherent in the other modes of labor mobilization that we know of.[3]

This leads me to my final point. Marxism is an effort to discover causality in the train of history. But what is the source of this causality? Essentially it seems to be the moving force of dialectics, expressed through the *predictable* activities of classes in conflict.

But how predictable are classes in their modes of be-

3. I cannot refrain from noting as well another theological attribute of Marxism in its horror of money and exchange, which so resembles that of the Church Fathers contemplating sexuality. The inadmissible thought is that trading and bargaining and "shopping," when conducted in an atmosphere free of duress, can be a source of pleasure for buyer and seller alike.

havior? Do we in fact know how various classes **"must"** behave in given circumstances? Bluntly, I do not think **we** do. It may well be (and herein again lies the power of Marxist analysis when applied to certain time periods or problems) that *some* classes in *some* situations are indeed "forced" to behave as they do. The classic example is the behavior of the nineteenth-century capitalist class in Marx's work—a class pressed by a destructive competition into the behavioral responses that would seal its own doom. But can we ascribe similar irresistible pressures to the economic environment of monopoly capitalism? Are all capitalist classes today pushed relentlessly to the same ideology, the same foreign policy, the same domestic measures? If so, how can we explain the diversity of manifestations of contemporary capitalism observable in different societies, from Sweden through South Africa to the United States, all of which are indisputably "capitalist"?

In this emphasis on the diversity of capitalist states, I do not wish to overlook the similarities of these societies which a Marxian scrutiny would stress—similarities of income distribution, industrial concentration, economic problems, etc. But the fact of difference remains, not only as an immensely important reality for the lives of people in these systems, but as a challenge to the underlying analytic concepts of Marxism itself. In a word, it suggests that the variables of geography and military tradition and national culture are at least as important—and at least as independent—as the variables of economics. To put it differently, we can say that the prime motive forces of history, in our day, seem to have moved from the relatively deterministic realm of economics to the relatively undeterministic realm of politics; perhaps we should simply say that after a period during which Marxian analysis was particularly cogent, the ruling determination of history has again reverted toward its original political base. Certainly when the history of the Vietnam war is finally written, the role of the military and the politicians will be far larger than that of the business interests.

Before this politicization (and militarization) of events Marxism is much reduced, not only in its specific predictive capability, but in its general historical relevance. It is surely significant, for example, that Mandel, who discusses the economic preconditions for and the difficulties of socialism so brilliantly, is mute before the problem which, more likely than any other, is apt to prove the undoing of socialism (or, for that matter, of capitalism)—the problem of political representation and responsibility. The word "democracy" recurs constantly throughout Mandel's book, but as a talisman, not as a term charged with specific meaning. A Marxist, I very much fear, is no more prepared to cope with the "contradictions" of individualism in a society of technologically imposed large-scale organization, or with the irrationalities and terrible dangers of the modern nation-state, than is anyone else.

It is for these reasons that I would find it cramping to call myself a "Marxist"—just as for the reasons previously cited I have no hesitation in expressing my agreement with much of Marxian analysis. What seems necessary now is to leave aside these categories and to search for an approach that both contains and goes beyond Marxism. No doubt such an all-embracing view will have to await another mind as penetrating and encyclopedic as that of Marx himself. In the meantime, however, we must begin to build our tentative syntheses from what knowledge social science has made available to us. For this purpose, the masterful re-presentation of Marxism by Ernest Mandel is as welcome as it will be indispensable.

CHAPTER 8

Technological Determinism

> The hand-mill gives you society with the feudal
> lord; the steam-mill, society with the industrial
> capitalist.—MARX, *The Poverty of Philosophy*

*T*hat machines make history in some sense—that the
level of technology has a direct bearing on the human
drama—is of course obvious. That they do not make all
of history, however that word be defined, is equally clear.
The challenge, then, is to see if one can say something
systematic about the matter, to see whether one can order
the problem so that it becomes intellectually manageable.

To do so calls at the very beginning for a careful specification of our task. There are a number of important ways
in which machines make history that will not concern
us here. For example, one can study the impact of tech-

nology on the *political* course of history, evidenced most strikingly by the central role played by the technology of war. Or one can study the effect of machines on the *social* attitudes that underlie historical evolution: one thinks of the effect of radio or television on political behavior. Or one can study technology as one of the factors shaping the changeful content of life from one epoch to another: when we speak of "life" in the Middle Ages or today we define an existence much of whose texture and substance is intimately connected with the prevailing technological order.

None of these problems will form the focus of this chapter. Instead, I propose to examine the impact of technology on history in another area—an area defined by the famous quotation from Marx that stands beneath our title. The question we are interested in, then, concerns the effect of technology in determining the nature of the *socioeconomic order*. In its simplest terms the question is: Did medieval technology bring about feudalism? Is industrial technology the necessary and sufficient condition for capitalism? Or, by extension, will the technology of the computer and the atom constitute the ineluctable cause of a new social order?

Even in this restricted sense, our inquiry promises to be broad and sprawling. Hence, I shall not try to attack it head-on, but to examine it in two stages:

1. If we make the assumption that the hand-mill does "give" us feudalism and the steam-mill capitalism, this places technological change in the position of a prime mover of social history. Can we then explain the "laws of motion" of technology itself? Or to put the question less grandly, can we explain why technology evolves in the sequence it does?

2. Again, taking the Marxian paradigm at face value, exactly what do we mean when we assert that the hand-mill "gives us" society with the feudal lord? Precisely how does the mode of production affect the superstructure of social relationships?

These questions will enable us to test the empirical content—or at least to see if there *is* an empirical content—in the idea of technological determinism. I do not think it will come as a surprise if I announce now that we will find *some* content, and a great deal of missing evidence, in our investigation. What will remain then will be to see if we can place the salvageable elements of the theory in historical perspective—to see, in a word, if we can explain technological determinism historically as well as explain history by technological determinism.

I

We begin with a very difficult question hardly rendered easier by the fact that there exist, to the best of my knowledge, no empirical studies on which to base our speculations. It is the question of whether there is a fixed sequence to technological development and therefore a necessitous path over which technologically developing societies must travel.

I believe there is such a sequence—that the steam-mill follows the hand-mill not by chance but because it is the next "stage" in a technical conquest of nature that follows one and only one grand avenue of advance. To put it differently, I believe that it is impossible to proceed to the age of the steam-mill until one has passed through the age of the hand-mill, and that in turn one cannot move to the age of the hydroelectric plant before one has mastered the steam-mill, nor to the nuclear power age until one has lived through that of electricity.

Before I attempt to justify so sweeping an assertion, let me make a few reservations. To begin with, I am fully conscious that not all societies are interested in developing a technology of production or in channeling to it the same quota of social energy. I am very much aware of the different pressures that different societies exert on the direction in which technology unfolds. Lastly, I am not unmindful of the difference between the discovery of a given machine and its application as a technology—for example, the invention of a steam engine (the aeolipile) by Hero of Alexandria long before its incorporation into a steam-mill. All these problems, to which we will return in our last section, refer however to the way in which technology makes its peace with the social, political, and economic institutions of the society in which it appears. They do not directly affect the contention that there exists a determinate sequence of productive technology for those societies that are interested in originating and applying such a technology.

What evidence do we have for such a view? I would put forward three suggestive pieces of evidence:

1. THE SIMULTANEITY OF INVENTION

The phenomenon of simultaneous discovery is well known.[1] From our view, it argues that the process of dis-

1. See Robert K. Merton, "Singletons and Multiples in Scientific Discovery: A Chapter in the Sociology of Science," *Proceedings* of the American Philosophical Society, CV (October, 1961), pp. 470–486.

covery takes place along a well-defined frontier of knowledge rather than in grab-bag fashion. Admittedly, the concept of "simultaneity" is impressionistic,[2] but the related phenomenon of technological "clustering" again suggests that technical evolution follows a sequential and determinate rather than random course.[3]

2. THE ABSENCE OF TECHNOLOGICAL LEAPS

All inventions and innovations, by definition, represent an advance of the art beyond existing base lines. Yet, most advances, particularly in retrospect, appear essentially incremental, evolutionary. If nature makes no sudden leaps, neither, it would appear, does technology. To make my point by exaggeration, we do not find experiments in electricity in the year 1500, or attempts to extract power from the atom in the year 1700. On the whole, the development of the technology of production presents a fairly smooth and continuous profile rather than one of jagged peaks and discontinuities.

2. See John Jewkes, David Sawers, and Richard Stillerman, *The Sources of Invention* (New York, 1960, paperback edition), p. 227, for a skeptical view.

3. "One can count 21 basically different means of flying, at least eight basic methods of geophysical prospecting; four ways to make uranium explosive; . . . 20 or 30 ways to control birth. . . . If each of these separate inventions were autonomous, i.e., without cause, how could one account for their arriving in these functional groups?" S. C. Gilfillan, "Social Implications of Technological Advance," *Current Sociology*, I (1952), p. 197. See also Jacob Schmookler, "Economic Sources of Inventive Activity," *Journal of Economic History* (March, 1962), pp. 1–20; and Richard Nelson, "The Economics of Invention: A Survey of the Literature," *Journal of Business*, XXXII (April, 1959), pp. 101–119.

3. THE PREDICTABILITY OF TECHNOLOGY

There is a long history of technological prediction, some of it ludicrous and some not.[4] What is interesting is that the development of technical progress has always seemed *intrinsically* predictable. This does not mean that we can lay down future timetables of technical discovery, nor does it rule out the possibility of surprises. Yet I venture to state that many scientists would be willing to make *general* predictions as to the nature of technological capability twenty-five or even fifty years ahead. This too suggests that technology follows a developmental sequence rather than arriving in a more chancy fashion.

I am aware, needless to say, that these bits of evidence do not constitute anything like a "proof" of my hypothesis. At best they establish the grounds on which a prima facie case of plausibility may be rested. But I should like now to strengthen these grounds by suggesting two deeper-seated reasons why technology *should* display a "structured" history.

The first of these is that a major constraint always operates on the technological capacity of an age, the constraint of its accumulated stock of available knowledge. The application of this knowledge may lag behind its reach; the technology of the hand-mill, for example, was by no means at the frontier of medieval technical knowledge, but tech-

4. Jewkes, et al. (see n. 2) present a catalogue of chastening mistakes (p. 230f.). On the other hand, for a sober predictive effort, see Francis Bello, "The 1960s: A Forecast of Technology," *Fortune,* LIX (January, 1959), pp. 74–78; and Daniel Bell, "The Study of the Future," *Public Interest,* I (Fall, 1965), pp. 119–130. Modern attempts at prediction project likely avenues of scientific advance or technological function rather than the feasibility of specific machines.

nical realization can hardly precede what men generally know (although experiment may incrementally advance both technology and knowledge concurrently). Particularly from the mid-nineteenth century to the present do we sense the loosening constraints on technology stemming from successively yielding barriers of scientific knowledge— loosening constraints that result in the successive arrival of the electrical, chemical, aeronautical, electronic, nuclear, and space stages of technology.[5]

The gradual expansion of knowledge is not, however, the only order-bestowing constraint on the development of technology. A second controlling factor is the material competence of the age, its level of technical expertise. To make a steam engine, for example, requires not only some knowledge of the elastic properties of steam but the ability to cast iron cylinders of considerable dimensions with tolerable accuracy. It is one thing to produce a single steam-machine as an expensive toy, such as the machine depicted by Hero, and another to produce a machine that will produce power economically and effectively. The difficulties experienced by Watt and Boulton in achieving a fit of piston to cylinder illustrate the problems of creating a technology, in contrast with a single machine.

Yet until a metal-working technology was established —indeed, until an embryonic machine-tool industry had taken root—an industrial technology was impossible to

5. To be sure, the inquiry now regresses one step and forces us to ask whether there are inherent stages for the expansion of knowledge, at least insofar as it applies to nature. This is a very uncertain question. But having already risked so much, I will hazard the suggestion that the roughly parallel sequential development of scientific understanding in those few cultures that have cultivated it (mainly classical Greece, China, the high Arabian culture, and the West since the Renaissance) makes such a hypothesis possible, provided that one looks to broad outlines and not to inner detail.

create. Furthermore, the competence required to create such a technology does not reside alone in the ability or inability to make a particular machine (one thinks of Babbage's ill-fated calculator as an example of a machine born too soon), but in the ability of many industries to change their products or processes to "fit" a change in one key product or process.

This necessary requirement of technological congruence[6] gives us an additional cause of sequencing. For the ability of many industries to cooperate in producing the equipment needed for a "higher" stage of technology depends not alone on knowledge or sheer skill but on the division of labor and the specialization of industry. And this in turn hinges to a considerable degree on the sheer size of the stock of capital itself. Thus the slow and painful accumulation of capital, from which springs the gradual diversification of industrial function, becomes an independent regulator of the reach of technical capability.

In making this general case for a determinate pattern of technological evolution—at least insofar as that technology is concerned with production—I do not want to claim too much. I am well aware that reasoning about technical sequences is easily faulted as *post hoc ergo propter hoc*. Hence, let me leave this phase of my inquiry by suggesting no more than that the idea of a roughly ordered progression of productive technology seems logical enough to warrant further empirical investigation. To put it as concretely as possible, I do not think it is just by happenstance that the steam-mill follows, and does not precede, the hand-mill, nor is it mere fantasy in our own day when

6. The phrase is Richard LaPiere's in *Social Change* (New York, 1965), p. 263f.

we speak of the coming of the automatic factory. In the future as in the past, the development of the technology of production seems bounded by the constraints of knowledge and capability and thus, in principle at least, open to prediction as a determinable force of the historic process.

II

The second proposition to be investigated is no less difficult than the first. It relates, we will recall, to the explicit statement that a given technology imposes certain social and political characteristics upon the society in which it is found. Is it true that, as Marx wrote in *The German Ideology,* "A certain mode of production, or industrial stage, is always combined with a certain mode of cooperation, or social stage," [7] or as he put it in the sentence immediately preceding our hand-mill, steam-mill paradigm, "In acquiring new productive forces men change their mode of production, and in changing their mode of production they change their way of living—they change all their social relations"?

As before, we must set aside for the moment certain "cultural" aspects of the question. But if we restrict ourselves to the functional relationships directly connected with the process of production itself, I think we can indeed state that the technology of a society imposes a determinate pattern of social relations on that society.

We can, as a matter of fact, distinguish at least two such modes of influence:

7. Karl Marx and Friedrich Engels, *The German Ideology* (London, 1942), p. 18.

1. THE COMPOSITION OF THE LABOR FORCE

In order to function, a given technology must be attended by a labor force of a particular kind. Thus, the handmill (if we may take this as referring to late medieval technology in general) required a work force composed of skilled or semiskilled craftsmen, who were free to practice their occupations at home or in a small atelier, at times and seasons that varied considerably. By way of contrast, the steam-mill—that is, the technology of the nineteenth century—required a work force composed of semiskilled or unskilled operatives who could work only at the factory site and only at the strict time schedule enforced by turning the machinery on or off. Again, the technology of the electronic age has steadily required a higher proportion of skilled attendants; and the coming technology of automation will still further change the needed mix of skills and the locale of work, and may as well drastically lessen the requirements of labor time itself.

2. THE HIERARCHICAL ORGANIZATION OF WORK

Different technological apparatuses not only require different labor forces but different orders of supervision and coordination. The internal organization of the eighteenth-century handicraft unit, with its typical man-master relationship, presents a social configuration of a wholly different kind from that of the nineteenth-century factory, with its men-manager confrontation, and this in turn differs from the internal social structure of the continuous-flow, semi-

automated plant of the present. As the intricacy of the production process increases, a much more complex system of
internal controls is required to maintain the system in working order.

Does this add up to the proposition that the steam-mill
gives us society with the industrial capitalist? Certainly the
class characteristics of a particular society are strongly
implied in its functional organization. Yet it would seem
wise to be very cautious before relating political effects exclusively to functional economic causes. The Soviet Union,
for example, proclaims itself to be a socialist society although its technical base resembles that of old-fashioned
capitalism. Had Marx written that the steam-mill gives you
society with the industrial *manager,* he would have been
closer to the truth.

What is less easy to decide is the degree to which the
technological infrastructure is responsible for some of the
sociological features of society. Is anomie, for instance, a
disease of capitalism or of all industrial societies? Is the
organization man a creature of monopoly capital or of all
bureaucratic industry wherever found? These questions
tempt us to look into the problem of the impact of technology on the existential quality of life, an area we have
ruled out of bounds for this chapter. Suffice it to say that
superficial evidence seems to imply that the similar technologies of Russia and America are indeed giving rise to
similar social phenomena of this sort.

As with the first portion of our inquiry, it seems ad-
visable to end this section on a note of caution. There is a
danger, in discussing the structure of the labor force or the
nature of intrafirm organization, of assigning the sole causal

efficacy to the visible presence of machinery and of over-looking the invisible influence of other factors at work. Gilfillan, for instance, writes, "engineers have committed such blunders as saying the typewriter brought women to work in offices, and with the typesetting machine made possible the great modern newspaper, forgetting that in Japan there are women office workers and great modern newspapers getting practically no help from typewriters and typesetting machines." [8] In addition, even where technology seems unquestionably to play the critical role, an independent "social" element unavoidably enters the scene in the *design* of technology, which must take into account such facts as the level of education of the work force or its relative price. In this way the machine will reflect, as much as mold, the social relationships of work.

These caveats urge us to practice what William James called a "soft determinism" with regard to the influence of the machine on social relations. Nevertheless, I would say that our cautions qualify rather than invalidate the thesis that the prevailing level of technology imposes itself powerfully on the structural organization of the productive side of society. A foreknowledge of the shape of the technical core of society fifty years hence may not allow us to describe the political attributes of that society, and may perhaps only hint at its sociological character, but assuredly it presents us with a profile of requirements, both in labor skills and in supervisory needs, that differ considerably from those of today. We cannot say whether the society of the computer will give us the latter-day capitalist or the commissar, but it seems beyond question that it will give us the technician and the bureaucrat.

8. Gilfillan (see n. 3), p. 202.

III

Frequently, during our efforts thus far to demonstrate what is valid and useful in the concept of technological determinism, we have been forced to defer certain aspects of the problem until later. It is time now to turn up the rug and to examine what has been swept under it. Let us try to systematize our qualifications and objections to the basic Marxian paradigm:

1. TECHNOLOGICAL PROGRESS IS ITSELF A SOCIAL ACTIVITY

A theory of technological determinism must contend with the fact that the very activity of invention and innovation is an attribute of some societies and not of others. The Kalahari bushmen or the tribesmen of New Guinea, for instance, have persisted in a neolithic technology to the present day; the Arabs reached a high degree of technical proficiency in the past and have since suffered a decline; the classical Chinese developed technical expertise in some fields while unaccountably neglecting it in the area of production. What factors serve to encourage or discourage this technical thrust is a problem about which we know extremely little at the present moment.[9]

9. An interesting attempt to find a line of social causation is found in E. Hagen, *The Theory of Social Change* (Homewood, Ill., 1962).

2. THE COURSE OF TECHNOLOGICAL ADVANCE IS RESPONSIVE TO SOCIAL DIRECTION

Whether technology advances in the area of war, the arts, agriculture, or industry depends in part on the rewards, inducements, and incentives offered by society. In this way the direction of technological advance is partially the result of social policy. For example, the system of interchangeable parts, first introduced into France and then independently into England, failed to take root in either country for lack of government interest or market stimulus. Its success in America is attributable mainly to government support and to its appeal in a society without guild traditions and with high labor costs.[10] The general *level* of technology may follow an independently determined sequential path, but its areas of application certainly reflect social influences.

3. TECHNOLOGICAL CHANGE MUST BE COMPATIBLE WITH EXISTING SOCIAL CONDITIONS

An advance in technology not only must be congruent with the surrounding technology but must also be compatible with the existing economic and other institutions of society. For example, labor-saving machinery will not find ready acceptance in a society where labor is abundant and cheap as a factor of production. Nor would a mass production technique recommend itself to a society that did not have a mass market. Indeed, the presence of slave labor seems

10. See K. R. Gilbert, "Machine Tools," in Charles Singer, et al. (eds.), *A History of Technology* (Oxford, 1958), Vol. IV, Ch. 14.

generally to inhibit the use of machinery and the presence of expensive labor to accelerate it.[11]

These reflections on the social forces bearing on technical progress tempt us to throw aside the whole notion of technological determinism as false or misleading.[12] Yet, to relegate technology from an undeserved position of *primum mobile* in history to that of a mediating factor, both acted upon by and acting on the body of society, is not to write off its influence but only to specify its mode of operation with greater precision. Similarly, to admit we understand very little of the cultural factors that give rise to technology does not deprecate its role but focuses our attention on that period of history when technology is clearly a major historic force, namely, Western society since 1700.

IV

What is the mediating role played by technology within modern Western society? When we ask this much more modest question, the interaction of society and technology begins to clarify itself for us:

1. THE RISE OF CAPITALISM PROVIDED A MAJOR STIMULUS FOR THE DEVELOPMENT OF A TECHNOLOGY OF PRODUCTION

Not until the emergence of a market system organized around the principle of private property did there also emerge an institution capable of systematically guiding the

11. See LaPiere (see no. 6), p. 284; also H. J. Habbakuk, *British and American Technology in the 19th Century* (Cambridge, 1962), *passim*.
12. As, for example, in A. Hansen, "The Technological Determination of History," *Quarterly Journal of Economics* (1921), pp. 76–83.

inventive and innovative abilities of society to the problem of facilitating production. Hence the environment of the eighteenth and nineteenth centuries provided both a novel and an extremely effective encouragement for the development of an *industrial* technology. In addition, the slowly opening political and social framework of late mercantilist society gave rise to social aspirations for which the new technology offered the best chance of realization. It was not only the steam-mill that gave us the industrial capitalist but the rising inventor-manufacturer who gave us the steam-mill.

2. THE EXPANSION OF TECHNOLOGY WITHIN THE MARKET SYSTEM TOOK ON A NEW "AUTOMATIC" ASPECT

Under the burgeoning market system, not only the initiation of technical improvement but its subsequent adoption and repercussion throughout the economy were largely governed by market considerations. As a result, both the rise and the proliferation of technology assumed the attributes of an impersonal diffuse "force" bearing on social and economic life. This was all the more pronounced because the political control needed to buffer its disruptive consequences was seriously inhibited by the prevailing laissez-faire ideology.

3. THE RISE OF SCIENCE GAVE A NEW IMPETUS TO TECHNOLOGY

The period of early capitalism roughly coincided with and provided a congenial setting for the development of an independent source of technological encouragement—the rise of the self-conscious activity of science. The steady expansion of scientific research, dedicated to the exploration of nature's secrets and to their harnessing for social use, provided an increasingly important stimulus for technological advance from the middle of the nineteenth century. Indeed, as the twentieth century has progressed, science has become a major historical force in its own right and is now the indispensable precondition for an effective technology.

It is for these reasons that technology takes on a special significance in the context of capitalism—or, for that matter, of a socialism based on maximizing production or minimizing costs. For in these societies, both the continuous appearance of technical advance and its diffusion throughout the society assume the attributes of autonomous process, "mysteriously" generated by society and thrust upon its members in a manner as indifferent as it is imperious. This is why, I think, the problem of technological determinism—of how machines make history—comes to us with such insistence despite the ease with which we can disprove its more extreme contentions. *Technological determinism is thus peculiarly a problem of a certain historic epoch—* specifically that of high capitalism and low socialism—*in which the forces of technical change have been unleashed, but when the agencies for the control or guidance of technology are still rudimentary.*

The point has relevance for the future. The surrender of society to the free play of market forces is now on the wane, but its subservience to the impetus of the scientific ethos is on the rise. The prospect before us is assuredly that of an undiminished and very likely accelerated pace of technical change. From what we can foretell about the direction of this technological advance and the structural alterations it implies, the pressures in the future will be toward a society marked by a much greater degree of organization and deliberate control. What other political, social, and existential changes the age of the computer will also bring we do not know. What seems certain, however, is that the problem of technological determinism—that is, of the impact of machines on history—will remain germane until there is forged a degree of public control over technology far greater than anything that now exists.

CHAPTER 9

Is Economic Theory Possible?

Just forty years ago, as a young professor at Kiel, Adolph Lowe asked the question *"Wie ist Konjunktur- theorie überhaupt möglich?"* [1]—how is a theory of the business cycle possible?—and answered that it was possible because the underlying economic process was, after all, determinable and dependable. Now, after a lifetime of reflection, he asks, "How is a theory of the underlying economic process itself possible?" and answers, to the discomfiture of his earlier self, that it is not—at least in the traditional sense of the word "theory"—for reasons which, among others, the

1. *Weltwirtschaftliches Archiv,* Vol. 24, 1926.

vagaries of the business cycle illustrate. Thus, as with many another philosopher, the outcome of a long process of investigation has been to fasten on the key premise of an earlier architecture of thought as constituting not an a priori from which analysis could proceed with assurance, but a proposition whose validity was to be the first to be called into question.

Already by the mid-1930's this trend of thought was visible in the interstices of Lowe's book *Economics and Sociology*. There the surface problem was to discover the mutual interests of, and the proper line of demarcation between, two rival disciplines for social analysis. But just below the surface one discerned an uneasy awareness of a fading relevance of what passed for economic theory to the complexities of the industrial process:

> . . . [N]ational, social and racial canons of behavior . . . obscure the single principle of money incentive. The ultimate result of all these transformations is the very opposite of the classical state of objective equilibrium; the deviations have become larger and longer-lasting, the readjustments slow and incomplete; the circular chain breaks periodically. Economic behavior has ceased to be the model of perfect social interaction.[2]

In the case of *Economics and Sociology* the uneasiness was resolved by making the supposed regularities of the cyclical process, rather than the linearities of the traditional "equilibrium path," the foundation for economic systematizing.[3] But now, in Lowe's latest book, *On Economic*

2. *Economics and Sociology* (London: Allen & Unwin, 1935), p. 76.
3. *Op. cit.,* p. 98: "[O]ur result [of placing cyclical analysis at the center of inquiry] is of even greater importance for the theoretical construction of a realistic scheme of the industrial circular flow. As long as the primary causes of the trade cycle persist, the economic process will produce its own data irrespective of other independent influences. The

Knowledge,[4] the premise of a dependable cycle has finally been relegated to the same limbo as that to which he had earlier assigned the idea of a "natural equilibrium," and the industrial process has been portrayed as subject to wholly unforeseeable twists stemming from its changed psychological and structural attributes. One might expect, in the circumstances, that the very act of theorizing would thereby be regretfully relinquished as well, the venerable relic of a simpler but, alas, vanished world. On the contrary, the abandonment of a belief in the empirical and historical regularities of the economic process has spurred Lowe to produce a final apologia for economic theory. Inevitably, however, its formulation—even its underlying rationale—has now changed decisively. No longer is theory to unravel for us a process, linear or cyclical, emerging spontaneously from the fixed interplay of human nature and the social and physical environment. Now theory becomes the means by which the economic process is consciously directed, or even generated, from a deliberately contrived interaction of manipulated participants and a controlled environment. As a result, the economist must abandon the luxury of an Olympian detachment from the spectacle he observes and elucidates. Willy-nilly he has been plunged into the mêlée and forced to become a critical actor in—more than that, a director of—the economic process.

Such a radical refashioning of the role of theory in the most "advanced" of the social sciences surely calls for com-

---

trade cycle will not be deflected from its typical course, and the fixed sequence of the cyclical phases represents the basic form of the circular flow and the theoretical system of coordinates of any realistic analysis."

4. *On Economic Knowledge: Toward a Science of Political Economics* (New York: Harper and Row, 1965). Numbers in parentheses in the text refer to pages in the book.

ment and re-exposition. As a long-standing student and disciple of Lowe's thought, that is what I seek to do here. Let me only say that I hope this desperately condensed, and personally interpreted, summary of the main argument of his recent work will be taken for no more than a gist of the original, to which interested readers must repair.

I

Let me begin an exposition of the argument with a brief glimpse at the state of contemporary methodology. It cannot be said that a passion for the subject is a mark of contemporary economics. Inquiries into the nature of economic theorizing, or into the relation between economic inquiry and science proper, are not only difficult to find these days, but when found rarely exhibit that zeal for exactitude so characteristic of other branches of contemporary economics. Mainly the attempt to discover a foundation for economics rests content with a more or less perfunctory statement about the role of scarcity as an "indispensable" condition for economic science, or in more sophisticated formulations, with an exposition of the "logic of choice" that emerges as a behavioral characteristic from the fact of scarcity.

Yet it is clear that economics, as we know it, does not embody *any* logic of choice selected at random, but a particular kind that is presumably dictated by scarcity. This is the logic of maximization. As a recent writer on the question has described it:

> Maximization provides the moving force of economics. It asserts that any unit of the system will move toward an equilibrium position as a consequence of universal efforts to maxi-

mize utility or returns. Maximization is a general basic law that applies to the elementary units and, by the rules of composition, to larger and more complicated collections of those units.[5]

I think it is fair to state that idea of maximizing, more or less as expressed above, constitutes the bedrock on which conventional economic theory rests. The reasons for this are twofold. In the first place, no other conception of human behavior yields as precise, determinable results as does the imaginary interplay of maximizing units. Secondly, the idea of maximizing corresponds to the ideas of "making money" or "profit-seeking" that we personally experience or are told about as basic attributes of the system in which we live.[6]

Yet the idea of maximizing, when we scrutinize it closely, is a curiously difficult one. For exactly what is it that we maximize? If we answer "utility"—that elusive ether of economics—we are soon hoisted by the petard of meaninglessness; as Samuelson has said, the claim that utility is maximized "is consistent with all conceivable behavior, while refutable by none." [7] But we face similar problems when we try to replace the "soft" word "utility" with various "harder"

5. Sherman Roy Krupp, "Equilibrium Theory in Economics and in Functional Analysis as Types of Explanation," in *Functionalism in the Social Sciences* (Philadelphia: American Academy of Political and Social Science, February, 1965), p. 69. The article goes on to describe "functional"—i.e., goal-seeking—systems as an alternative to "mechanical" maximizing systems. However, the behavior that generates the requisite feedbacks, etc., of these functional systems results from individuals and firms following the conventional maximizing courses of action.

6. Cf. Frank Knight, *On the History and Method of Economics* (Chicago: Phoenix edition, 1963), p. 164.

7. *Foundations of Economic Analysis* (1947 ed.), pp. 91–92. Despite its title, this book is more concerned with the conditions and consequences of a "given" economic model than with establishing the roots of that model in the real world. See discussion of maximization, *op. cit.*, pp. 15, 19, and especially 21–23. There is also no consideration of the empirical validity of maximization as the acknowledged underlying behavior postulate.

words, such as "returns." For example, so far as the individual is concerned, no one suggests that he seeks to maximize his gross cash revenue, but rather that he balances the benefits thus received against the pains of earning them—a formulation that quickly leads us to the conclusion that if the individual maximizes anything, it is still "utility." The situation is better in regard to firms where we can forget about nonpecuniary aspects and speak unambiguously about maximizing net cash income. This clarity holds, however, only for the firm in a purely competitive market. Once we enter the world of oligopoly, maximization of returns becomes an aim that can be translated into practice through the most contradictory activities—a fact that again makes the word "maximizing" disconcertingly empty of precise meaning.

Thus most attempts to find a "foundation" for economics quickly bring us to concepts that are as recalcitrant as they seem to be indispensable. It is not surprising that T. C. Koopmans, commenting on the diverse but equally unsatisfying methodological efforts on the part of Lionel Robbins and Milton Friedman, ends his essay with the lament: "One is led to conclude that economics as a scientific discipline is still somewhat hanging in the air." [8]

We shall return in due course to the problems raised in this very cursory introduction. The difficulties we have encountered serve a purpose for us here in setting the stage for an examination of Lowe's work. For Lowe in fact squarely challenges the prevailing methodological approach. First, he denies the operative reliability of maximization as a working principle of economic life. And beyond that, he proceeds to locate the foundations of economics in relation-

8. T. C. Koopmans, *Three Essays on the State of Economic Science* (New York: McGraw-Hill, 1957), p. 141.

ships quite different from those that place maximization, in its conventional sense, at the center of theoretical concern.

Not surprisingly, therefore, *On Economic Knowledge* begins from a different angle of entry than is commonly encountered. Rather than commencing with a prioris on the scarcity of nature or the logic of choice, the work begins with a question along another line: can economics be a science? Or to put it somewhat differently, since the question is meant rhetorically, if economics is to be a science, what qualifications must it have?

Lowe begins to answer the question by taking as his definition of science that put forth by Ernest Nagel in *The Structure of Science:* a science reveals "repeatable patterns of dependence" in which various properties of a subject stand to one another.[9] Note that this imposes none of the usual constraints on economics. A concern with "repeatable patterns of dependence" brings Lowe not to a consideration of a stingy nature and its effect on Man, but only to the much more general dependence of Man on the physical and chemical characteristics of the material world. In a word, it focuses initially on the traditional, if now sometimes overlooked, view of economics as a science of production. What is "scientific" in this man-matter relationship, however, are only those general laws of nature that affect human provision—of human behavior we have as yet nothing to say. Thus a part of the claim of economics to "patterns of repeatable dependence" rests on the fact that economic activity involves man with the regularities of the material world,

9. Ernest Nagel, *The Structure of Science* (New York: Harcourt, Brace and World, 1961), p. 4.

including not least those arising from the technology by
which nature is made to serve man.[10]

But these material realities serve only as a series of
boundary conditions or constraints on human activity, sad-
dling it, for example, with the problems of diminishing
returns, or endowing it with economies of scale. There is,
however, a second area in which "repeatable patterns of
dependence" can also be discerned. This is the relation, not
of Man and Matter, but of Man and Man, which is to say,
the necessity, in all economies above the Crusoe level, for
individual acts of production or distribution to be integrated
into a viable social whole.

Here the problem is quite different from that posed by
nature and its laws. The functioning of an economic society
requires that human activities, separated not only by the
division of labor, but by the various "micro-goals" that its
members may aspire to—be they leisure, or accumulation,

---

10. This concern with Man-Matter, and with production or provisioning, as a necessary, if not yet sufficient, condition for a definition
of economics brings Lowe into substantial disagreement with those who
define it solely as a study of "choice." Boulding, for instance, in a long
review of Lowe's book in *Scientific American,* May, 1965, takes the view
that economic man "is more interested in decisions than in provisions.
His economics rises out of scarcity simply because it is scarcity that
forces him to make decisions. If there were no scarcity he would not
have to make any choices. On this basis economics emerges as a generalized theory of choice." Per contra, Lowe would argue that the act
of choice, like the act of consumption, is in itself a psychological phenomenon about which economics has little or nothing to say. The
psychic riches of a hermit, or the psychological problems of a Buridan's
ass, do not enter into the economist's purview. Only insofar as consumption claims a known *quantity of goods* (or purchasable services), or
when choice involves the allocation of resources or of marketable labor,
does the economic problem enter. Choice is, no doubt, a creature of
scarcity—although the latter is a culturally conditioned and not an
absolute attribute of existence. But choice is *economically* meaningful
only to the extent that it affects the provisioning problem, just as a
"logic" of choice is interesting only if it follows consistent patterns,
preferably of maximization. Of this, more later.

or high consumption, or whatever else—be combined both vertically, in sequences of production, and horizontally, in relations of exchange. For this dependability of social relations, however, although it is as necessary as that of the physical world for human survival, we cannot look to "nature" as our guarantor. Rather, some system of social cooperation, enforced by generally observed sanctions and rewards, and coordinated by universally recognized signals, must bring about a sufficient degree of behavioral regularity for adequate social provisioning to ensue.

Thus the arrogation of a "scientific" status for economic analysis rests on two "repeatable patterns of dependence"— one the workings of nature, and the other a reliable system of behavioral coordination. But this analysis only opens, rather than closes, the problem of economic theory. As Lowe points out (p. 28), it suggests that economic science might quite properly follow a taxonomic orientation, concerning itself with the changing characteristics of the operation of economic systems under different technical conditions, such as preindustrial, or developing, or highly industrialized societies, or with the behavioral regularities characteristic of feudalism, laissez faire, collectivism, etc. In fact, however, Lowe emphasizes, "economic theory, as it is laid down in textbooks or is explored at the frontiers of research, concerns itself almost exclusively with market economies" (p. 28). This suggests that economics finds its main *theoretical* challenge not in the tasks of historical description or analysis, but in the exploration of the special problems of market systems. For it is here that we find a unique case of the "repeatable patterns" on which economic science rests. In market systems, in contradistinction to those obedient to tradition or command, there arises a "mysterious" synchronization of freely chosen micro-goals with an apparently unchosen, but nonetheless adequate, macro-goal for the entire society. In the spontaneous dovetailing of this freely chosen behavior into a more or less successful outcome for the community as a whole lies the unique problem to which economic investigation is naturally attracted, and which in fact raises economic theory from a taxonomic effort to the status of a genuine "explanatory" science.

II

Thus regularities of behavior as they exist in, affect, and are produced by, a market society become the central problem for economic theory. Lowe states these preconditions, however, only to move to his next and more important step. This is the contention that whereas market society in its earlier states did indeed produce the kinds of behavior that satisfy the needs of traditional theory, the organized capitalism of today does not.

The crucial point here is not that organized capitalism somehow interferes with the freedom of occupational choice, or movement, or with the free act of economic participation. It is rather that the general incentive of the actors —the behavioral force directed toward their substantive ends—is no longer strictly enjoined, as it is in classical market society. This incentive, or "action directive" in Lowe's term, on whose strict observance ultimately rests the orderliness of the aggregate provisioning process, is in fact none other than the maximization principle. It is expressed here, however, not in terms of a certain psychic state of satisfaction to which marketers "naturally" tend, but as *a set of behavioral rules* which they are forced to obey. Buyers must go to the cheapest market, sellers to the dearest; and there each must seek to complete his economic transaction at a price that represents the greatest economic advantage of which he is aware (p. 36). Lowe calls this behavioral pattern "the extremum principle"; from it indeed there follows —in a market of pure competition—the Paretian optimality situation in which each has maximized his provisions to the degree that the preferences of others allow.

This all-important governor of an orderly economic market process is encapsulated in the so-called Law of Supply and Demand. The law, whose tenets are familiar enough to every freshman economics student, is usually taken as a generalization concerning *actual* "normal" economic behavior. Lowe's position leads him instead to scrutinize the behavioral *requirements* for such a law to operate. One of these is extremum behavior, as above defined. A second requirement is a certain interpretation of future developments, abbreviatedly known as stabilizing elasticities of expectations. Only when the buyer or seller expects that a new level of prices will continue (or return to former levels) will his buying or selling behavior be appropriate for the law to yield its expected results. It is well known that the expectation that a change in prices will continue in the same direction will induce behavior contrary to that required by the law.

But the critical proposition is yet to follow. It is that conditions making for the economic behavior required by the law of supply and demand were in fact present during the era in which the classical conception of the market originated, whereas today's conditions lead to kinds of behavior incompatible with its normal operation. For this crucial contention Lowe relies mainly on two sources. Turning to the "business reports, autobiographies, correspondences, and governmental bluebooks" of the era of the industrial revolution, he finds a "widespread tendency toward the systematic extremum incentive . . ." (p. 45). This in turn can be traced back to a still deeper-lying socioeconomic constellation of forces. "The combined pressures of mass poverty, of social isolation of the individual in a competitively organized civil order, and of a cultural climate in which economic success had become the prime source of power and prestige make it easy to understand that the extremum principle became the supreme maxim of market behavior" (p. 69).

But it was not alone unbridled acquisitiveness coupled with the sharp proddings of need that provided the behavior requisite for a determinate economic system. Lowe finds as well reason to believe that the existing technical conditions also promoted a framework of expectations conducive to the appropriate action patterns. Here the main consideration is the small scale of the capital required for the budding manufacturing operations. In a passage cited from Adam Smith, Lowe cites the "stock" which will be promptly "withdrawn" if conditions prove unpromising and which will be as promptly reoffered if conditions improve (p. 72). He infers the prevalence of a highly mobile and fluid capital structure, in which working capital available on short notice from dealers is of more importance than heavy fixed equipment. Such a flexible state of affairs would contribute importantly to a quickly adjustable economic system in which deviations or "convulsions" in trade are short-lived, and in which, accordingly, short-run time horizons and stabilizing expectations should prevail.

By way of contrast, Lowe confronts us with the condition

of the psychological action directives and the state of expectations in the present stage of capitalism. The old-fashioned extremum principle has yielded to a bewildering variety of behavioral possibilities. Since the point is an important one, I shall quote at length:

> Attitudes such as the striving for fixed rates of return or business policies directed toward maintaining rather than increasing the value of assets or the share of the market seem in many a large corporation to take precedence over, or to modify in significant ways, the traditional struggle for maximum profit. These "homeostatic" tendencies are strengthened and at the same time transformed by the concern of modern business with public relations and also by its growing regard for wider social interests. No less striking as a symptom of new attitudes is a certain insensitivity on the part of major consumer strata to price fluctuations over time or to price differentials for physically homogenous products at one and the same time. There the traditional incentive of minimizing expenditure seems to give way to a preference for routinized purchases of branded goods at favorably located sellers (p. 47).

To this growing looseness of the extremum principle as a behavioral guide Lowe now adds a second characteristic of the contemporary economy. This is the high order of technical specificity and the large bulk of its fixed capital assets, with the ensuing reluctance—or inability—to establish the short run as the relevant profit horizon. To quote again:

> Not only does [the] growing "viscosity" of the industrial market exclude the short run as the proper horizon for calculation, but the diversity in the technical and organizational setup of agriculture, industry, and trade precludes the selection of any one time span as a basis for a general maximization rule. Indeed, practically any output decision must today be justified as satisfying some standard of pecuniary advantage duly interpreted. In other words, considering the state of uncer-

tainty in the modern industrial market, opposite actions such as increasing or decreasing output, raising or lowering prices, can be defended in one and the same situation as the most promising step for profit maximization (pp. 47–48).

This progressive deterioration of the conditions insuring predictable behavior patterns can of course be traced a considerable distance back into the nineteenth century. The amelioration of living conditions and the satiation of acquisitive appetites, as well as the stiffening of the capital structure, can be observed at least as early as the era in which Marx wrote. How did it happen, then, that the system as a whole maintained an essential orderliness, and that economic theorizing, however wide of the mark in instances of specific predictions, was yet not so far from observable reality as to be discarded out of hand?

The answer, according to Lowe, lies in the presence of "escapements," which together with the prevailing behavior patterns and the existing state of technology define the matrix within which the economic process unfolds. These escapements—such as a wave of suitable inventions, a population impulse, or geographic expansion—provide sufficient "extra-systemic" stimulus to override and correct the disequilibria that might otherwise be produced by sluggish action directives or cramping technical constraints (pp. 65–66, 77). Throughout the period of maturing capitalism, just such escapements, in the form of rising population, a steady stream of innovations, and, not least, wars, provided the necessary external boost. "It was extra-systemic forces making for continuous growth that reduced the risks of investment and created an expectational climate conducive to maintaining self-balancing tendencies, at least over the long run. In focusing attention on these tendencies, neo-classical

Economics maintained a hold, even if a tenuous one, on the real world" (p. 78).

Only when the pressure of these extra-systemic forces came to a halt in the late 1920's did we discover what the growing internal changes in behavior and technical structure could mean in terms of the massive dysfunction of the Great Depression. As a result we see in every Western economy the expansion of controls and public demand whose function—at least to the economic theorist—is to serve as a substitute for the "automatic" escapements of the late nineteenth century.

What does this trend of events mean for economic theory? It is clear that the results of contemporary predictive attempts have been highly unsatisfactory. Lowe instances the sorry record of economic forecasts starting with the erroneous expectation of a post-World War II depression, down through the miscalculation of the Korean inflation, the failure to read the 1958 recession correctly, the premature concern about a general decline in 1962. No one would deny that the short-run forecasting ability of economics is still very poor and that its ability to predict drops off precipitously over longer stretches of time. This Lowe attributes mainly to the weakening behavioral regularities of the system, and to its inflexible technical structure.

But a still more fundamental question is posed. In the new environment of organized capitalism, is it still meaningful to speak of economic "theory" as a method of predicting future states of the economic system from the knowledge of an initial stage and of the prevailing patterns of action? According to Lowe, it is not. The volatility of the micro-units' motivations leads to paradoxical consequences not only for economic theory but for economic policy. As Lowe writes:

[T]he contemporary dilemma—a dilemma no less frustrating for practice than it is for theory—can be precisely stated. If it is true that economic theory can be built only on observations of or speculations about actual behavior, and if it is also true that, to be amenable to theoretical generalizations, the patterns of actual behavior must be regular and stabilizing, the prevailing variety of conflicting action directives and the climate of expectational uncertainty are incompatible with any theory, and there can then be no scientific knowledge on the primary level. The dilemma can be stated in another way. We do have an economic theory, but it refers to situations in which there is no practical need for theoretical guidance, since the automatism of the system assures that all goes well. However, once this automatism begins to fail, scientific prediction turns into an indispensable condition for restoring the viability of the market process. But with the failure of the automatism the empirical basis for such prediction—the regularity of micro- and macro-movements—seems lost (p. 98).

III

The dilemma requires for its solution nothing less than the recasting of theory, making it explicitly and deliberately an arm of practice, and consciously adapting it for an economic model in which the previous foundation for theory—known behavior patterns—is lacking. This task leads Lowe into a still closer examination of the formal principles of traditional theory. In a highly original section he examines the mechanical, engineering, and organismic analogies and metaphors contained in traditional economic conceptualizing—that is, the more or less explicit borrowing for the purposes of economic abstraction of various features of classical mechanics (e.g., atomism, least action, or the conservation principle), or of engineering feedback systems (e.g., demand and supply adjustments), or of biological-organismic conceptions (e.g., the long-term evolution of economic systems).

All of these models—a "hybrid" version of which underlies traditional theory—offer certain valid insights into the market interaction of the human particles, but they still leave open the question of the extra-systemic, environmental forces that give rise to the particular micro-activities with which theory is to deal.[11] And since these external forces are neither immune from historical change nor so all-powerful that they make it impossible for any individual to resist them, the hybrid model at best describes economic processes over a highly limited range of experience. Once we exceed that range—roughly the age of the industrial revolution, when the environment came as close as it ever did to providing precisely the pressures needed for obedience to the canons of economic extremum behavior—we are faced with the problem of how to deal theoretically with the economic system that evolved out of this virtually closed and self-sustaining state of affairs.

This problem leads Lowe beyond the traditional model to

11. What the traditional models show with considerable clarity is that the supposed "good working order" that emerges spontaneously from the interplay of free economic particles is a misconstruction of the problem. "Indeed the market as envisaged by traditional theory is in good working order, but it is far from 'free' in the sense of resulting from spontaneously chosen modal micro-goals. Rather the choice of goals is imposed on the individual marketer by a very peculiar state of his environment. Conversely, experience during the laissez-faire stage of industrial capitalism demonstrated only too clearly that increasing spontaneity of decision-making by no means guarantees the good working order of the market. Rather the need for securing the minimum of stability required for continuous provisioning has made it imperative to counteract such spontaneity by contrived pressures of economic policy" (p. 132).

the formulation of a new theoretical analogue capable of explaining more adequately the relation of theory and actuality in the present. A specification of theoretical prerequisites adequate for the environment of early capitalism must somehow be transformed into one more closely congruent with the attributes of mature capitalism. To put it differently, the structural attributes and environmental conditions which could be taken as fixed and neutral in the theoretical models appropriate for early capitalism must give way to a new conception in which structure and environment themselves become subsumed as active, nonneutral factors in the economic processes of industrial capitalism. But this explicit inclusion of the environment rules out the critical conception implicit in traditional theory—that of a fixed mode of economic behavior. For if we once admit the environment as a changing and active factor, it is impossible to believe that micro-activity will thenceforth remain unchanged.

To sum up, the environment of growing affluence, of large-scale units, and of widened horizons of uncertainty progressively weakens the reliability of extremum action and negative feedbacks on which was built the stability of the system, both for the participants and for the observing economists. Hence, both practice and theory fall into the peril of indeterminacy. But both can be rescued, albeit at a very considerable price: "[T]*he principle of unlimited micro-autonomy must yield* to a new operational principle of decision-making" (p. 130). And, "Economics as a medium of passive contemplation, observing and systematizing autonomous processes, [must be] converted into *Political Economics,* namely, into an instrument of active interference with the course of these processes" (p. 91).

IV

The new operational principle by which determinacy is to be restored both to theory and to reality is designated *Control*.

As a principle, Control is not to be confused with the existing controls that already seek to stabilize affairs. "It is of the essence of the latter," says Lowe, "that they take the behavior of the micro-units for granted, confining themselves to modifying the natural and institutional framework within which micro-actions take their course. . . . In contrast, Control as here understood refers to a public policy that concerns itself with the shaping of the behavioral patterns themselves—by influencing the purposive and cognitive motivations of the actors immediately, or in a roundabout way through reorganization of the system's structure" (p. 131). This deliberate introduction of Control gives rise to a new phase of economic theory in which participation is indissolubly melded with observation. This Lowe calls Political Economics.

But the explicit elevation of Control, with its inextricable concern for the goals of economic activity, also works a fundamental change in the nature of theory itself. With the rejection of behavior as a fixed datum, it is no longer possible for the economist to rely on the hypothetico-deductive method traditional to economics, in which we extrapolate from a given state, through the postulate of fixed behavioral responses, to a successive state. Now that behavior has been explicitly relegated to the unknowns and that Control has been explicitly moved from the background, where it resulted from the quiet pressures of environmental conditions, to the foreground of conscious policy-making, a new "logic of goal-seeking" is required. This Lowe finds in the replacement of the traditional deductive process with a new "Instrumental" approach.

By Instrumentalism Lowe means *the use of economic reasoning*—i.e., knowledge about technical constraints, laws of production, structural or other incompatibilities in the provisioning process, etc.—*to infer behavior patterns appropriate for the achievement of deliberately selected terminal states*. Thus the destination of the economy ceases to be the unknown which is deduced from an initial state by the application of standard economic responses to given stimuli, and becomes instead the postulated *datum* which serves as the goal to which successive stages of technical interlocking and behavioral response must be adapted and accommodated. The Law of Supply and Demand, for instance, now ceases to be an a priori of human behavior which can be applied in all market situations, and becomes instead a set of "instructions" to be followed by sellers and buyers if a desired goal of "market equilibrium" is to be attained. In similar fashion the propensity to consume would cease to be a behavioral constant to be mechanically used for the determination of the multiplier, and becomes a pattern toward which consumer behavior must be guided, provided that such and such a multiplier is needed to achieve a certain economic macro-target.

This introduction of political direction into the very heart of economic theory changes the theoretical procedure in still other ways than in inverting the established chain of syllogisms. It destroys once and for all any claims to timelessness for economic theory, instead explicitly relating each act of theorizing to the particular constellation of events for which it is intended. This follows because each act of inference in the instrumental chain can be verified only when the desired terminus is in fact achieved or missed. Thus, as the data of environment change, or as knowledge of behavioral stimuli improves, the theoretical work of the economist must change *pari passu*.

Lowe analyzes this theoretical work needed for an economy of Control in a threefold way: first, as the political problem of defining goals; second, as the scientific step of elaborating the "path" of the system from a given to a terminal state; and third, as the administrative problem of securing the requisite micro-behavior to achieve the desired end. For societies that retain economic micro-autonomy as an independent high-ranking value the crucial variable amenable to public manipulation will be that of expectations. Lowe suggests that modified extremum behavior (not too different perhaps from that blend of profit-seeking and "statesmanlike consideration" characteristic of the more public-minded large corporations today), guided by government policies planned to stabilize the general business outlook, may permit a reasonable degree of social control during these years in which we grope our way toward "the next stage in which the social process will be the manifestation of responsible action rather than an inexorable sequence of events" (p. 160).

V

It remains only to add a few comments and observations on the main theme of Lowe's book.[12] These must surely begin with some reflections on the essential thesis of the work—that the erstwhile determinacy of economic behavior is weakened to such an extent that it is no longer capable of supporting a superstructure of traditional theory.

It may be that this central thesis will prove as difficult to verify or refute as the Weber-Tawney hypothesis. Like the latter, Lowe's contention has a prima facie plausibility— but again like the Weber-Tawney hypothesis, it is far from an uncontestable proposition. Take, for instance, Lowe's assumption about the prevalence of extremum behavior during the industrial revolution. It is true, of course, that the general level of affluence was then much lower than now, and as a result we would expect a corresponding sharpening of economic appetites. And yet the matter is not cut-and-dried. There were not only the avaricious manufacturers but the gentlemanly farmers, and not only the starving working class but a well-to-do middle class with whom we must reckon. In fact, we know very little about actual modes of behavior in that period, but it is likely that extremum actions were liberally interlaced with other kinds of action directives.

12. I have omitted entirely any consideration of a long central section on Instrumentalist foreshadowings among the major economists from Smith to Keynes, as well as any mention of a final section where Instrumentalism is applied in the paradigmatic cases of stabilization and balanced growth. For these and many peripheral matters the reader must have recourse to the book itself.

Nor can we assert without hesitation that the expectations of businessmen were mainly stabilizing in an earlier era. It is true that Adam Smith talks of "dealers" in capital, and describes as being of some significance a pin factory employing only ten men; but it is also true that large amounts of capital were already "sunk" in the great textile establishments of Arkwright and Strutt, and in the works of Boulton and Watt and of Wilkinson. For such large capitalists, at least, the horizon of planning and the immobility of capital were probably not too different from that in similar industries today. Moreover, the "bubbles" and panics of the eighteenth and early nineteenth centuries hardly argue for a general stability of expectations, but rather for a sense of uncertainty not too different from that of today.

Turning to the present, I would similarly qualify the sharp contrast between yesterday and today explicit in Lowe's formulations. It is admittedly difficult to find classic maximizing activity in certain key areas of the economy such as the short-run behavior of large corporations, but if we look to other areas—agriculture or small business or the labor market—we can still observe traditional patterns in operation. More than that, predictions based on the assumptions of traditional theory still yield acceptable results in many cases: location theory, for instance, quite accurately predicts the movement of capital according to the principle of maximum economic advantage; generalizations based on the assumption of declining demand curves yield useful results in market analysis; and the theory of comparative advantage, itself founded on an assumption of maximizing behavior, enables us to project roughly accurate flows of international and interregional trade.

If contemporary extremum behavior is not quite passé,

neither are all current expectations adversely affected due to the immobility of capital. It is true that the large firms of today are typically saddled with vast quantities of fixed capital, but it is also true that they enjoy large cash flows that allow them to reshape the direction of their economic efforts within short periods—the prime instances being conversion to war, or in time of peace the adaptive efforts of the chemical companies. Moreover, studies show that the capital-output ratio in the economy at large has been falling —that is, that a given dose of capital yields a larger flow of output than formerly. This too argues against, rather than for, an increasing immobility of capital.

Such observations make me wish to soften Lowe's contrast between a "deterministic" past and an "indeterministic" present. We do not yet live in a world in which Macy's can ignore Gimbels, or in which men seek to buy dear and sell cheap, or where corporations act without thought of maximizing profits. On the other hand it is equally undeniable that consumers no longer buy to take the last penny of advantage, and that corporate "maximum" profits become increasingly defined in terms of long-run market power rather than in terms of short-run money income. In a word, we seem to span two worlds, one of the past, to which established theory applies, and one of the future, to which Instrumentalist considerations are more germane, and our situation is rendered doubly difficult in that we are willing neither to rely on the appositeness of traditional theory nor to consign ourselves to the ministrations of Control. Indeed, it may be that the most striking contrast between past and present (so far as economic behavior is concerned) lies not in the altered environment but in the changed public view of that environment, especially in the growing public unwillingness to tolerate a degree of instability once accepted without complaint.

These reflections bear on the rationale, rather than on the relevance, of Instrumentalism. They touch as well, however, on the practicality of the objective of Instrumentalist Control. As we have seen, Lowe gives short shrift to programs that constitute the "escapement mechanisms" of contemporary capitalism, since these are based on the expectation of traditional system-stabilizing behavior, and urges in their place programs that will set out directly to reshape behavior itself.

In fact, however, the contemporary mechanisms, such as fiscal policy, monetary policy, etc., work fairly well during periods of economic calm. This suggests that the theoretical premises on which they are constructed are not wholly wide of the mark, and that traditional theorizing continues to have both importance and reliability during "normal" times. There remain, of course, the all-important abnormal times when behavior *is* unreliable and when standard actions taken on the expectation of standard responses can backfire. Presumably, however, at just such moments of crisis, the government—even though operating on traditional theoretical assumptions—resorts to "crash programs," "emergency measures," etc., whose purpose, albeit unwittingly, is indeed Instrumental in aiming to restore normal stabilizing activity.

Whether or not such programs, informed by a traditionalist view of the economic process, will be powerful or persuasive or adroit enough to realize their intended results is a moot point. But it is likely to remain moot, even under the aegis of an avowedly Instrumental approach. For Instrumentalism asks us to substitute one kind of prediction—the prediction of the effect on economic activity of a certain political program—for an older kind of prediction: the attempt to foresee the effect of supposedly "fixed" behavioral patterns within a given set of conditions. The old system may be untenable because we know that its behavioral postulates are unreliable. But the new kind of prediction involves us in an attempt to make cause-effect statements about social processes as to whose outcome we can do little more than guess. The links between policy and behavior, between signal and cognition, between stimulus and action, are still so little understood that the guidance of a better "basic" theory may not offer much by way of better practice. Indeed, the likelihood is that the policies of a government following the ideas of Instrumentalism would probably vary but little from those based on traditional economics—at least, so long as one macro-goal of the planners was to preserve the market system itself.

But must Instrumentalism restrict its programmatic ideas to those that rely on the unreliable stimuli and signals by which a government authority might try to manipulate its marketers? Might not Instrumentalism be used more effectively to promote control by command rather than by persuasion?

The question raises difficult issues, of which Lowe is thoroughly aware. By elevating micro-autonomy to the status of a macro-goal in itself, Lowe admittedly limits the practical reach of Instrumental theory to those adjustments, such as stability or balanced growth, for which the requisite marketing behavior can, with some good fortune, be adduced. On the other hand, other goals, perhaps of greater significance in the long run—the radical redistribution of income or the substantial curtailment of property rights or the

de-commercialization of large areas of life—may lie quite
beyond the limits of market adjustment. In a word, there
are apt to be important objectives that would require the
abrogation of the market mechanism for their achievement,
and which are ruled out of reach by the elevation of micro-
autonomy to a cardinal position in the hierarchy of goals.

Lowe is concerned with this possibility and with the
fact that powerful forces making for social change and for
administrative centralization may cause the demands of the
future to exceed the adaptive capabilities of a market society.
If this is so, then Instrumentalism may indeed be taken over
by the protagonists of a command system, and its relevance
to a society of micro-freedom forgotten.

Yet in admitting the possibility that a micro-autonomous
society may not survive the stresses of the future, Lowe also
offers a theoretical insight on which may be built the strong-
est possible "last ditch" defense of the values which such
a society seeks to preserve. In a sense, the final import of
Lowe's book is the possibility of a new alternative to the
time-honored ways in which economic societies have maintained that minimum of orderliness without which the provisioning chain would be broken. Tradition, command, and
the marketplace have hitherto provided the pressures by
which the individual has been subordinated to the community. Now Lowe offers a fourth way—the regularization
of behavior through the use of the faculties of reason,
welded, to be sure, to the remaining only partially tamed
forces of acquisitiveness, prestige, etc. For it is Lowe's
implicit hope that a new understanding of the requirements
of economic order—not only on the part of the directing
authorities but equally on the part of the obliging economic

citizens—can provide a new basis for that voluntary discipline that must come from all if it is not to be imposed on all.

Thus the plea for Instrumentalism is not merely a plea for a reconstitution of economic theory. It is also a weapon specifically forged for the preservation of "free" societies, to whatever extent their freedom proves to be historically viable and morally defensible.

CHAPTER **10**

On the Limits of
Economic Prediction

*T*he uses of economics are many, as are also the method-
ologies by which its various purposes can be defended or
elucidated.[1] In this essay I shall confine my attention, however, to but one of its many aims—the predictive intent

1. There is a considerable literature on the matter. Let me mention
as standard references Milton Friedman, *Essays in Positive Economics,*
J. M. Keynes, *Scope and Method of Political Economy,* and Lionel Robbins, *An Essay on the Nature and Significance of Economic Science.*
Especially germane to this essay are Tjalling Koopmans, *Three Essays on
the State of Economic Science,* Adolph Lowe, *On Economic Knowledge*
and essays in *Economic Means and Social Ends* (ed. R. Heilbroner),
and Fritz Machlup, "Operational Concepts and Mental Constructs in
Model and Theory Formation," *Giornale degli Economisti e Annali di
Economia,* September–October, 1960.

that constitutes a distinguishing characteristic of so much economic work. Lest I be accused of claiming that prediction is an integral part of *all* economics, let me explicitly point out that the discipline has taxonomic, structural, purely formal, normative, and still other aspects, none of which involves prediction, and all of which have their useful roles to play. Nonetheless, I do not think that most economists would disagree with my contention that a predictive purpose lies at the heart of much of economic science today, in particular when that science is used on behalf of policy.

The question I then wish to pursue is whether we can discern—admittedly in a general rather than a particularistic way—any *inherent* boundaries or limits to this predictive capability. It may be objected at the outset that in putting the matter in this way I have already begged the crucial question by assuming that economics *has* a predictive capability. Since the bulk of this paper will be devoted to establishing the reasons for believing that this capability is severely bounded, perhaps I had best begin by discussing how economic science can lay claim to the very possibility of prediction in the first place.

I

As with all the sciences, economics asserts its capabilities for prediction on one of two grounds. The first we may call *correlational*. Correlational prediction establishes that certain relationships have been regularly observed in the past, and predicts that they will again be observed in the future *without positing any causal explanations of the ob-*

served relationship. For example, Friedman observes that individuals are "extraordinarily stubborn about the real amount of money they want to hold." He suggests that "Part of the explanation is the currency held by business enterprises. I do not know what the rest of the explanation is." He predicts that if the amount of nominal money in the community is increased, "people can and *will* [my emphasis] try to reduce their cash balances and the process of trying . . . will bid up the prices of all sorts of goods and services." [2]

In some realms of pure science, where the notion of causality disappears into a mathematical cloud, it may be that correlational prediction is an ultimate terminus for inquiry. This is a matter of current controversy, but it is not relevant to our concerns. For in the applied natural sciences, or in the sphere of social science, correlational forecasts must be taken as no more than a makeshift substitute for a more "solid" basis for prediction: the construction of a model in which a special kind of *functional relationship* is established among the variables in the process.

This special relationship consists in identifying the interaction of the variables as specific instances of a general case, or if we will, as instances of the workings of a "law." For example, if we are asked to predict whether a certain profit-seeking firm will hire another worker, and if we know that the marginal cost of that worker will be greater than the marginal revenue attributable to him, few economists would hesitate to predict that the worker will not be hired. Why? Because the prediction follows logically as a

2. Milton Friedman, *Inflation, Causes and Consequences,* pp. 10, 11, 12.

conclusion from the "law-like" premise about the short-run maximizing behavior of entrepreneurs.

In view of the higher status of this second kind of prediction, I will concern myself in the remainder of this essay exclusively with problems that affect what we may call predictive model-building, or more conveniently, predictive theorizing. Perhaps I should add to my opening caveat that not all theorizing need be predictive in purpose, and that not all prediction—*vide* correlational analysis—need be based on theoretical models. But economics certainly abounds with models constructed with predictive intent, and it is the properties of these models that we must now examine.

All predictive models, economic or other, rest ultimately on two preconditions. The first is the ability to conceive fruitful categories of generalization with which to bring intellectual order into the world of raw data. This obvious precondition is more important than might at first appear, for it determines what it is that we wish to predict. That problem will not concern us until our conclusion; instead let us note that to be useful for a predictive model this concept- or construct-forming activity must be accompanied by the *practical possibility of fleshing out the construct with data*. The theory of income determination, for example, awaited both the conceptual formulation of such relevant categories as consumption, investment, etc., and the establishment of the means of compiling the data in question. In much the same way, predictive models of the natural world depend not only on the gradual evolution of the appropriate "paradigms," but on the subsequent development of the data required to make the new constructs statistically operational.[3]

The second aspect of the predictive model-building process is no less essential than the first. It is the ability to formulate so-called "higher-level" hypotheses capable of embracing the data that have been compiled as potential "evidence" under the guidance of the initial constructs. The success of the predictions that are thereafter made by deductive logic depend, therefore, on the extent to which the overarching hypothesis succeeds in summarizing the "repeatable patterns of dependence" of the events themselves.[4] In a word, the model will predict successfully, provided that its higher-level hypotheses are "right."

I do not think there is much disagreement as to the general nature of predictive theorizing that I have just described. Now I wish, however, to proceed to my central theme, which is to inquire into the limitations of this process when it is applied to the specific universe of events denoted as "economic." More precisely I wish to show (1) that there are indeed limits to the predictive capability of economic model-building, imposed both by the nature of the data and by difficulties in framing hypotheses capable of "anticipating" events in the real world; and (2) that the nature of these limits is very different in the short run and in the long— using these words, as we shall see, in a rather special (and non-Marshallian) sense. At the conclusion I will venture a word as to the handicaps that this predictive limitation imposes on economic science.

3. Thomas S. Kuhn, *The Structure of Scientific Revolutions,* Chs. 7–8.
4. Ernest Nagel, *The Structure of Science,* p. 4.

II

At first glance, economics seems unusually well-adapted to the predictive tasks it undertakes because it builds its predictive theories on two well-defined hypotheses, both of which give every promise of yielding reliable results. The first of these concerns the physical nature of the production process with which economics is largely (although not exclusively) concerned. By the physical nature of the production process, I mean the engineering sequence of inputs and outputs, or the technical combination or coordination of different kinds of inputs to achieve a desired output. The act of predictive theorizing begins with the premise that these physical requirements of production can be described in functional terms that will enable us to know *how changes in inputs will affect outputs*. These functional relationships may be very complex, but it is assumed that they will not be arbitrary or unknowable. If we are to forecast the economic process, in other words, there must be no "surprises" in the production process. The production function need not be linear or smooth, but it cannot change without warning into a step function, or display sudden discontinuities, without making the act of prediction *ipso facto* impossible.

We shall revert shortly to the plausibility of this essential precondition for economic prediction. But first we must consider a second and no less necessary condition. This is the assumption that we can make reliable statements of a functional kind concerning the *behavioral response to economic stimuli*. These responses need not necessarily be "maximizing" (or even acquisitive), for perfectly adequate hypotheses concerning behavior can be based on the assumption of homeostatic responses (as in some aspects of traditional societies), or potlatch behavior, or whatever. The only requirement, clearly similar to that applicable to the production process, is that whatever the behavioral response, it must be related in a determinable manner to the stimuli that produce it. We must know, before the fact, how human actors will react to economic incentives or sanctions if we are to foretell the movements of the economic system.

I do not think there can be much question that the *possibility* of predictive theorizing in economics rests on these two premises. More to the point, there is not much question, either, that the two premises are "validated" in the real world. For it is not merely the possibility of economic theory but the continuity of industrial market societies that rests on these basic assumptions. If most production functions were in actuality irregular or discontinuous, the smallest changes in the organization of the productive process could lead to a breakdown of the economic system. In the same way, if behavioral reactions were generally unreliable and "lawless," the web of interactions that binds together the market mechanism would have broken down long ago. Thus in the very persistence of the economic system we can find common-sense support for—although not, of course, strictly logical proof of—the validity of the two hypothetical pillars of economic prediction.

The failure of the real world to falsify our basic hypotheses must be qualified, however, by the time span and degree of fineness of our predictions. It is one thing to "predict" the continuity of the system, based on our suppositions of regular production and behavior functions, and another thing to use these presumed functions to predict precise rates of growth, levels of employment, frequency and amplitude of cyclical deviations, etc. It is clear enough from experience that our capability for precise prediction is, to say the least, somewhat less than perfect. The question must then be asked as to whether this failure to produce finely timed and exactly quantified predictions is due to a failure to allow for extraneous factors (comparable to gusts of wind that might disturb a projectile's flight path), or whether it reflects deeper-rooted shortcomings in the data-gathering or hypothesis-making constituents of the theorizing process.

It will be useful if we begin to examine this critical question by dividing the aims of predictive theory into a short-run and a long-run aspect. By the short-run, we mean a period of time during which the fundamental constituents of the two functions do not change. In the case of the production function this requires that we hold technology "constant" and focus our attention on changes in the input mix and in the input-output relationship within a "given" level of technique for the economy as a whole.[5] With behavior, we also take as invariant the fundamental determinants of the underlying motivation, assuming that the maximizing or homeostatic or other drives continue to hold sway during the period in question. In a word, we confine our attention to movements along, rather than of, the production and behavior curves.

Turning now to the production function, and asking what obstacles it poses to accurate numerical prediction, we im-

5. A "given" level of technique is not an easy concept to specify. We will use it in the sense that no changes in the production process affecting the main items of output during the period in question would require the replacement of large quantities of capital or the retraining of substantial numbers of the labor force.

mediately encounter the problem of the adequacy of the data from which our higher-level hypotheses must be formed. To predict the effect of every possible small change in inputs on outputs, even assuming that techniques are un-altered, we would have to know the slope and shape of isoquants for every important commodity, which is to say the physical, chemical, and engineering requirements for an enormous array of products and services.

Here we enter a world in which there exists a vast litera-ture in the abstract and a very small one in the concrete. Although we have a clear understanding of the notions of marginal elasticities of substitutions, variable returns to scale, increasing and diminishing returns, etc., the clear fact is that we do not know the shape of the actual produc-tion functions for most commodities, as is demonstrated all too plainly in our inability to construct a dynamic input-output matrix.

Thus there are obvious limitations on our ability to make fine predictions arising out of our sheer ignorance of the nature of the production process. Yet, even if it takes a heroic act of faith, it is not inherently implausible that such knowledge could be attained. There are, as far as we know, physical and chemical properties of materials that determine the proportions in which they can be combined, and given the constraint of an unchanged technology, there are also limits established by mechanics as to the minimum amounts of labor energy of different kinds that are required to work a given process. Thus it seems within the bounds of plausibil-ity that it would be possible to construct a set of production functions that would mirror with a fair degree of accuracy the actual production possibilities open to society in the short run; or to put it differently, we would expect the degree of

precision of our predictions to increase concomitantly with
our grasp of the available facts.

Quite a different situation faces us, as Lowe emphasizes,
when we look into the requirements for a reliable behavior
function for the short run.[6] For here, the matter to be predicted is a psychological rather than a physical reaction.
In order to predict the behavior of economic actors (1) we
must know whether a given stimulus—a price rise, a change
in income, a government directive, etc.—will give rise to
"positive" or "negative" behavior, that is, to buying or selling, to investing or disinvesting, to compliance or disobedience; and (2) we must also be able to estimate how "intense" will be the response called forth by the stimulus.

It is obvious that the compilation of the necessary data to
support our behavioral hypotheses is intrinsically much
more difficult than is the case with the world of production.
Yet if we again make a heroic effort of belief, it seems possible to venture an affirmative estimate as regards at least
one of the wanted sets of behavioral data, that of the intensity of reactions to given stimuli. Assuming that we know
the direction of response, it is plausible to expect that a study
of sufficient quantities of data could yield fairly reliable
patterns of elasticities of substitution among commodities,
or of the marginal propensities of different groups to consume or invest, etc. If we had such data—and there seems
no inherent reason why we could not steadily improve our
knowledge of such behavioral traits—we could then predict,
for example, by how much our purchases of x would rise (or
fall) if the price of x or y were to change by such-and-such
a percentage, or by how much a change in the rate of interest would induce or restrict the flow of investment.

6. *On Economic Knowledge, op. cit.,* pp. 34–39.

Hence, whereas there is a practical limitation to the capability of short-term prediction in the collection of data (no doubt much more difficult in the case of behavior than in the case of production), here too we find no inherent limit to the erection of usable higher-level hypotheses. Moreover, economic predictions can be very useful even if they are not wholly accurate. I do not have to be able to foretell the degree of change within a fraction of one percent to render a useful service in predicting that the effect of an increase in government spending is likely to be a rise in the volume of output. Or to put the case even more generously, it may be enough that I can make negative predictions, such as that the effect of a rise in interest rates is very unlikely to bring about an investment boom.

The problem of short-run prediction takes on a graver aspect, however, when we turn to the remaining component of behavioral regularity on which a reliable model would have to be based. This is the question of whether a given stimulus will induce "positive" or "negative" behavior on the part of the actor. As is well known, a price rise, interpreted as a precursor to further price rises, will induce additional rather than decreased buying. A penalty for, say, hoarding, read as the sign of worse to come, may bring about a rush to hoard, etc.

This indeterminacy in the "direction" of economic response is more or less confined, it should be emphasized, to critical moments or turning points in the economic process —indeed, the presence of "perverse" behavior may be a major factor in bringing about such turning points. But perverse reactions, although few enough not to endanger the market process during periods of normality, bulk very large when the validity of predictive theory is at stake. For the purpose of prediction, as we have already said, is hardly to confirm that the normal processes will continue, but to alert us to the moments when it will not. And it is, of course, just at these points that the labile behavior patterns of the economic actors undermine the very possibility of prediction itself. If, for example, I know that a rise in the rate of government spending *may* affect expectations adversely, then I cannot predict whether more spending will be accompanied by a larger or smaller volume of output. It follows as well that this uncertainty as to behavior makes it impossible even to make negative predictions, for I can no longer be sure that a rise in interest rates—interpreted as a harbinger of a still tighter monetary policy to come—will not induce corporations to increase their borrowings or their capital expenditures before the government "cracks down."

Is the problem of the potential perversity of behavior also a matter that can be repaired by the accumulation of sufficient data? The question ultimately resolves to untestable beliefs in determinism or free will. But even if we take an extreme determinist point of view, it is clear that the problem of amassing the relevant data is qualitatively different in this case from the previous one. The difference is metaphorically suggested by the contrast between a rheostat and a switch. When we are seeking to predict the intensity of behavioral response, we are taking for granted the direction of the flow of current and confining ourselves to estimating its strength and the strength of the resistances it meets. When we are seeking to predict the direction of response, we need to know whether we will encounter a critical threshold of response at which the current reverses itself. Although we could probably learn a good deal about the nature of the environmental conditions that are propitious for "perverse" reactions, it seems probable that there will remain an inner core of the decision-making process that will be for all intents and purposes beyond any possible information retrieval system. The difficulties of forecasting movements in the stock or commodity markets, or the reactions of businessmen to monetary or fiscal policy are therefore grounded at a deeper level than the difficulties of forecasting the extent of the response, once we know what its "sign" will be.

III

Thus, in the short run, we encounter a fundamental and impassable limit to the powers of predictive theorizing in the interpretational (or expectational) strand of economic behavior. The practical importance of this limit obviously depends on the frequency and pervasiveness of "perverse" interpretations, a matter to which we will refer subsequently. First, however, let us turn to the problem of the limits of predictive theorizing over very long periods, for here we find an instructive and surprising change. The possibility of long-run prediction, like prediction in the short run, is also based on the possibility of discovering regular patterns of material and behavioral functions, but now we find that the breakdown in the predictive possibilities lies not in the realm of behavior but in that of technics and engineering.

How can behavior, the quicksand for short-run analysis, become a bedrock for hypotheses from which we can deduce conclusions about the long run? The answer is that we are now concerned with periods longer than those that will be affected by the indeterminacy of reactions that troubled us in the short run. Indeed, it is characteristic of the perturbations of behavior that are so disastrous for short-run prediction that they are self-limiting or of brief duration. The reason for this is clear. Perverse market behavior, being non-self-equilibrating, is exceedingly difficult to sustain for extended periods of time. Although such behavior may be rationally justified and therefore self-reinforcing for short periods (when buyers, expecting higher prices, increase their rate of purchasing and find that prices are in fact higher), the pursuit of these perverse patterns must sooner or later lead to a breakdown of the market mechanism. At this juncture, when expectations must be newly formulated, we typically find a resumption of normal marketing behavior. In the meantime, the path of the system will have "jumped," which will have upset short-run predictions, but when the regularity of the behavioral element resumes, the possibilities for prediction will be restored.

A second and no less important reason for the long-run stability of behavior is that the underlying drives or mixture of drives on which it is based—acquisitiveness, homeostasis, obedience, etc.—are cultural manifestations that change only very gradually and over long periods of time. Basically the functional behavior-links between economic stimulus and response express the "habits," customs, traditions, and usages of societies, and display all the inertia characteristic of social institutions. Thus, whereas we cannot prophesy whether behavior will be normal or perverse in any particular instance, it is very safe to prophesy that the patterns associated with normality will tend to predominate over the long run, resisting even revolutions in their viscosity.

Curiously, it is now the other attribute of the behavior function—the intensity rather than the direction of reaction —that augurs difficulties for long-run prediction. Acquisitiveness may remain, but tastes change. The question that must be faced for long-run behavior functions is whether we can hazard, no matter how great our intellectual heroism, informed generalizations as to the "drift" of tastes or as to the effect of new commodities on the general shape of economic behavior.

This problem might in the end prove fatal for the hopes of describing behavioral reactions in terms that would continue to be confirmed over several decades or generations, were it not for the presence of an even larger and more intransigent issue. This is the fact that the long-run production functions of the economy are as awkward or impossible to predict "in principle" as those of behavioral responses in the short run. It is one thing to pretend that we can imagine the slopes of existing production functions so that we can construct a model of an economy adjusting itself to these relationships in response to changes in the environment, but it is another to think that we can say anything about the nature of long-run shifts in these production functions. All that we know from experience is that the production possibilities of industrial society display rapid, and seemingly unpredictable, changes that are the exact opposite of the sluggish consistency of the functions representing long-run behavior. It may be that some day we will discover laws of scientific evolution, but until that day the advance of the scientific and technological frontiers takes place in a manner that is beyond our capacity to foresee, with the result that it is still totally impossible to establish long-run production functions for any of the major commodities of society today, much less to predict what may be the major commodities of society tomorrow.

IV

Thus we discover that there are inherent limitations to the power of predictive theorizing in economics—limitations that are rooted in the nature of the real world and that are, therefore, beyond the power of remedy by improvements in economic technique alone. In the short run, economic prediction is limited by the residue of behavioral indeterminacy that escapes scientific scrutiny, either directly or indirectly. To be sure, to the extent that the external world can be "regularized" so that expectations are steady and the occasions for perverse behavior accordingly reduced, the performance of economics as a short-run predictive science will be enhanced. Such is the thrust of Lowe's Political Economics, whose purpose is to restore the reliability of predictive theory by making behavior itself the direct object of manipulative policy, rather than taking the behavioral function as one of the "givens" in the economic process.[7] Short of a wholly controlled world, however, there must remain an element of behavioral uncertainty that restricts the reach of even the most highly informed prediction.

In the long run there is also a limit to the reach of economic prediction, revealed not so much in an inability to forecast movements of prices, etc., as in an inability to predict the secular evolution of economic systems, capitalist or any other. The failure of all the great models of economic evolution, from Smith to Marx, has always been attributable primarily to an inability to foresee the nature of technological change, or the results, behavioral as well as

7. Lowe, *op. cit.*, Part I, p. 9.

material, that a rapidly evolving technology would bring to economic society. To the extent that the evolution of science and technology still remain largely unpredictable, higher-level hypotheses concerning the physical processes of production are ruled out, and with them the chance for models that will accurately display the changing structure of society over long periods of time.

A final word. To establish that there are intrinsic limits to economic prediction is not to declare that predictive theorizing is therefore a useless activity. The formulation of reliable higher-level hypotheses remains the most powerful lever we have for the control of our destinies. The functional relationships on which these hypotheses are based are far from fully explored, so that the predictive possibilities *within* the limits of behavioral and technological uncertainty are by no means wholly exploited. In the short run, for example, we may be unable to predict turning points, but there remain long stretches of smooth running for which it should be possible to specify, with far greater quantitative accuracy than today, the propensities and elasticities and coefficients that describe the underlying continuities of behavior and production.

As to the long run, the situation is less clear. In the short run we are confronted with fluctuations; in the long run with trends. What are the economic prospects fifty years hence? What are the social implications of these prospects? Insofar as these questions hinge on the elusive element of technological development, they seem inherently further from our grasp than the vagaries of the short period. The evolutionary models of the classicists, Marx included, appear in retrospect to owe their impressive dynamics to behavioral and technical assumptions of a fixity that would no longer be admissible. The temptation, therefore, is to avoid entirely the risky, and necessarily uncertain, enterprise of seeking to establish long-term paths of socioeconomic development. Indeed, if there is any single besetting sin of contemporary economic investigation, it is its studious avoidance of any "historic" perspective on the problems it investigates.

Thus we are caught in a dilemma: on the one hand, there is the clear inability to erect higher-level hypotheses that will successfully cover the technological evolution of the system; on the other hand, there is the peculiar inutility of a social science that is unable to consider long-term evolutionary forces and processes. The solution, insofar as I can see one, is perhaps easier to describe than to carry out. In part it suggests the deliberate search for new constructs that may open up previously overlooked functional relationships and thereby somewhat extend our predictive reach. In particular one wonders whether the introduction of class relationships and behavior patterns might not bring to attention functional connections that escape notice in a model built solely on individual behavioral reactions.[8] In another part, the existing predictive limitations might be overcome by the investigation of long-run trends of technological evolution and of patterns of technological interaction with economic and social phenomena—matters that have barely been looked into as yet. Until such new constructs or functional relationships are developed, however, present-day economic science will predict the long-term future at its peril—and will suffer the consequences for its inability to do so.

8. For an interesting effort to provide such new constructs, both having to do with technology and with class behavior over the long run, see Paolo Leon, *Structural Change and Growth in Capitalism.*

Alternative
Futures

CHAPTER 11

Transcendental Capitalism

> A society in which production is governed by blind economic forces is being replaced by one in which production is being carried on under the ultimate control of a handful of individuals. The economic power in the hands of the few persons who control a giant corporation is a tremendous force which can harm or benefit a multitude of individuals, shift the currents of trade, bring ruin to one community and prosperity to another. The organizations they control have passed beyond the realm of private enterprise—they have become more nearly social institutions.

*I*t is thirty-odd years since Adolf A. Berle and Gardiner C. Means published *The Modern Corporation and Private Property* (whence the quotation above), but three intervening decades have not outmoded this extraordinary book. To be sure, some of the names included on their famous list of the two hundred largest nonbanking corporations have been displaced by other names, and the economic power of the list itself has not grown quite so alarmingly as Berle and Means feared (in a moment of fantasy they suggested that by the year 2300 the two hundred giants might be fused into one single immense corporate organism with a business life expectancy of over 1,000 years). But the issues posed by

The Modern Corporation and Private Property are no less resonant and no less contemporary on that account. For as the title of the book made clear, this was not just an inquiry into economic performance. It was also, and perhaps more profoundly, an inquiry into economic philosophy. In a fundamental sense it questioned not only the practices of the great concentrate of economic power, but the very right of that concentrate to exist. Having revealed traditional economic theory to be little more than a pious theology, it asked what was left to describe the American economic system except a *Realeconomik* of privilege for privilege's sake.

For Gardiner Means, economist and statistician, the economic problems raised by the concentrate—market power, price-fixing, collusion, and competition—marked out the road to be followed in later work. But for Berle, professor of law, diplomatist, and amateur politician, it was the philosophic issue which was the more attractive. "It is conceivable—indeed it seems almost essential if the corporate system is to survive—" he wrote at the conclusion of the book "that the 'control' of the great corporations should develop into a purely neutral technocracy, balancing a variety of claims by various groups in the community and assigning to each a portion of the income stream on the basis of public policy rather than private cupidity."

"Is this suggestion of a responsible business community merely a dream?" he asked elsewhere. Thirty years later, *The American Economic Republic* constitutes his answer.

It is not, unhappily, the best of his books. *The 20th Century Capitalist Revolution* (1953) is tighter and sharper; *Power without Poverty* anticipates what is to come later and is more interesting. By contrast with these, *The American Economic Republic* sprawls and repeats and vaporizes. Nonetheless, it is a book worth careful consideration, for the problems it raises are of utmost importance.

The book begins where *The Modern Corporation and Private Property* ended: with the issue of property itself. Clearly, says Berle, the traditional conception of property as personal chattels—the property which Locke said belonged to a man because he had "mixed his labor" with it —has little relevance to the "property" of an industrial system. Property must now be seen as an aspect of power; it is not merely things, but organization, momentum, the capacity to command resources. This kind of property, which is the central reality of the economic process, is controlled by a small group of more or less self-perpetuating managers who are subject to various pressures which we shall consider in a moment.

But note that the rationale for the existence or use of these great blocs of power-property cannot be found under the traditional view of property as proprietorship. The managers do not "own" the power complexes they direct; the "owners" are holders of another kind of property—"passive property" which entitles them to an uncertain claim on the earnings of the great concentrate and to the chance to make money by dealing in their certificates of "ownership" shrewdly. This kind of property may be a great convenience, but it has virtually nothing to do with assuring the successful operation of the real power-property for which it is presumably a counterpart.

Thus the concepts of the nineteenth century dissolve under Berle's acidulous intelligence, and along with them dissolves the comfortable justification for property as things made by and used by their owners. We are left with the much more pragmatic calculus of results rather than premises: property is legitimate, not in and of itself, but to the extent that it is used as society wishes and to the extent that it yields results of which society approves.

But let us not linger here. Having subjected the standard rationale of property to this disenchanted analysis, Berle now asks similarly disconcerting questions of two other hoary underpinnings of the traditional capitalist rationale. One of these is capital, which he has no trouble in dissociating from its beatified progenitor, the thrifty capitalist. Capital is not created by thrifty capitalists in the American economic republic—at least not in important measure. Capital is created by extracting it from the consumer, who is quite unaware when he buys a consumer durable good that part of his payment will end up as the corporate "saving" which is made out of profits. In like manner, the free market—that holy of ideological holies—is given short shrift. The market, Berle makes plain, is not a state of nature but a state-created, state-sustained institution, and beyond that, one which "has been completely displaced as an infallible god, has been substantially displaced as universal economic master, and increasingly ceases to be, or to be thought of, as the only acceptable way of economic life."

Is there left, then, only a refined neofeudalism—a naked system of power responsible only to itself? In an earlier book, *The 20th Century Capitalist Revolution,* Berle had indeed placed his corporate giants in a position of untrammeled power. "The only real control which guides and limits their economic and social action," he wrote, "is the real, though undefined and tacit, philosophy of the men who compose them. . . . To anyone who studies and even remotely begins to apprehend the American corporate system, the implications of the line of thought here sketched have both splendor and terror. The argument compels the conclusion that the corporation, almost against its will, has been compelled to assume in appreciable part the role of conscience-carrier of twentieth-century American society."

The prospect was clearer in its terror than in its splendor, for it implied that the American system was to be ultimately responsible to men—hopefully, to enlightened men—over whom no political, and very little economic, control existed. But in the subsequent *Power with Property* Berle sought to amend this dictatorial interpretation of affairs. For the conscience of the corporation was, he claimed, not the product "of the centers of power and responsibility directing the economic machinery." Rather it emanated from the universities, the press, the professions—the "spiritual elite." In turn, this core of economic power had to be responsive to the democratic process itself. For the economic republic, Berle emphasized, was essentially a *political* entity. Its economic institutions, no matter how powerful, were always subservient to its political institutions; its economic powers, no matter how seemingly impregnable, were always subject to check—and in the long run, to control—by the democratic will.

Much of *The American Economic Republic* is taken up with a description of the various political agencies by which private power is curtailed, and to a description of the ways in which business, labor, government, and public welfare sectors interact and counterbalance to bring about the "republic" itself. But this is not yet the capstone to the system. For behind the corporate conscience, behind the spiritual elite and the democratic process, Berle now discovers a final set of values which impels and sustains the American political economy. He calls it the Transcendental Margin, meaning by this the capacity of the system to create a surplus of creative energy, a drive over and above that adduced by mere selfish considerations. It is the presence of a transcendental margin which made Utah flourish while Nevada stagnated, which propelled Israel but not Iraq, the Netherlands but not Bulgaria.

"Let us not claim that the transcendental margin is peculiar to the American social-economic system . . . ," concludes Berle. "But in the United States the transcendental margin was continuously greater, and expanded more consistently, than in most other contemporary systems. It generated greater productivity, and greater intellectual resources for still further expansion. In the post World War II period, it has become the decisive influence."

Therewith, in desperate condensation, is Adolf Berle's answer to the question he posed thirty years ago: Is a responsible business community possible? His answer is clearly: Yes, it is; it exists here in America; it can be examined in the still unfinished American economic republic.

One characteristic immediately lifts this analysis far above the level of any other conservative appraisal of the system. It is Berle's capacity to divorce his defense from the usual deceits and rationalizations. The massive concentration of private power, the indispensable role of the state, the make-believe of laissez-faire economics—these stumbling blocks for the ordinary conservative are no problem to Berle. On the contrary, he is one of the discoverers of the extent of corporate power and of the necessity of a mixed economy. *Fortune* magazine may rhapsodize over a new textbook by the very conservative Wilhelm Roepke; Berle cites Roepke's name only to associate it with the do-nothing policies which plunged Germany into the depths of her 1931 misery. Thus when Berle deals with the institutions of the present system, with the sheer facts of power, the realities of the "market," the interplay of public and private power, he is without peer, liberal or conservative.

Unfortunately, however, this is not where matters end. Berle is not content to demolish the shaky ideology of the past, to demonstrate that the system works according to different rules from those of the textbooks and that the existing system seems to respond to some kind of "social control," albeit of a weaker kind than envisaged in classical economic thought. Instead he goes on to dress this essentially neutral judgment in an ideological garb of its own—not only to explain it but to justify it. And here, I fear, the sharp and particularistic and fearless intelligence of the analytic Berle gives way to a soft, uncritical, and complaisant view.

I note, to begin, a tendency to use some "facts" in curious ways to make a point. Thus, speaking of stock ownership, Berle writes: "The wealth-distribution process . . . goes steadily and implacably forward. . . ." Does it? Berle's own source, the study by Robert J. Lampman on wealth ownership, shows an *increasing* concentration of share-ownership between 1922 and 1953; and recent income distribution studies have shown *no* perceptible improvement in income distribution (and some worsening) since the great World War II redistribution.

Or again, he claims: "Current statistics [for 1961] indi-

cate a total unemployment of slightly over 4,000,000. . . .
Under the definitions of 'unemployed' applied to Western
Europe the American unemployed would be counted more
nearly at 2,500,000. . . ." And later: "There are, at a sophisticated guess (no figures are available), about 4,000,-
000 in [Russian] concentration camps of forced residence
now. These equate to the American figure of unemployed.
. . . The communist system did not eliminate unemployment, but merely gave it another name."

This is a misuse of figures to the point of irresponsibility.
Given all statistical adjustments, U.S. unemployment rates
have run about double to triple those of Europe during the
decade of the 1960's. And if there are "no figures," how
does Berle blandly assume that four million Russians are in
concentration camps? I know of no authority from whom
such an estimate could have been obtained. And even assuming that there *were* four million Russians in concentration camps, by what logic can these be equated with the
victims of the *economic* malfunction of the American republic? Is Berle claiming that our economic casualties are
matched by the victims of political malfunction in Russia?
Then what of our own political victims: the Negroes condemned to half the average income of the whites, or the unemployed for whom we are unable to muster the votes
which will bring economic relief?

This prettifying of the figures, this minimizing of evils,
this false analogizing and easy glossing over of unpleasantness ("A tolerable, not to say comfortable, situation exists
for nine-tenths of the population of the United States") reveal an unwillingness to probe into matters of overall performance as searchingly as into matters of legal definition.
And this tendency to whitewash is made the more evident

when we consider not only what is in the description of the economic republic but what is left out. Thus we find no mention of the misbehavior of important sections of the managerial elite, as for instance in the electrical conspiracy. No thoughtful analysis is made of the morality of Ralph Cordiner or the intelligence of Roger Blough. The level of comprehension or compassion to be intuited from the speeches of our business leaders, from the pieties and platitudes of the business press, from the editorials of our mass media, from the congressional testimony of our trade associations—none of this is weighed in the balance. Nor is there mention, in discussing the "successful" operation of our system, of its dependence on an armaments industry huge in size and not easy to excise or replace. Nor did I find in a description of the American economic republic any discussion of the extent to which the "consensus" which supports (and supposedly judges) the business manager is itself constantly pumped up by the deliberate efforts of the managers themselves.

And then, what are we to make of the transcendental margin—that driving force behind the American economy? I could imagine attributing this force to the thirst for profits which, at least in the late nineteenth century, drove some men to prodigies of effort. But the drive after profits is specifically excluded by Berle from the ultimate propulsive values. What are they then?

> Two values would emerge high on the list. One would be the value known in philosophical language as "truth." By this I mean truth in the large, in all aspects, from individual interest in not telling lies and in personal sincerity, to the frontiers of scholarly search. . . . A second enduring value is beauty. . . . The constant conflict by the more honorable portion

of the American community against sordid murder of the
esthetics of an open road by advertisers, or to maintain the
dignity of an honorable main street against dollar-chasing
real-estate schemes, testifies to that fact.

Are these the dynamic forces of our nation? As I wander
about the American republic, watching the slums move out,
not in, witnessing the exposure of my children to the "sin-
cere," "truth-telling" voices on the great silver screen, contemplating the dreary spectacle of payola and fix, delin-
quency and crime, racket and cynicism, of passivity before
evil and acquiescence in ugliness, I must confess that I find
it difficult to assert that Berle's values are in control.

Not that these values do not exist. I think the problem is
that there is not one American Economic Republic but two.
One is inhabited by those on whom fortune has smiled. It begins at the Pan Am building and ends on Park Avenue and
96th Street. It is the view from the top, the view in which
things work, in which flaws seem small and relatively unimportant, in which reasonable men, lunching comfortably,
can come to reasonable agreement about how to decide
reasonable things, in which the impotence of the unlettered,
the unimportant, the unskilled is never experienced at first
hand, in which—with full recognition of the exceptions
which must, of course, be borne in mind—all's right with the
world. But there is also another republic, which begins at
96th Street and continues north into the wynds of Harlem
and the dreariness of the Bronx and Yonkers, and from this
republic there is another view, more constricted, less Olympian, meaner, poorer, unhappier. We fortunate citizens may
never have to visit, much less live in, the commonwealth of
the less fortunate, but a book which aims to describe and to
judge the American economic republic as a whole must give

just as much weight to each miserable and unprivileged citizen as to each contented and favored one, if it is to be, in fact, a description of the way things are, and not merely the way we hope they are.

CHAPTER **12**

The Industrial State

John Kenneth Galbraith has not enjoyed the regard of his fellow economists to anything like the degree that he has enjoyed the acclaim of the public. Indeed, to a substantial number of economists, particularly those of the conservative and prestigious "Chicago school," his name is very nearly anathema. One of the deans of this school saw fit recently to write an editorial column for *The New York Times*, the only purpose of which seemed to be to attack Galbraith. The authors of a recent textbook found it useful to include as a student exercise a quotation from "an economist serving as American ambassador to India," instructing the student to "Explain why every sentence of that quotation—except the third and fourth—is wrong, nonsensical, or irrelevant." A colleague of mine, discussing a list of books that might be useful for a graduate seminar in Political Economics, simply shrugged off *American Capitalism* and *The Affluent Society* as works that serious people could not take seriously.

This virtual rejection of Galbraith by his peers[1] is offset only by their general admiration for his style, even when, as is often the case, they are the objects of its shafts.

> Corporate executives with an overacute sense of persecution [Galbraith writes] have sometimes supposed that economists, in the ideas they advance, are their enemies. In fact, the economics profession is strongly in the service of the beliefs they most need. It would, *prima facie,* be plausible to set a limit on the national product that a nation requires. The test of economic achievement would then be how rapidly it could reduce the number of hours of toil that are needed to meet this requirement. Were economists to advocate this goal, with the revolutionary effects that it would have on the industrial system, there would be grounds for complaint. None have been so uncooperative.

There are few economists who will not wince at these sentences, and fewer still who would not like to write their rejoinders in prose as cutting.

Yet I think the academic critics are wrong on both counts. To my mind, Galbraith is an economist of considerable merits, who seeks to infuse economics with a social relevance that is, on the whole, egregiously missing from most of its

1. After *The Affluent Society* appeared Elmo Roper polled the economic community to ascertain its feelings about the book. A slightly larger percentage (10%) "disagreed totally" with Galbraith than "agreed totally" with him (8%); almost as many (28%) "mainly disagreed" as "mainly agreed" (33%); while 21% found as much to disagree as to agree with (*Saturday Review,* June 6, 1959).

current output, particularly from that of the Chicago school. At the same time, I believe that the celebrated style, far from being an expression of Galbraith's power and boldness, is in fact his fatal weakness.

I shall return to the matter of style in due course. Meanwhile, *The New Industrial State* comes as an interesting outgrowth of Galbraith's previous books. In all of them Galbraith has been wrestling with a major problem of great difficulty, although, alas, of little interest to most economists. This has been to find a systematic explanation for the way in which American capitalism operated in fact, rather than an explanation of how it was supposed to operate in theory. To put it differently, he has been searching for a new theory that would handle the realities of corporate power as satisfactorily as the prevailing textbook theory handled the make-believe world in which that corporate power was largely ignored.

In his first major book, *American Capitalism,* Galbraith explained the workings of the system in a way that incorporated his emphasis on bigness and power with the orthodox view of the system as a self-regulating mechanism. *American Capitalism* was traditional in its picture of the economy as a self-regulating entity, but it struck out on its own in describing the regulative force as no longer that of the competitive market. Instead Galbraith placed at the center of his analysis a supposed tendency of the system automatically to balance off masses of power in one area with the creation of "countervailing" masses elsewhere.

The book was in many ways a perceptive appraisal of capitalism. (It contained, for example, the stunning sentence: "The foreign visitor, brought to the United States, visits the same firms as do the attorneys of the Department of Justice in their search for monopoly.") But its "theory" was not very successful. Various economists, including the aforementioned dean of the Chicago school, ripped into it with relish, losing sight in the process of the intransigent problem that lay behind Galbraith's effort: Was it possible to describe the operation of the economic system in terms closer to reality than the orthodoxies of classical economics?

The Affluent Society dropped the problem of the balance of power among industrial giants to examine the balance between the industrial sector as a whole and the public agencies. The "theory" was that the economic order bred a persistent imbalance between overproduction of private wares and the underproduction of public ones, leading to many of the malaises peculiar to "affluent" societies. Unlike the first book, *The Affluent Society* did not claim to discover an internal balancing mechanism, but frankly left the redress of this inherent tendency to deliberate public intervention. It was this, of course, that again earned for Galbraith the distaste of the Chicago school.

The New Industrial State goes a step further in this unwelcomed direction. The traditional line of demarcation between public and private, says Galbraith, is in economic fact, if not in economic theology, rapidly becoming blurred or even erased. "Men will look back in amusement," he writes, "at the pretense that once caused people to refer to General Dynamics and North American Aviation and A.T.&T. as *private* business." The reality is that a new economic order is emerging, characterized by very large industrial organizations that maintain economic order among themselves, and between their interests and those of the government, by an even more nearly complete, albeit carefully camouflaged and stoutly denied, network of planning.

This planning does not take the form of the social and economic blueprints dear to the reformer. Rather, it consists of the more or less uncoordinated efforts of each of these corporations to secure for itself an environment of order and stability in which it can work effectively. Thus planning assumes many disguises. In part it is visible in the union contracts that eliminate for the corporation the uncertainties of a free or unruly labor market. In part it is visible in the highly developed arts of advertising, through which the corporation creates a state of consumer "demand" sufficiently reliable and loyal to enable it to plan ahead with reasonable confidence. In part it is manifest in a curiously symbiotic relationship with the government, to which, however ritually berated (although the ritual is diminishing in fervor, Galbraith notes), the corporation looks for assurance of a continuing level of high aggregate demand.

In other words, the reality of the Industrial System, Galbraith shows us, is the opposite of everything that is highlighted in the textbooks. The play of the market is carefully and effectively minimized, not maximized. Enterprises are no longer passive entities impinged upon by the all-powerful and independent activities of consumers and suppliers of services, but corporations that radiate lines of power to create orderly and acceptable behavior of both suppliers and buyers. In a word, "the corporation" is more and more the name for an integrated sequence of operations that converts resources into salable commodities, and this sequence is insulated as much as possible by the controllers of the corporation from the disruptive force of the marketplace.

Needless to say, this kind of planning is not the deliberate creation of a social engineer. "The imperatives of technology and organization, not the images of ideology, are what determine the shape of economic society," writes Galbraith. The "imperatives of technology" are clear enough: the long integrated sequence of operations requires time, capital, specialized manpower, and an assurance of stability if it is to be used efficiently. But what are the "imperatives of organization"?

This brings us to Galbraith's view of the entrepreneurial function in the semiplanned Industrial System—or, rather, to his explanation of what now fills the role of the entrepreneur, who is still represented as the active agent of the system in the standard textbook accounts. There are such entrepreneurs left, Galbraith admits, but they are no longer typical of the mature corporation, which is the bastion of the system. The locus of power is no longer a single person, but a "technostructure," an interlocking structure of specialists, technicians, experts, and organization men who collectively guide the giant corporation. It is part of the mythology of capitalism, says Galbraith, that we still cling to the notion that power is wielded most effectively and efficiently by the single entrepreneur. In fact it is the committee system, with its combination of impersonality, specialization, and bureaucratic procedure, that has proven indispensable to the corporation's goals.

What are these goals? First, autonomy—freedom from interference either by "the owners" or government (as far as this is possible). Second, safety and longevity for the enterprise. Third, growth of the institution with which their lives, as well as their material fortunes, are identified. Note that among these goals, the textbook paradigm of simple "maximizing of profits" is notably absent.

Thus the Industrial System appears as an almost self-contained system within the larger society. Its operation moves toward an ever more highly organized society, responsive to the direction of an ever more independent "technostructure." To be sure, the entire operation depends for its success on the acceptance of the final products that emerge. But this is more or less assured by the management of product demand through advertising, and the support of total demand through government policy.

At the same time, of course, the system, by virtue of its efficiency, also enhances the level of productivity, so that along with the endless force-feeding of the consumer comes the possibility of using the energies of the economy for other, nonindustrial purposes—"the expansion of public services, the assertion of the aesthetic dimension of life, widened choice as between income and leisure, the emancipation of education." If these ends are to be superimposed on the state, however, it will have to be done by some force outside the Industrial System. Galbraith suggests that this force can be provided by the entrance into politics of a group that is perhaps the ultimate source of power in the modern world —the scientific and educational estate that is, in the end, responsible for the creation of the technostructure itself. Thus finally we are left with an undecided question. In the default of effective leadership by the enlightened members of society, there is the specter of the self-sustaining, self-justifying industrial state to whose purposes the rest of society will have to be fitted, willy-nilly. If the enlightened minority can seize control, however, the industrial state may yet fall into its proper role as the servant rather than the master of man.

This is a difficult book to deal with critically: in part, because the book contains more than I have indicated—a discussion of the integration of the Industrial System and the Cold War, a theory of motivation, a disquisition on the relevance of classical profit maximizing to the actions of the giant firm, and more besides. The book thus invites piecemeal criticism (of which I do not doubt it will receive more than its share from the economics profession), especially in its attack on the maximizing of profits, where I must say Galbraith is not very convincing.[2]

But there is a more fundamental difficulty. It lies, I think, in the level of abstraction of the work, which hovers between a very generalized schema and an empirical study, and is not quite either. As a result it suffers on the one hand from the absence of the solid empirical demonstration that would convince us of the conceptual validity of the technostructure as the new power center of capitalism, while on the other it is not quite reduced to the fundamental level of generaliza-

---

2. Let me add a footnote for economists. Galbraith demonstrates (or rather, asserts) that corporations do not act so as to maximize their profits in the *short run*. But the goals he specifies (security, autonomy, and, mainly, growth of sales) are by no means incompatible with profit-maximizing in the long run. The issue here is the time-horizon over which profits are calculated. Profit-maximizing is an operational concept only insofar as it allows us to predict behavior. If the time-horizon is short, as in very competitive firms, the maximizing postulate allows us to predict price and output decisions. But if the horizon lengthens, it is no longer possible to declare that one and only one policy will maximize net revenues. The critical issue, in other words, is not that of the motive, but of the actions that will be taken to achieve a given end. See A. Lowe, *On Economic Knowledge*, pp. 47–48.

tion that served to make Schumpeter's theory of capitalism so impressive.

Take, for example, the central contention of the book— that the strategic group within the economic system has shifted from the possessors of wealth to the possessors of collective expertise. I do not doubt that Galbraith is right in stressing this basic trend and in assigning its cause to the fundamental forces of technology and science. The trouble is that this tendency is treated as if it were already an accomplished fact, and this is doubtful. It is my belief that even in the most "mature" corporations (i.e., those in which the technostructure is most clearly visible), there is still a final level of decision-making power that is lodged firmly at the top, and this top upon examination often turns out to be a small group of powerful stockholding interests or their representatives. The technostructure may propose, but in the end it is the directors, or a small number of top officers, who dispose.[3]

Thus the technostructure is much too diffuse a term to describe hierarchies and groups within which there continue to reside all-important distinctions of power. Further, it masks the fact that there is going on within American capitalism a contest between the forces of science and technology and the older forces of wealth and ownership. I believe, with Galbraith, that the future lies with the ascendancy of the professional elites, but the tension between the Old Guard and the New needs to be brought to the fore, not hidden behind the undifferentiated screen of the technostructure.

3. Let me refer to two studies of this subject: Gabriel Kolko's *Wealth and Power in America* (pp. 61–62) and Don Villarejo's "Stock Ownership and the Control of Corporations," *New University Thought* (Autumn, 1961, and Winter, 1962).

I am not convinced either by Galbraith's prescription for social reform. Surely if history teaches us anything it is the futility of appeals to the educated elite. As Galbraith himself lamely writes, following his advice to the educational community to cut itself free from the industrial system:

> The first inclination of most educators will be to dismiss these pages as another hortatory exercise. It can only be hoped that reflection will lead to a more useful response.

It is, I fear, a frail hope. If, as Galbraith so boldly (and I think correctly) maintains, the "imperatives of technology and organization" will shape society, then he must have the courage to carry his theoretical model into the future, whatever its course. It was precisely this that gave to Schumpeter's analysis its power, for he unflinchingly extended the implications of his analysis to the end, even though he disliked the conclusions to which it led. Galbraith's model is important and original, and by comparison with the pale stuff of so much contemporary economics, powerful. But his grand outline is weakened by an unwillingness to press home his analysis to its bitter conclusion—a conclusion touched on lightly in the vision of a self-perpetuating and self-serving Industrial System, but then blurred by conclusions that are, I believe, just "another hortatory exercise."

This final reluctance to allow the model to reach its ultimate destination may well be related to the curious problem of Galbraith's style. Last summer, in Raymond Williams' *Culture and Society*, I came across a telling critique of R. H. Tawney, one of the master stylists of historical exposition and a towering figure of Fabian Socialism. Calling attention to Tawney's predilection for irony and to a certain "filigree" in his marvelously constructed sentences, Williams discovers a weakness in Tawney's stance. "It is," he writes, "a device for lowering tensions, when, however, tension is necessary. It is a particular estimate of the opposition to be expected, and it is, of course, an underestimate."

So, many times magnified, with Galbraith. The much-envied style is aphoristic, terse, above all, mocking. But just as Tawney's magisterial prose causes him ultimately to hold back expression of the anger he feels, so Galbraith's mocking irony causes him in the end to avoid a clear moral commitment with regard to the problems he raises.

Is such commitment necessary? "The economy for its success requires organized public bamboozlement," writes Galbraith flatly. The word "bamboozlement" is the clue. Any other—"deception," "fraud," "untruth"—would amount to a declaration of war. "Bamboozlement" allows an issue of the most searching importance to be passed over in a mood of raillery. The next sentence in the text reads: "And at the same time it nurtures a growing class which feels itself superior to such bamboozlement and deplores it as intellectually corrupt." Galbraith is himself a member of that class —and, indeed, in his public life has lived up to his own prescription in speaking out for ends and ideas that differ considerably from those of the technostructure. Yet in this book, as indeed in his previous books, his position vis-à-vis the society he criticizes remains essentially ambiguous. Rather than producing clear judgment, the moral power of his argument is, finally, dissipated in wit.

CHAPTER 13

A Marxist America

Until his death in 1964, Paul Baran was virtually the only left-wing Marxist economist in the United States who held a full-time academic appointment. Since he was nothing if not outspoken in his beliefs, he was undoubtedly a trial for the authorities at Stanford, who, to their credit, resisted continual pressure from patriotic organizations to fire him. Somewhat less to their credit the university repeatedly passed over him for salary increases until finally the Economics Department protested in his behalf. Nevertheless when he died, people of many political opinions paid tribute to his personal courage and warmth as well as to his intellectual penetration.

Paul Sweezy, too, has suffered because of his Marxist ideas. Sweezy's career began brilliantly at Harvard, where he was a protégé of the great Joseph Schumpeter. Following the war, Sweezy was harassed during the McCarthy days by a zealous State district attorney whose efforts were finally curbed only by the United States Supreme Court. Since then he has been asked to teach only on rare occasions by a few audacious institutions including, I am happy to report, my own, and he has mainly devoted himself to publishing (with the late Leo Huberman) the left-wing Marxist magazine *Monthly Review,* together with books from the same press.

I mention these biographical details to provide a setting for a book that is so far from the run-of-the-mill of American social science as to require an introduction of this kind. Working in an isolation from the academic community which was partly enforced, and partly self-imposed, Baran and Sweezy have produced an appraisal of American society, at once bitter and perhaps embittered, that is totally at odds with the interpretation of American society we find in the books of most professors. This flavor of academic heresy is unusual only in America, however. If I judge correctly, the image of American society that arises from their pages approximates (and gives additional substance to) the way our society is seen and understood not only in Russian and Chinese intellectual circles, but in many important centers of thought in Europe, Latin America, Africa, and Asia. If for no other reason, this fact should be sufficient to justify a careful study of this book.[1]

But there is another reason. I would also strongly urge every non-Marxian economist in America to study this book as a test of his own beliefs. This is not because I believe the

1. *Monopoly Capital* by Paul A. Baran and Paul M. Sweezy.

Baran-Sweezy analysis to be essentially correct—indeed, as I hope to make clear, I think in important respects it is deeply flawed. It is, rather, that unlike most books we read, this one attacks prevailing beliefs at their roots. The book may arouse an emotional defensiveness in the reader, as it does in me, but at least it forces him to spell out his defense, rather than allowing him the complacency of unchallenged assumptions.

Baran's and Sweezy's book can be best considered, I think, in three ways: as a moral indictment, as an economic model, and as a theory of power. Of the three I find the first to be the most effective. This is not because the material is new—we are all familiar with the dreary statistics of poverty, misallocation of resources, aborted education, etc. What in most books, however, are only complaints, are in this book particulars of one central accusation: that the social order peculiar to capitalism is irrational. By this Baran and Sweezy mean that, at bottom, it is the institution of private property that inhibits, deflects, or simply defeats efforts to undo the social inequities we all learn to live with and not to think about.

This stress on the systemic roots of our failure to repair the slums, to relieve poverty, to improve our educational efforts, is something to be mulled over by those all-too-many social scientists who have ignored the most elementary social judgments in the name of "value-free" inquiry, or as theologians of pure competition. Unfortunately, I fear that Baran's and Sweezy's accusations will not be very effective with most of them. I think there is a core of important truth in their argument, but the authors push their claims too far —so far, in fact, that finally their indictment arouses skepticism rather than indignation.

In part this failure of persuasion lies in the avowedly

exaggerated argument of the book. Every bit of available evidence is brought to bear against the system, but not a word is said in its defense. Nor are the charges scrutinized with anything like scholarly care. To take one instance that may stand for many, when I read (p. 364n.) of Leo Srole's study showing a high incidence of mental disturbance in New York City, I want to know first whether there is any evidence that mental illness is *increasing* (I know of no studies proving this), and second, what a similar study would reveal in Calcutta, Paris, and Moscow. Until I know that, I cannot accept Srole's study as "evidence" that the outlook for capitalism is "the spread of increasingly severe psychic disorders leading to the impairment and eventual breakdown of the system's ability to function even on its own terms."

The argument backfires for another reason. Whereas capitalism is portrayed as a system of class relations which does nothing but foist irrationality upon social action, socialism is pictured as the very paradigm of sweet reason. Thus, "Militarism and conquest are completely foreign to Marxist theory, and a socialist society contains no group or class which, like the big capitalists of the imperialist countries, stands to gain from a policy of subjugating other nations and peoples." This after Hungary, and at a time when we face the threat of a major Russo-Chinese conflict!

But the main failure of the moral indictment lies elsewhere in the authors' refusal to allow for any causes of social evil outside the realm of economic relations. Behind every instance of human weakness, indifference, or cruelty they

show us the underlying cause to be the defense of class interests. In the end, this insistence, valid enough when thought-
fully applied, becomes invalid because it is indiscriminately
used. Baran and Sweezy set out to demonstrate that capitalism is an irrational system because of the insurmountable
barriers of property relations; they end up by proving that
it is possible to be irrational even in the defense of such a
proposition.

However much I share their concern for social morality,
I suspect that the authors are more interested in their description of monopoly capitalism as a system. And this is
indeed a provocative aspect of their book. For what they
have presented is nothing less than a neo-Marxian theory of
capitalism—a theory in which those time-honored categories of Marxian analysis, surplus value and the falling rate
of profit, have been excluded and in which a new central
tendency takes their place.

This central tendency they call the Law of Rising Surplus.
By this the authors mean two somewhat different things.
The first is that in an industrially progressive society there
will be a steadily increasing capacity to produce more than
is needed simply to sustain the working population at mini-
mally acceptable levels and to replace worn-out equipment.
This concept in itself is not particularly different from our
ordinary ideas of rising productivity, except that by focusing
on the mass of available "surplus product," we are forced
to examine qualitatively as well as quantitatively the ends
to which society applies its wealth. As Baran argued very
brilliantly in a previous book, *The Political Economy of
Growth,* the nature and use of this surplus gives us profound
insights into the values of a social order. In an appendix to
the Baran-Sweezy book, Joseph D. Phillips estimates the

amount of surplus in the United States in 1963 as $327,725,-000,000, or fifty-six percent of GNP. As to its application, we have but to look at Park Avenue—below 96th Street, and above it.

But Baran and Sweezy are more interested in a second use of the term surplus. To give a somewhat inexact parallel, the word is used as a kind of expanded version of "savings-and-investment," referring to those particular flows of revenue and outlay as they exist in a capitalist economy. Surplus can then be looked at (as can savings) as the money accruing to various individuals or businesses in a capitalist economy, or (like investment) as those economic acts which constitute the "real" counterpart of these financial changes. Specifically, in the Baran-Sweezy model, surplus becomes on the one hand a series of gains, such as monopoly profits, excess depreciation, property income, etc., and on the other, a series of activities, namely, investment, luxury consumption, and capitalist waste into which those gains are absorbed.

Here the authors discover a deep-seated problem. For they maintain that the amount of financial surplus will tend to grow, in large part because of an alleged tendency of corporate profits to rise, whereas the modes of expenditure available to mop up this surplus—the investment, waste, and luxury consumption needed to offset the rising stream of property and privileged income—will, for various reasons, lag behind. Indeed, Baran and Sweezy believe that a condition of chronic stagnation must therefore be the norm for a highly developed monopoly capitalism—a condition from which it has been rescued only by the fortuitous advent of epochal inventions (the steam engine, the railroad, and the automobile) and by the stimulating effects of wars.

These are interesting and potentially important propositions that deserve the careful attention of non-Marxian economists. I am myself not entirely easy with many of Baran's and Sweezy's definitions of "surplus," in particular their treatment of taxes and their failure to include any wage or middle-class salary payments as part of surplus. In addition, I am not convinced of their argument that corporate profits tend to grow within the economy, since I believe they overlook the prevailing permissive corporate attitude toward wage raises, and ignore the possibility, recently raised by Victor Fuchs, that corporate output is a declining proportion of total national output.[2]

Meanwhile, however, the Baran-Sweezy model brings us to the third, and in my view the weakest, aspect of the book. This is their theory of the structure and exercise of power within monopoly capitalism. For essentially their argument as to the inability of the system to absorb its surplus hinges on a political rather than an economic obstacle. This is the refusal of the ruling oligarchy to utilize the surplus for non-military purposes.

This is not a willful or arbitrary refusal. According to Baran and Sweezy, the ruling oligarchy is *unable* to pour the surplus of society into housing or education or other such things because expenditures for these purposes would jeopardize its economic and social interests. As they put it,

> It would be possible to run through the gamut of civilian spending objects and show how in case after case the private interests of the oligarchy stand in stark opposition to the satisfaction of social needs. Real competition with private

2. *The Service Economy*, p. 192.

enterprise cannot be tolerated . . . undermining of class privileges or of the stability of the class structure must be resisted at any cost. And almost all types of civilian expenditure involve one or more of these threats.

What is wrong with this assertion? To begin with, it treats the oligarchy as if it were a compact body of men who acted in concert with one will and one aim. Yet studies of the interests of the big corporations reveal profound divisions of interest among them. For example, Victor Perlo has shown that the big companies divide into two groups, one that benefits from arms spending, and another, equally big, that suffers from it.[3] Similarly, I have written on the wide differences that characterize big-business ideology, making it possible for Thomas J. Watson, for example, to say things that would strangle Ralph Cordiner.[4]

Second, Baran and Sweezy credit the oligarchy with immense operative power: "In constitutional theory the people exercise sovereign power; in actual practice a relatively small moneyed oligarchy rules supreme." If this were true, one would ask why—until the debacle of Vietnam—no Republican had been elected to the Presidency since Herbert Hoover, the sole exception being the "national" candidate, Eisenhower.

Finally, the oligarchy that emerges from the Baran-Sweezy analysis strikes me as a deceptive stereotype. There have been, I know, ruling classes so set in their ways, so blind to reality, that they have been unable to make those accommodations needed to assure their own survival: the French aristocracy comes to mind. But there have been other ruling classes—the English—who have managed their affairs

3. *Militarism and Industry*, p. 199f.
4. *The Business Establishment* (ed. Earl Cheit), Ch. 1.

very adroitly. Thus anyone in, say, 1750 who characterized the aristocracy as "incapable" of reconciling itself to the demands of the bourgeoisie would have obscured under this "class analysis" the very cultural and national traits that in the end spelled the all-important differences between the fate of the English and the French nobility.

This same objection must be brought to bear against Baran's and Sweezy's portrait of the capitalist class. Could not, after all, such a class learn to consume its surplus through public housing on the grand scale? Baran and Sweezy tell us flatly that it cannot: "Such planning and such action . . . will never be undertaken by a government run by and for the rich, as every capitalist government is and must be." How, then, are we to explain the slum clearance programs in Sweden or Norway; the family allowances in Germany; the medical programs in England? If these kinds of remedial action are possible in America, what we need to understand are the reasons why capitalists here are different from those abroad. It is the principal defect of Baran's and Sweezy's analysis that they provide no means of answering this critical question.

The reason for this seriously distorted argument lies, I think, in a fatal Marxian predilection for "closed systems" of thought that can then proceed with a delicious inexorability to their assigned destinations. In such systems, it is very hard to incorporate models of thought or action that partake of uncertainty, indeterminateness, or changeability. As a result, beliefs and attitudes that are perfectly correct as first approximations of social behavior—such as the predisposition of the American government and business class to defend its system of privileges—are frozen in ways that leave no room for compromise, retreat, adaptation, or learning. No wonder, then, that the historic drama has so often defied Marxist predictions—the "hopeless" English Tories of the 1930's becoming the most enlightened Conservative party in Europe, the "militant" unionists of the New Deal becoming the fat cats of the 1960's, the "reactionary" middle class leading the revolutions of the underdeveloped world.

These failures of prediction—based, I believe, in large measure on an overly abstract conception of power and class—lead me to discount much of the future Baran and Sweezy envisage. At home they see a static monopoly capitalism, suffering from increasing psychic malaise, while abroad the champions of liberty and freedom rally mankind under the banners of national liberation. What they do not see are possibilities for a long-run emergence of rationality in America, as the new elites of science and social science gradually emerge; or the chances that retrograde movement may follow from the revolutionary tendencies of the underdeveloped world. I would agree with them that capitalism as a system of function and privilege will be and should be eventually replaced by a more rational system, and that revolutions will be needed in the underdeveloped world before those miserable peoples can achieve the national will to make the enormous developmental effort required of them. But I am certain that the road to the future will not run as straight to heaven or hell as the one that Baran and Sweezy describe.

CHAPTER 14

The Power Structure

*I*s there an American upper class? Of course there is, although the admission may go against the American grain. (It is interesting to reflect that the only other country with as much difficulty in admitting to a class structure is the Soviet Union.) But is the American upper class a *ruling* class? That is, does it, by virtue of its social and economic position, also hold the reins of political power? That is a more difficult problem, for it is possible to contend that power in America is exercised not by a class but by various elites who may not be members of a superior class, and whose allegiance to or alliance with it may be temporary or subject to change. It is over this question that the two books here discussed differ sharply. G. William Domhoff argues in *Who Rules America?* that the upper class is a governing class; the late Arnold M. Rose maintains, in *The Power Structure,* that this is not the way power is exercised at all.

Domhoff's book is lean and precise, and largely devoid of the animus one expects in books that set out to demonstrate a thesis of its kind. It marshals its facts carefully and presents, on the whole, a convincing case that there exists an identifiable group

> . . . which receives a disproportionate amount of [the] country's income, owns a disproportionate amount of [the] country's wealth, and contributes a disproportionate number of its members to the controlling institutions and key decision-making groups of [the] country.

Who constitutes the group? Domhoff's criteria are both social and economic. Membership in the upper class is attested by one or more of the following: (1) listing in the *Social Register;* (2) attendance at one of a fairly small number of prep schools (Choate, Groton, Lawrenceville, etc.); (3) membership in one of the small number of exclusive men's clubs (in New York, the Brook, Knickerbocker, Harmonie); (4) family wealth (a millionaire entrepreneurial father or a $100,000 corporate executive or lawyer father); or (5) by marital or close family attachment to the above.

One can of course criticize such a list which, like any attempt to set forth formal criteria, fails to take into account every case. There are certainly some products of prep schools who are by no stretch of the imagination upper class, and there are millionaires who would never be allowed into the Knickerbocker. But it would be foolish to fault the effort because of its inadequacies. To my mind Domhoff has correctly identified a "crowd" that certainly has high social status, in large part derived from just these qualifications. It is, Domhoff hastens to add, an *open* class to which new recruits are constantly added, largely through advancement within the large corporations or other upper-class-controlled institutions.

Finally we should note that, although Domhoff defines his upper class as a social group (whose members freely mix and intermarry), the characteristics he uses to define them include the all-important nonsocial element of business wealth. Later he uses the words "business aristocracy" (the term is taken from the work of Digby Baltzell) as synonymous with the upper class—meaning by this not that all members of the upper class are businessmen, which they are not, but that a tie of business interest underlies and unifies most of the upper class.

This is all preliminary to the main argument. Having established the existence and the peculiar marks of an upper class, Domhoff now must show that in the hands of this class reside the control of the corporate economy, the shaping of the American polity, and the basic direction of the Federal government, including its military policy.

There are two ways of demonstrating such a claim. One is to prove that the key *decisions* within these areas of power are in fact made by members of the upper class—to establish that it is they who call the shots. The other is simply to show that the institutions within which these decisions are made—the corporations, the State and Defense Departments, the White House, etc.—are headed or staffed by upper-class members who can therefore be *presumed* to control the policies that flow from these institutions. That is, instead of showing who makes decisions, one analyzes the "situations" in which decisions are made. Domhoff chooses the second method for several reasons, some having to do with the accessibility of the data (it is much easier to find out who sits where than to ascertain who says what), and partly, I suspect, because this method is more congenial to establishing what he wants to establish.

What does Domhoff's analysis reveal? It is hardly surprising to discover that the upper class is intimately connected with the corporate structure and with the system of wealth based on that structure. Wealth and income in America may be more equally divided than in the past, but the share going to the very top remains very large: 45,000 families (0.1 percent of all families) receive an average income of $110,000 a year, and some 90,000 families own between two-thirds and three-quarters of *all* corporate stock. There is no proof that this *propertied* elite is identical with the *social* elite, but all evidence points to a very large overlap. Moreover, there is no doubt that the social upper class provides more than fifty percent of the directors of the topmost companies, while many of the remaining directors are members of various elites (lawyers, professional men of various kinds, college presidents), some of whom are on the road to entering the upper class.

The American polity—i.e., its political will—is a more difficult matter to analyze by Domhoff's method. Essentially what he shows is that the upper class has a predominant voice (or, more accurately, a predominant representation) in many of the organizations that seek to influence American thought. The big foundations, the Council on Foreign

Relations, the Foreign Policy Association, the National Association of Manufacturers and the Committee for Economic Development, the universities, the important media, etc., are by and large run by members of the upper class. Whereas Domhoff does not maintain that these institutions can "make" public opinion at will, he agrees with Richard Rovere that the Establishment has "very nearly unchallenged power in deciding what is and what is not respectable opinion in this country."

Moving on to the Federal government, Domhoff shows that the upper class provides the main financial backing of both the Republican and the Democratic parties, that it is an important source of recruitment for Cabinet posts, that it furnishes Presidents (who are usually not members of the upper class themselves) with their coteries of advisers, that it permeates the diplomatic corps and the regulatory agencies, at least at the top. The military, too, are usually subject to the leadership of the upper class, as evidenced by a study of the personnel heading the Department of Defense: "Of eight men who have served in the [Secretaryship of Defense] since it was created in 1947, five were listed in the *Social Register* and the remaining three were a corporation lawyer, a president of General Motors, and a president of the Ford Motor Company."

Thus, in area after area, Domhoff succeeds in showing that the command posts are filled by representatives of a small, socially identifiable group. Quite properly he does not push this claim too far. There are loci of power in American life—mainly Congress, and state and local government, and certain agencies such as the FBI—where the representation of the upper class is missing and its influence, presumably, minimal. "The national upper class . . . does

not control every aspect of American life," Domhoff con-
cedes, but weighing the evidence as a whole he is led to conclude that "the income, wealth, and institutional leadership
of . . . 'the American business aristocracy' are more than
sufficient to earn it the designation 'governing class.'"

This is, of course, a radical analysis—radical not in the
sense of advocating wholesale social change (Domhoff's
book has no programmatic intent) but by virtue of its description. Domhoff quotes C. Wright Mills that, "when
little is known, or only trivial items publicized, then plain
description becomes a radical fact—or at least is taken to be
radically upsetting." Hence Domhoff's position is apt to
provoke stiffened attitudes from many readers, and a reception which is less interested in assessing his findings as
a whole than in taking exception to this or that aspect of
them.

That would be unfortunate, for as far as it goes the book
sheds a good deal of light on an aspect of American society
where the floodlights of publicity can hardly be said to play.
The designation of an "upper class" and its association with
power are attributes of reality that it is well to call to our
attention, if only because these attributes are politely or
pointedly overlooked by most social analysts. Yet, having
made this important identification, one can legitimately ask
what else Domhoff has shown.

Here the book displays two weaknesses. The first, which is
perhaps inherent in his mode of analysis, is a failure to
specify exactly what is meant by the "control" that the
upper class wields. Take, for example, the least disputable
fact—that the upper class controls the corporate economy.

Certainly it is true that the upper class holds the director-
ships and that it receives a large share of the dividends. But
what is the "control" that it exercises? The corporate economy is not a single machine to be steered at will, but rather
a congeries of semicompetitive institutions whose activities
impinge on each other. Certainly individual boards of directors control the course of their corporations (within the limits
allowed them by pressure of the market), but it is difficult
to see what is meant by the "collective" control of the upper
class when each board of directors is out to undercut—certainly not to augment—the income and prerogatives of the
boards competing with it.

The meaning of the key word *control* becomes even more
elusive when we turn to other sectors of the nation. "Control of America's leading universities by members of the
American business aristocracy is more direct than with any
other institutions which they control," writes Domhoff. In
so far as "control" means occupancy of certain seats (here
designated as Trustees) this is undoubtedly true. But what
is the limit or effectiveness of this "control"? Occasionally,
as in Berkeley, the Trustees will assert their right to hire or
fire a president. But it is one thing to fire a president, and
another to interfere with or to shape the curriculum, the expression of faculty views, the temper of the student body,
etc. Here it would be my judgment that the Trustees are
much less powerful. Or to turn from the university to the
Federal government, it is again one thing to note that advisers
and Secretaries are noticeably of upper-class background,
but another to demonstrate that specific interests, policies,

and decisions follow from this class domination which would not take place were another class to have those positions.

To this it may be said that the interests, decisions, and policies of the government (or of the universities, etc.) need be no more than those that generally protect the United States as a social order in which there can be an upper class based mainly on wealth—that the "control" of the upper class need consist in no more than maintaining the general compass setting that steers us toward social, economic, and political objectives compatible with the maintenance of property as the basis of the social order.

As a general historical statement this is true, and important to say. But once we have said it, the course of history is still left indeterminate. For Domhoff is careful to stress that the upper class is not a unified group with a single defined strategy or goal. It includes among its members civil libertarians as well as segregationists, hard-line anti-Communists as well as advocates of rapprochement, supporters of Eugene McCarthy as well as of Joseph McCarthy. *In a word, the identification of an upper class, and the demonstration that it occupies the seats of power, do not allow one to make essential predictions as to the future course of American national behavior.* If we withdraw from Vietnam or advance there, if we disengage from the Cold War or intensify it, if we rebuild the cities or allow them to rot, in each case and on each side we will be able to discern the "controlling" influence of the upper class. What we have, then, is an analysis that cannot be put to practical use. Domhoff's analysis cuts through much obfuscation with a sharp knife, but just when that knife is applied to the purposes for which we need it most, it loses its cutting edge.

This brings us to Arnold Rose's *The Power Structure,* a much longer, less well-organized, and generally more polemical book, but one that contrasts with it almost perfectly —for Rose reaches (or should I say, begins from) conclusions totally different from those of Domhoff. For one thing, the concept of class structure does not really enter Rose's book at all. He is not interested in the question that absorbs Domhoff: Is there a *social* group whose interests are dominant? Rose wants to know what the elites are up to, and elites—the outstanding members of any profession or occupation or function—need not belong to a given *class.* Rose pursues the question of power along lines that take him away from an examination of the social position of institutional leaders into the smoke-filled back rooms where somebody, very likely not in the *Social Register,* is deciding what policy is really going to be.

This leads Rose into the investigation of particular struggles, such as the Kennedy nomination or the passage of the Medicare bill or the local political structure of Texas. These stories do not enlist much new information, but they all arrive with considerable persuasiveness at a common conclusion—that businessmen do not constitute a power elite of any overriding importance: or, conversely, that the power of the business elite is effectively hedged or countered by that of other elites, such as the military or the political elites. "The relationship between the economic elite and the political authorities," writes Rose, "has been a constantly varying one of strong influence, cooperation, division of labor, and conflict. . . . Further, neither the economic elite nor the political authorities are monolithic units which act with internal consensus and coordinated action with regard to each other. . . . In fact there are several economic elites which only very rarely act as units within themselves and among themselves, and there . . . are actually four political parties, two liberal ones and two conservative ones. . . ." In other words, Rose seeks to substantiate (with "facts that leave no significant areas of omission") the hypothesis that the power structure must be defined as a product of many influences rather than as the result of the domination of a single economic elite.

Thus Rose's book provides in some detail—although not really on a broad national scale—a sense of the clash of interests from which emerges the determination of actual issues. Yet, to my mind, as an overall attempt to explain how America is ruled, it suffers from a fault as vitiating as those in Domhoff's book. The trouble is that Rose does not explain the nature of the interests that *bind* the contestants, over and above the issues that divide them. He does not see, as Domhoff does, that the politician who struggles against a businessman, especially on a national rather than a local issue, may also be a representative of the interests of the upper class. To bring this point out clearly would require a wider canvas than Rose has used. An analysis of the forces which were for and against such measures as the attempt to regulate the auto industry, or to control business-caused pollution, or, for that matter, an analysis of the politics of the entire New Deal or the New Economics, would clearly reveal that certain members of the upper class were ranged *against* the business community, because those sectors of the upper class saw their long-term interest in broader terms than immediate profits.

But the weakness of Rose's book goes deeper than that.

In portraying America as a society ruled by the clash of elites, he loses sight of the fundamental fact that America is also a class society—that is, a society in which a certain form of privilege, reward, ideology, and interest has emerged to surround and protect a particular social and economic hierarchy. As a result, whereas Domhoff's analysis has no predictable direction, Rose's has no center of gravity. If C. Wright Mills were alive he would criticize Rose's effort for failing to give his elites "coherence as an historical force" (*The Power Elite,* p. 16), and I think in this instance he would be right.

Is it possible to define the nature of the American social and economic structure, and its relation both to history and to political events, more clearly than this? I would think that we need to combine the two approaches, beginning with Domhoff's essential identification of the hegemony of a national upper class based on private property, and then proceeding along Rose's lines, first to specify the divisions of this upper class into factions, and then to trace the influence of these factions in the processes of politics. Such a composite approach, combining historicity and particularism, would constitute a major contribution to American sociology. I wonder if anyone will succeed in producing a book that will be at once so objective and so radical.

CHAPTER 15

Futurology

Ours is not the first age to believe it could foretell the future. The Greeks consulted the oracles; the Middle Ages the clergy; the Enlightenment the philosophers and historians. The difference is that we ask the scientists. Of the forty-odd contributors to the first report of the Commission on the Year 2000, a group established by the American Academy of Arts and Sciences to predict the next thirty-two years, three-quarters are social or natural scientists: economists, sociologists, political scientists, psychologists, physicists, and the like. Gone are the soothsayers, the clergymen, the philosophers, and all but two historians. No less revealing, we find on the Commission no artists or writers, no politicians or soldiers, no architects or engineers, no businessmen or students.

But of course. What would *they* know about the year 2000? We are carried toward the future on the momentum of impersonal social and natural forces whose nature it is the business of scientists to investigate. Other kinds of people may have a hand in making the future, but they are not the ones we turn to when we seek to predict it.

The United States is not alone in the belief in the possibility of scientifically exploring the future. In England there is a similarly constituted Committee on the Next Thirty Years; in France the project *Futuribles;* in Oslo last year assembled the First International Future Research Congress. The scientific study of the future, with its dashed lines and pictographs, is part of the worldwide culture of our time.

One reason for this widespread interest in futurology, as Daniel Bell, Chairman of the American Commission, points out in his introductory essay to this volume,[1] is simply the millennial appeal of the Great Year that is already in sight. On the occasion of the last millennium crowds gathered on hilltops in Europe to await the end of the world; on this one they will gather to search for the first signs of the coming of a new world. The idea of progress, unknown in the year 1000, burns strong for the year 2000, and the Sunday supplements of that fabulous New Year's celebration will certainly turn more toward what is yet to come than to what has been left behind.

But there is a deeper reason for the prevailing interest in the future. It is that we have come more and more to *define*

1. *Toward the Year 2000: Work in Progress,* Volume XI of the Daedalus Library, edited by Daniel Bell.

the future by those social changes whose causes we can identify and whose course we can, with some degree of certainty, project forward. The rise of population, the steady advance and diffusion of technical knowledge, the ubiquitous national commitment to economic growth and, to some degree, national planning, all give rise to tremendous hydraulic pressures that push society into the future in more or less foreseeable ways.

Thus the act of prediction, as we conceive it, is concerned less and less with the forenaming of specific events, and more and more with the delineation of those processes that mark the boundaries of the shape of things to come. Indeed, it is clear from papers in the commission's report that the "harder" or more specific the prediction, the less interesting or plausible it is. For example, Ithiel de Sola Pool writing (in 1965) on "The International System in the Next Half Century" foresaw as the most likely among many possibilities that "Major fighting in Viet-Nam will peter out about 1967; and most objective observers will regard it as a substantial American victory," and Herman Kahn and Anthony Wiener, writing "A Framework for Speculation" about the next third of a century, predict 100 technical innovations that include such delightful fantasies as human hibernation and programmed dreams.

Such "hard" predictions are invariably titillating or sensational, but they are rarely interesting because we cannot see the logic behind the predicted event. No doubt Dr. de Sola Pool thought it consistent with his "predictive game" to prophesy the likelihood of an American "victory" against an Asian revolution, but lacking his chain of reasoning we are merely left with a bad joke; perhaps Kahn and Wiener may be right even in their most far-out technical prognostications, but without their underlying process of selection, their prediction has no more than amusement value. (This is not true, by the way, of their interesting projections for GNP and population, also contained in this essay and elaborated in their full-length book, *The Year 2000*.)

Happily, most of the papers steer clear of this sort of fortune-telling. Indeed, their titles speak for themselves. "Can Social Predictions Be Evaluated?" "Forecasting and Technological Forecasting," "The Life Cycle and Its Variations," "Notes on Meritocracy," "The Need for a New Political Theory." As can be seen, these papers predict problems rather than solutions, establish limits rather than targets, depict interactions rather than clear-cut trajectories. Meanwhile, knitting the papers together are more or less verbatim reports of the Working Sessions themselves, whose titles describe even more clearly the conception of the task as it appeared to the participants: "Baselines for the Future," "Alternative Futures," "Centralization and Decentralization," "The Need for Models."

All this is the very paradigm of the scientific—as contrasted with an earlier prescientific—mode of prevision. Indeed, never was an exercise in forethought undertaken with such wry awareness of the pitfalls of prediction. As Daniel Bell remarked toward the end of one of the working sessions:

> Since we have been concerned with the nature and limitations of forecasting, I would like to conclude this session with a prediction I found in going through an old file. It pictures a future world, and the text reads: "From the train of moving seats in the darkest building, a visitor looks down upon a

miniature landscape far away . . . and finally he beholds
the city itself with its quarter-mile high towers, huge glass,
and soaring among them four-level, seven-lane directional
highways on which you can surely choose your speed—100,
200 miles per hour. The city of 1960 has abundant functions: fresh air, fine green parkways, recreational centers,
all results of plausible planning and design. No building's
shadow will touch another. Parks will occupy one third of
the city area." "Who can say," whispers a voice, "what new
horizons lie before us. We have both the initiative and the
imagination to penetrate them." The text and the voice are
from Futurama, the elaborate scale-model of the ideal city
of the future, which was presented at the General Motors'
exposition at the 1939 World's Fair. There you have 1939
looking at 1960, and see where we are today.

With so much intelligence focused on a problem of such
importance one would expect *Toward the Year 2000* to be a
fascinating document. Yet, except as an exhibit in the
history of ideas, it is not. There are, to be sure, many excellent papers, among which I particularly liked an essay
on Violence by James Q. Wilson, parts of the aforementioned piece by Kahn and Wiener, and above all the introductory and concluding pieces by Bell himself, distinguished
both in style of language and structure of thought. Yet,
taken as a whole the collection seems curiously bland, in-
conclusive, unimpressive.

One reason for this lies in the symposium format itself. It
is no doubt part of the scientific approach to believe that
many expert minds can elucidate a complicated question
better than one mind can, but the price of the gain in expertise is a telling loss of impact. Perhaps I exaggerate, but I
cannot recall ever having read a collective intellectual effort
that left a profound impression on me, and this one is no
exception. The individual essays, each aimed in a different

direction, scatter light rather than focus it; the transcripts of the working sessions, included to give a sense of the struggle for insight, read only like disjointed conversation. The whole enterprise would have been infinitely better had one person, preferably Bell, woven all the background papers into a single coherent view, but then of course it would not have been so scientific.

The second reason for my disappointment goes considerably deeper. It lies in a point of view, explicitly stated by Bell, but tacitly endorsed by all, that "many of our problems do not derive from capitalism, but from the fact that we have a national society where changes of all sorts have immediate impact, economically and otherwise, on all other parts of our society." Now I do not doubt that a tightening of our social bonds is a very important phenomenon of the present and future. Yet a concentration on this politically "neutral" attribute of our times leads one all too easily to overlook the far-from-neutral historical implications of the fact that the society whose bonds are being tightened is a *capitalist* society.

Indeed it is astonishing to read so many essays dealing with the forces that propel us into the future and to find no mention of the specifically capitalist nature or form of some of those forces. For instance, in a consideration of America's role in the international world nowhere do we find a discussion of whether American corporations will continue to pour their profits abroad, although there are few international forces more important today than the Americanization of European business and the interweaving of the prosperity of certain large American corporations and the preservation of the status quo in Latin America.

The same curious blindness affects the discussion of

domestic issues. There is much talk of planning and the market system, but no real analysis of the degree to which they are compatible. Again, this is because the "market system" is considered wholly as a functional mechanism for pushing land, labor, and capital to their points of highest return—which is of course compatible with planning; but there is no consideration of the fact that the mechanism is also a social and institutional system closely linked with the existing distribution of income. From this point of view it is a good deal less easy to claim that the market system is indifferent to the imposition of public goals.

Again, a failure to place the specific problems of capitalism in the foreground leads to an all-too-undiscerning treatment of the central question of growth. Growth is assumed to be a self-evident benefit for society. Perhaps it is— yet there are disturbing consequences of growth for a capitalist economic system. For one effect of growth is virtually certain to be a weakening of the motivational base on which capitalism, or, for that matter, every other Western system, has always depended—the existence of a large body of propertyless workers who do the work that society offers them, not because they want to but because they have to. But if the projections of the Commission are to be taken seriously, that source of motivation will be severely eroded by the year 2000. Kahn and Wiener project a "post-industrial" world by that date with family incomes (for a family with two children) of between $16,000 and $64,000. At these levels of well-being, will the normal incentives of the market suffice to recruit the working force? Already the complaint is that young people do not want to enter many lower-middle-class occupations, despite the fact that they pay well. The rise of widespread affluence thus promises to strain the recruitment process of a market society to the point at which nonmarket methods of labor allocation may be necessary. But problems of this sort disappear in a view of the "post-industrial" future that ignores the particular problems associated with our capitalist jumping-off point.

Yet, in a report which is by no means restricted to economic problems, it would be unfair to belabor the Commission for what I consider to be a kind of economic naïveté. And in fact my disappointment ultimately derives from another source altogether. It arises from a feeling that the Commission, for all its scientific air, has not really performed its task in a scientific way. For not one but two approaches can be discerned through many of the papers and most of the discussion in this volume. In one, the participants stand "above" the system, seeking to analyze and report its trends with all the aloofness of the astronomer plotting the movement of the planets. In the other, however, the participants stand "within" the system, working *for* social change—that is, not predicting the course of the planets but seeking to alter it.

Both of these are useful, even necessary tasks, but both of them are not scientific tasks. When it comes to designing the future we need many more points of view than those of the scientist, and in particular of the rather Establishmentarian scientists on this Commission. As Fred Charles Iklé points out in his essay, there is a disconcerting similarity between the agenda of the Commission and the Great Society program of President Johnson. If the task of the Commission is to imagine a better world—even a "scientifically imaginable" better world—it will need the radical and bold outlook of those outside the Establishment quite as much as the measured banalities of the professordom.

But is it the task of the Commission, as a specifically *scientific* enterprise, to imagine such a world? I do not think it should be. Although it may be only a delusion of our time, I believe that the scientific exploration of the future does in fact open startling and powerful new possibilities. By this I do not mean those of an imaginary better world, but those of the existing real world as it is likely to be if the trends of the present should continue into the future. In the systematic projection of technological, demographic, and economic probabilities, and in the absolutely disinterested— but not, let me emphasize again, ahistoric—examination of the consequences of these trends, the scientists and social scientists have a great deal to offer us. To be sure, we accept their predictions in the hope that we can, if need be, disprove them by acting on the information they have given us, but even this hope rests on the confidence we can place in the scientific validity of what we have been advised we shall have to struggle against. *In turn, however, this validity, on which so much depends, can only be assured if those who have been entrusted to make the observations of the future have been relieved of any responsibility for whatever actions may take place, or may be inhibited, because of what they report.* It is up to the scientists to make their forecasts with the utter objectivity of scientists, but this is exceedingly difficult to do once prediction and advocacy become mingled.

It is precisely this failure to adhere rigorously and courageously to their competence as scientists that I miss in *Toward the Year 2000.* Out of the very best of motives the Commission has fallen into an ambiguous position—as at once the predictor and the maker of the future. In the end, I fear, this mixture of aims is bound to weaken the potential achievement of the project. Forewarned against the possibility of constructing another Futurama, the Commission nonetheless risks the same outcome by repeating, albeit in much more sophisticated ways, the mistakes of the General Motors designers.

CHAPTER 16

Ecological Armageddon

*E*cology has become the Thing. There are ecological politics, ecological jokes, ecological bookstores, advertisements, seminars, teach-ins, buttons. The automobile, symbol of ecological abuse, has been tried, sentenced to death, and formally executed in at least two universities (complete with burial of one victim). Publishing companies are fattening on books on the sonic boom, poisons in the things we eat, perils loose in the garden, the dangers of breathing. The *Saturday Review* has appended a regular monthly Ecological Supplement. In short, the ecological issue has assumed the dimensions of a vast popular fad, for which one can predict with reasonable assurance the trajectory of all such fads—a period of intense popular involvement, followed by growing boredom and gradual extinction, save for a diehard remnant of the faithful.

This would be a great tragedy, for I have slowly become convinced during the last twelve months that the ecological issue is not only of primary and lasting importance, but that it may indeed constitute the most dangerous and difficult challenge that humanity has ever faced. Since these are very large statements, let me attempt to substantiate them by drawing freely on the best single descriptive and analytic treatment of the subject that I have yet seen, *Population, Resources, Environment,* by Paul and Anne Ehrlich of Stanford University. Rather than resort to the bothersome procedure of endlessly citing their arguments in quotation marks, I shall take the liberty of reproducing their case in a rather free paraphrase, as if it were my own, until we reach the end of the basic argument, after which I shall make clear some conclusions that I believe lie implicit, although not quite overt, in their work.

Ultimately, the ecological crisis represents our belated awakening to the fact that we live on what Kenneth Boulding has called, in the perfect phrase, our Spaceship Earth. As in all spaceships, sustained life requires that a meticulous balance be maintained between the life-support capability of the vehicle and the demands made by the inhabitants of the craft. Until quite recently, those demands have been well within the capability of the ship, both in terms of its ability to supply the physical and chemical requirements for continued existence and to absorb the waste products of the voyagers. This is not to say that the earth has been generous —short rations have been the lot of mankind for most of its history—nor is it to deny the recurrent advent of local ecological crises: witness the destruction of whole areas like the erstwhile granaries of North Africa. But famines have passed and there have always been new areas to move to. The idea that the earth as a whole was overtaxed is one that is new to our time.

For it is only in our time that we are reaching the ceiling of earthly carrying capacity, not on a local but on a global basis. Indeed, as will soon become clear, we are well past that capacity, provided that the level of resource intake and waste output represented by the average American or European is taken as a standard to be achieved by all humanity. To put it bluntly, if we take as the price of a first-class ticket the resource requirements of those passengers who travel in the Northern Hemisphere of the Spaceship, we have now reached a point at which the steerage is condemned to live forever—or at least within the horizon of the technology presently visible—at a second-class level; or at which a considerable change in living habits must be imposed on first class if the ship is ever to be converted to a one-class cruise.

This strain on the carrying capacity of the vessel results from the contemporary confluence of three distinct developments, each of which places tremendous or even unmanageable strains on the life-carrying capability of the planet and all of which together simply overload it. The first of these is the enormous strain imposed by the sheer burgeoning of population. The statistics of population growth are by now very well known: the earth's passenger list is growing at a rate that will give us some four billion humans by 1975, and that threatens to give us eight billions by 2010. I say "threatens," since it is likely that the inability of the earth to carry so large a group will result in an actual population somewhat smaller than this, especially in the steerage, where the growth is most rapid and the available resources least plentiful.

We shall return to the population problem later. But meanwhile a second strain is placed on the earth by the simple cumulative effect of *existing* technology (combustion engines, the main industrial processes, present-day agricultural techniques, etc.). This strain is localized mainly in the first-class portions of the vessel where each new arrival on board is rapidly given a standard complement of capital equipment and where the rate of physical- and chemical-resource transformation per capita steadily mounts. The strain consists of the limited ability of the soil, the water, and the atmosphere of these favored regions to absorb the outpourings of these fast-growing industrial processes.

The most dramatic instance of this limited absorptive power is the rise in the carbon dioxide content of the air due to the steady growth of (largely industrial) combustion. By the year 2000, it seems beyond dispute that the CO_2 content of the air will have doubled, raising the heat-trapping properties of the atmosphere. This so-called greenhouse effect has been predicted to raise main global temperatures sufficiently to bring catastrophic potential consequences. One possibility is a sequence of climatic changes resulting from a melting of the Arctic ice floes that would result in the advent of a new Ice Age; another is the slumping of the Antarctic icecap into the sea with a consequent tidal wave that could wipe out a substantial portion of mankind and raise the sea level by sixty to a hundred feet.

These are all "iffy" scenarios whose present significance may be limited to alerting us to the immensity of the ecological problem; happily they are of sufficient uncertainty not to cause us immediate worry (it is lucky they are, because it is extremely unlikely that all the massed technological and human energy on earth could arrest such changes once they began). Much closer to home is the burden placed on the earth's carrying capacity by the sheer requirements of a spreading industrial activity in terms of the fuel and mineral resources needed to maintain the going rate of output per person in the first-class cabins. To raise the existing (not the anticipated) population of the earth to American standards would require the annual extraction of great multiples of the quantities of iron, copper, lead, tin, etc., that we now take from the earth. Only the known reserves of iron allow us seriously to entertain the possibility of long-term mineral extraction at the required rates (and the capital investment needed to bring about such mining operations is enormous). And, to repeat, we have taken into account only today's level of population: to equip the prospective passengers of the year 2010 with this amount of basic raw materials would require a doubling of all the above figures.

I will revert later to the consequences of this prospect. First, however, let us pay attention to the third source of overload, this one traceable to the special environment-destroying potential of newly developed technologies. Of these the most important—and if it should ever come to full-scale war, of course the most lethal—is the threat posed by nuclear radiation. I shall not elaborate on this well-known (although not well-believed) danger, pausing to point out only that a massive nuclear holocaust would in all likelihood exert its principal effect in the Northern Hemisphere. The survivors in the South would be severely hampered in their efforts at reconstruction not only because most of the easily available resources of the world have already been used up, but because most of the technological know-how would have perished along with the populations up North.

But the threats of new technology are by no means limited to the specter of nuclear devastation. There is, immediately at hand, the known devastation of the new chemical pesticides that have now entered more or less irreversibly into the living tissue of the world's population. Most mothers' milk in the United States today—I now quote the Ehrlichs verbatim—"contains so much DDT that it would be declared illegal in interstate commerce if it were sold as cow's milk"; and the DDT intake of infants around the world is twice the daily allowable maximum set by the World Health Organization. We are already, in other words, being exposed to heavy dosages of chemicals whose effects we know to be dangerous, with what ultimate results we shall have to wait nervously to discover. (There is food for thought in the archeological evidence that one factor in the decline of Rome was the systematic poisoning of upper-class Romans from the lead with which they lined their wine containers.)

But the threat is not limited to pesticides. Barry Commoner predicts an agricultural crisis in the United States within fifty years from the action of our fertilizers, which will either ultimately destroy soil fertility or lead to pollution of the national water supply. At another corner of the new technology, the SST threatens not alone to shake us with its boom but to affect the amount of cloud cover (and climate) by its contrails. And I have not even mentioned the standard pollution problems of smoke, industrial effluents into lakes and rivers, or solid wastes. Suffice it to report that a 1968 UNESCO conference concluded that man has only about twenty years to go before the planet starts to become uninhabitable because of air pollution alone. Of course, "starts to" is imprecise; I am reminded of a cartoon of an industrialist looking at his billowing smokestacks, in front of which a forlorn figure is holding up a placard that says, "We have only 35 years to go." The caption reads, "Boy, that shook me up for a minute. I thought it said 3–5 years."

I have left until last the grimmest and gravest threat of all, speaking now on behalf of the steerage. This is the looming inability of the great green earth to bring forth sufficient food to maintain life, even at the miserable threshold of subsistence at which it is now endured by perhaps a third of the world's population. The problem here is the very strong likelihood that population growth will inexorably outpace whatever improvements in fertility and productivity we will be able to apply to the earth's mantle (including the watery fringes of the ocean where sea "farming" is at least technically imaginable). Here the race is basically between two forces: on the one hand, those that give promise that the rate of increase of population can be curbed (if not totally halted); and on the other, those that give promise of increasing the amount of sustenance we can wring from the soil.

Both these forces are subtly blended of technological and social factors. Take population growth. The great hope of every ecologist is that an effective birth-control technique —cheap, requiring little or no medical supervision, devoid of taboos or religious hindrances—will rapidly and effectively lower the present fertility rates which are doubling world population every 35 years (every 28 years in Africa; every 24 in Latin America). No such device is currently available, although the Pill, the IUD, vasectomies, abor-

tions, condoms, coitus interruptus, and other known techniques could, of course, do the job if the requisite equipment, persuasion (or coercion), instruction, etc., could be
brought to the 80 to 90 percent of the world's people who
know next to nothing about birth control.

It seems a fair conclusion that no such worldwide campaign is apt to be successful for at least a decade and maybe
a generation, although there is always the hope that a "spontaneous" change in attitudes similar to that in Hungary or
Japan will bring about a rapid halt to population growth.
But even in this unlikely event, the sheer "momentum" of
population growth still poses terrible problems. Malcom
Potts, Medical Director of International Planned Parent-
hood has presented a shocking statistical calculation in this
regard: he has pointed out that population growth in India
is today adding a million mouths per month to the Indian
subcontinent. If, by some miracle, fertility rates were to
decline tomorrow by 50 percent in India, at the end of
twenty years, owing to the already existing huge numbers of
children who would be moving up into child-bearing ages,
population growth in India would still be taking place at the
rate of a million per month.

The other element in the race is our ability to match
population growth with food supplies, at least for a generation or so, while birth-control techniques and campaigns
are perfected. Here the problem is also partly technological,
partly social. The technological part involves the so-called
Green Revolution—the development of seeds that are capable, at their best, of improving yields per acre by a factor of
300 percent, sometimes even more. The problem, however,
is that these new seeds generally require irrigation and fertilizer to bring their benefits. If India alone were to apply

fertilizer at the per capita level of the Netherlands, she would consume half the world's total output of fertilizer. This would require a hundredfold expansion of India's present level of fertilizer use. Irrigation, the other necessary input for most improved seeds, poses equally formidable requirements. E. A. Mason of the Oak Ridge National Laboratories has prepared preliminary estimates of the costs of nuclear-powered "agro-industrial complexes" in which desalted water and fertilizer would be produced for use on adjacent farms. It would require 23 such plants per year, each taking care of some three million people, just to keep pace with present population growth. Since it would take at least five years to get these plants into operation, we should begin work today on at least 125 such units. Assuming that no hitches were encountered and that the technology on paper could be easily translated into a technology *in situ,* the cost would amount to $315 billion.

There are, as well, other technical problems associated with the Green Revolution of an ecological nature—mainly the risk of introducing locally untried strains of plants that may be subject to epidemic disease. But putting those difficulties to the side, we must recognize as well the social obstacles that a successful Green Revolution must overcome. The new seeds can only be afforded by the upper level of peasantry—not merely because of their cost (and the cost of the required fertilizer) but because only a rich peasant can take the risk of having the crop turn out badly without himself suffering starvation. Hence the Green Revolution is likely to increase the strains of social stratification within the underdeveloped areas. Then, too, even a successful local crop does not always shed its benefits evenly across a nation but results all too often in local gluts that cannot be transported to starving areas because of transportation bottle-necks.

None of these discouraging remarks are intended in the slightest to disparage the Green Revolution, which represents the inspired work of dedicated men. But the difficulties must be kept in mind as a corrective to the lulling belief that "science" can easily offset the population boom with larger supplies of food. There is no doubt that supplies of food *can* be substantially increased—rats alone devour some 10 to 12 percent of India's crop, and insects can ravage up to half the stored crops of some underdeveloped areas, so that even very "simple" methods of improved storage hold out important prospects of improving basic life-support, quite aside from the longer-term hopes of agronomy. Yet, at best these improvements will only stave off the day of reckoning. Ultimately the problem posed by Malthus must be faced—that population tends to increase geometrically, by doubling, and that agriculture does not, so that eventually population *must* face the limit of a food barrier. It is worth repeating the words of Malthus himself in this regard:

> Famine seems to be the last, the most dreadful resource of nature. The power of population is so much superior to the power in the earth to produce subsistence for man, that premature death must in some shape or other visit the human race. The vices of mankind are active and able ministers of depopulation . . . [S]hould they fail in this war of extermination, sickly seasons, epidemics, pestilence, and plague, advance in terrific array, and sweep off their thousands and ten thousands. Should success still be incomplete, gigantic inevitable famine stalks in the rear, and with one mighty blow, levels the population with the food of the world.

This Malthusian prophecy has been so often "refuted," as economists have pointed to the astonishing rates of growth of food output in the advanced nations, that there is a danger of dismissing the warnings of the Ehrlichs as merely another premature alarm. To do so would be a fearful mistake. For, unlike Malthus, who assumed that technology would remain constant, the Ehrlichs have made ample allowance for the growth of technological capability, and their approach to the impending catastrophe is not shrill. They merely point out that a mild version of the Malthusian solution is already upon us, for at least half a billion people are chronically hungry or outright starving, and another one and a half billion under- or mal-nourished. Thus we do not have to wait for "gigantic inevitable famine"; it has already come.

What is more important is that the Ehrlichs see the matter in a perspective fundamentally different from Malthus', not as a problem involving supply and demand but as one involving a total ecological equilibrium. The crisis, as the Ehrlichs see it, is thus both deeper and more complex than merely a shortage of food, although the latter is one of its more horrendous evidences. What threatens the spaceship Earth is a profound imbalance between the totality of systems by which human life is maintained and the totality of demands, industrial as well as agricultural, technological as well as demographic, to which that life-support capacity is subjected.

I have no doubt that one can fault bits and pieces of the Ehrlichs' analysis, and there is a note of determined pessimism in their work that leads me to suspect (or at least hope) that there is somewhat more time for adaptation than they suggest. Yet I do not see how their basic conclusion can be denied. Beginning within our lifetimes and rising rapidly to crisis proportions in our children's, humankind faces a challenge comparable to none in its history, with the possible exception of the forced migrations of the Ice Age. It is with the responses to this crisis that I wish to end this essay, for, telling and courageous as the Ehrlichs' analysis is, I do not believe that even they have fully faced up to the implications that their own findings present.

The first of these I have already stated: it is the clear conclusion that the underdeveloped countries can *never* hope to achieve parity with the developed countries. Given our present and prospective technology, there are simply not enough resources to permit a "Western" rate of industrial exploitation to be expanded to a population of four billion—much less eight billion—persons. It may well be that most of the population in the underdeveloped world has no ambition to reach Western standards—indeed, does not even know that such a thing as "development" is on the agenda. But the elites of these nations, for all their rhetorical rejection of Western (and especially American) styles of life, do tend to picture a Western standard as the ultimate end of their activities. As it becomes clear that such an objective is impossible, a profound reorientation of views must take place within the underdeveloped nations.

What such a reorientation will be it is impossible to say. For the near-term future, the outlook for the most population-oppressed areas will be a continuous battle against food shortages, coupled with the possible impairment of the intelligence of much of the surviving population due to protein deficiencies in childhood. This pressure of population may lead to aggressive searches for *Lebensraum,* or, as I have frequently written, it may culminate in revolutions of desperation. In the long run, of course, there is the possibility of considerable growth (although nothing resembling the attainment of a Western standard of consumption). But no quick substantial improvement in their condition seems feasible within the next generation at least. The visions of Sir Charles Snow or Soviet Academician Sakharov for a gigantic transfer of wealth from the rich nations to the poor (20 percent of GNP is proposed) are simply fantasies. Since much of GNP is spatially nontransferable or inappropriate, such a massive levy against GNP would imply shipments of up to 50 percent of much movable output. How this enormous flood of goods would be transported, allocated, absorbed, or maintained—*not to mention relinquished by the donor countries*—is nowhere analyzed by the proponents of such massive aid.

The implications of the ecological crisis for the advanced nations are not any less severe, although they are of a different kind. For it is clear that free industrial growth is just as disastrous for the Western nations as free population growth for those of the East and South. The worship in the West of a growing Gross National Product must be recognized as not only a deceptive but a very dangerous avatar; Kenneth Boulding has begun a campaign, in which I shall join him, to label this statistical monster Gross National Cost.

The necessity to bring our economic activities into a sustainable relationship with the resource capabilities and waste-absorption properties of the world will pose two problems for the West. On the simpler level, a whole series of technological problems must be met. Fume-free transportation must be developed on land and in the air. The cult of disposability must be replaced by that of reusability. Population stability must be attained through tax and other inducements, both to conserve resources and to preserve reasonable population densities. Many of these problems will tax our ingenuity, technical and socio-political, but the main problem they pose is not whether, but *how soon,* they can be solved.

But there is another, deeper question that the developed nations face—at least those that have capitalist economies. This problem can be stated as a crucial test as to who was right—John Stuart Mill or Karl Marx. Mill maintained, in his *Principles of Economics,* that the terminus of capitalist evolution would be a stationary state, in which the return to capital had fallen to insignificance, and a redistributive tax system would be able to capture any flows of income to the holders of scarce resources, such as land. In effect, he prophesied the transformation of capitalism, in an environment of abundance, into a balanced economy, in which the capitalist, both as the generator of change and as the main claimant on the surplus generated by change, would in fact undergo a painless euthanasia.

The Marxian view is, of course, quite the opposite. The very essence of capitalism, according to Marx, is expansion —which is to say, the capitalist, as a historical "type," finds his raison d'être in the insatiable search for additional money-wealth gained through the constant growth of the economic system. The idea of a "stationary" capitalism is, in Marxian eyes, a contradiction in terms, on a logical par with a democratic aristocracy or an industrial feudalism.

Is the Millian or the Marxian view correct? I do not think that we can yet say. Some economic growth is certainly compatible with a stabilized rate of resource use and disposal, for growth could take the form of the expenditure of additional labor on the improvement (aesthetic or technical) of the national environment. Indeed, insofar as education or cultural activity are forms of national output that require little resource use and result in little waste product, national output could be indefinitely expanded through these and similar activities. But there is no doubt that the main avenue of traditional capitalist accumulation would have to be considerably constrained; that net investment in mining and manufacturing would likely decline; that the rate and kind of technological change would need to be supervised and probably greatly reduced; and that, as a consequence, the flow of profits would almost certainly fall.

Is this imaginable within a capitalist setting—that is, in a nation in which the business ideology permeates the views of nearly all groups and classes, and establishes the bounds of what is possible and natural, and what is not? Ordinarily I do not see how such a question could be answered in any way but negatively, for it is tantamount to asking a dominant class to acquiesce in the elimination of the very activities that sustain it. But this is an extraordinary challenge that may evoke an extraordinary response. Like the challenge posed by war, the ecological crisis affects all classes, and therefore may be sufficient to induce sociological changes that would be unthinkable in ordinary circumstances. The capitalist and managerial classes may see—perhaps even more clearly than the consuming masses—the nature and nearness of the ecological crisis, and may recognize that their only salvation (as human beings, let alone privileged human beings) is an occupational migration into governmental or other posts of power, or they may come to accept a smaller share of the national surplus simply because they recognize that there is no alternative. When the enemy is nature, in other words, rather than another social class, it is at least imaginable that adjustments could be made that would be impossible in ordinary circumstances.[1]

There is, however, one last possibility to which I must also call attention. It is the possibility that the ecological crisis will simply result in the decline, or even destruction, of Western civilization, and of the hegemony of the scientific-technological view that has achieved so much and cost us so dearly. Great challenges do not always bring great responses, especially when those responses must be sustained over long periods of time and require dramatic changes in life-styles and attitudes. Even educated men today are able to deny the reality of the crisis they face: there is wild talk of farming the seas, of transporting men to the planets, of unspecified "miracles" of technology that will avert disaster. Glib as they are, however, at least these suggestions have a certain responsibility when compared with another and much more worrisome response: *je m'en fiche*. Can we really persuade the citizens of the Western world who are just now entering the heady atmosphere of a high-consumption way of life that conservation, stability, frugality, and a deep concern for the distant future must take priority over the personal indulgence for which they have been culturally prepared and which they are about to experience for the first time? Not the least danger of the ecological crisis, as I see it, is that tens and hundreds of millions will shrug their shoulders at the prospects ahead ("What has posterity ever

1. Let me add a warning that it is not only capitalists who must make an unprecedented ideological adjustment. Socialists must also come to terms with the abandonment of the goal of industrial superabundance on which their vision of a transformed society rests. The stationary equilibrium imposed by the constraints of ecology requires at the very least a reformulation of the kind of economic society toward which socialism sets its course.

done for us?"), and that the increasingly visible approach of ecological Armageddon will bring not repentance but Saturnalia.

Yet I cannot end this essay on such a note. For it seems to me that the ecological enthusiasts may be right when they speak of the deteriorating environment as providing the *possibility* for a new political rallying ground. If a new New Deal, capable of engaging both the efforts and the beliefs of this nation, is the last great hope to which we cling in the face of what seems otherwise to be an inevitable gradual worsening and coarsening of our style of life, it is possible that a determined effort to arrest the ecological decay might prove to be its underlying theme. Such an issue, immediate in the experience of all, carries an appeal that might allow vast improvements to be worked in the American environment, both urban and industrial. I cannot estimate the likelihood of such a political awakening, dependent as these matters are on the dice of personality and the outcome of events at home and abroad. But however slim the possibility of bringing about such a change, it does at least make the ecological crisis, unquestionably the gravest long-run threat of our times, potentially the source of its greatest short-term promise.

Index

Index

Acquisitiveness, 33ff. (*see also* Maximization)
  and capitalism, 48–50, 207
  drive of, 36f.
  psychoanalytic basis, 39
Advertising, 46–7
African socialism, 70
Ambrose, Bishop, 34, 35, 42
Arrow, Kenneth, 120
Authoritarianism, 69f., 85–7, 108–11
Axelrad, Sidney, 107

Baran, Paul, 15n., 237–46

Behavior, 175ff., 203–5, 205–7 (*see also* Prediction)
Bell, Daniel, 152n., 260, 260n., 262–3, 264
Bello, Francis, 152n.
Bergson, A., 97n.
Berle, A.A., 213–23
Bettelheim, Chas., 15n., 96n.
Bible, 34
Bottomore, Thos., 97
Boulding, Kenneth, 172n., 270, 281
Business
  and state, 4f., 15ff.
  system, 79
  (*see also* Capitalism)

Capitalism
  defined, 79, 80–3, 144
  and human nature, 105–6
  ideology of, 81–2, 105–6, 283
  Marxian view of, 127ff.,
      144, 236ff., 282–3
  and production, 48–50, 282–5
  and state, 4f., 15ff.
  and technology, 147ff.
  (*see also* Marxism)
Carr, E. H., 9, 9n.
Central Planning Board, 88–9,
      93
China and development, 67–8
Christ, 41
Class struggle, 131, 140, 283–4
Class structure, 122, 243–5,
      247–57
Collectivist thought, 8, 10, 28, 30
Collectivism, 69f., 85–7
Commoner, Barry, 274
Communism, 59f., 68f., 85–7
  fundamentalist view of, 76–7
Control, instrumentalist, 183f.
Control over society, 253–7
Controls, over economy, 21–3
Cuba and development, 67–8

Delgado, Oscar, 63
Demand and supply, law of,
      175f., 184f.
Democracy, 110–1, 145
  and development, 69
Determinism, 147–64 (*see also*
      Technology)
Development
  agriculture and, 65n., 276–8
  communism and, 68f., 85–7
  and democracy, 69
  misconceptions of, 60–2

  and population problem, 62,
      65, 71, 271–2, 275–6
  revolutionary aspects of, 52–6,
      58, 60, 63f., 280
Domhoff, G. Wm., 247–57

Ecological problem, 100, 269–85
Economic development, *see*
      Development
Economic stability, 25
Economics
  and behavior, 175ff., 203–7
  and ecology, 269–85
  instrumental, 184–91
  Keynesian, 122, 123
  Marxian, 117, 123–5, 127–
      45, 168–70, 232n., 236ff.
  models, 121f., 180–1, 196ff.
  neoclassical, 117ff., 130–1
  political, xi, 182ff., 208
  prediction, 193ff.
  and privilege, 122
  and rigor, 124
  and theory, 166f., 193ff.
  and wealth, 35–6
Ehrlich, Paul and Ann, 270–1,
      274, 279, 280
Elites, emergence of, 30–1
Engels, F., 6, 155n.

Feinstein, C. H., 90n.
Fenichel, Otto, 36n.
Feudalism, 147
Foreign policy, U.S., 58–60, 72–8
Freedom, 6, 8, 43, 44, 69f.,
      85–7
Friedman, Milton, 13n., 43n.,
      170, 193n., 195

Freud, Sigmund, 141
Fromm, Eric, 97n., 105n.,
    111n.
Furtado, Celso, 11n.
Functional relationships, 195f.
Futurama, 262–3, 267
Futurology, 259–68

Galbraith, J. K., 52, 53, 54,
    225–35
Gary, Elbert, 12
General Electric Co., 27
Gilbert, K. R., 160n.
Gilfillan, S. C., 151n., 158,
    158n.
Government and capitalism,
    19f., 243f., 247ff.
Granma, 108–9
Green revolution, 65n., 276–8
Greenhouse effect, 272

Habbakuk, H. J., 161 n.
Hagen, E. E., 159n.
Handmill, 146–147
Hansen, Alvin, 161
Hayek, Friedrich, 5n., 6, 7, 7n.,
    8, 8n., 13n., 88
Hegel, 8
Heilbroner, R., 193n.
Hero of Alexandria, 150, 153
Hoffman, Paul, 52, 53, 54, 59
Huberman, Leo, 109n., 237
Human nature
    and capitalism, 105–6
    and socialism, 103–5, 107–11
    and wealth, 39
    (*see also* Acquisitiveness, Be-
        havior)

Ideology, *see* Capitalism,
        Socialism
Iklé, Fred, 266
Instrumentalism, 184–191
Inventions, simultaneous, 150

James, William, 38, 38n., 39,
    47, 158
Jewkes, John, 151n., 152n.

Kahn, Herman, 261–2, 263, 264
Keynes, J. M., 40, 41n., 122,
    123, 193n.
Knight, Frank, 5n., 6, 7, 8n.,
    11, 11n., 169n.
Kolko, Gabriel, 12n., 233n.
Koopmans, T. C., 170, 193n.
Krupp, Sherman R., 169n.
Kuhn, Thos., 197n.

Labor theory of value, 132–3,
    140
Lampman, Robert, 219
Land reform, 54, 63
Lange, Oskar, 88, 89, 90, 90n.,
    91, 92, 93
LaPiere, Richard, 154n., 161n.
Lenin, 87, 87n.
Leon, Paolo, 210n.
Leontief, W., 85n.
Lerner, Abba, 95n.
Liberal philosophy of history,
    16–18
Libertarian philosophy of his-
        tory, 5–9, 10–3
Lippincott, Benj., 89, 90n.

Lippmann, Walter, 5n., 8, 8n.
List, F., 8.
Locke, J., 215
Look, 67
Lowe, Adolph, 165–91, 193n., 202, 208, 232n.

Mably, Abbé, 117
Machlup, Fritz, 193n.
Malthus, T. R., 278–9
Mandel, Ernest, 96n., 104n., 129–46
Mannheim, 8
Marcuse, Herbert, 106, 107
Market mechanism
  failures of, 45
  and morality, 45–50
  and socialism, 94–7
Marx, Karl, 6, 8, 14n., 44, 48, 87, 117, 129, 133, 137, 140, 147, 148, 155, 155n., 157, 208, 210, 282
Marxian economics, 117, 123–5, 127–45, 236ff.
  limitations of, 139–42, 240–6, 281–2
Marxian philosophy of history, 5–9, 13–16, 30, 96n., 127ff., 147–9, 159–64
Mason, E. A., 277
Maximization, 168–70, 232n.
Means, Gardiner, 213–4
Merton, Robert, 150n.
Military expenditure, 20, 22, 23
Mill, J. S., 106, 110, 281–2
Miliband, R., 15n.
Mills, C. Wright, 252, 257
Mises, Ludwig von, 13n., 88
Models, economic, 121f., 180–1, 196ff.

Money, 109f., 143, 143n. (*see also* Wealth)
Monopoly capitalism, 236–46
Moorstein, Richard, –5n.
Motivation, problem of, 107–9

Nagel, Ernest, 171, 197n.
Negro problem and development, 61
Nelson, R., 151n.
New York Times, 67
Neisser, Hans, 27n.
Niel, Mathilde, 105n.

Paradigm, xii–xiii
Perlo, Victor, 244
Phillips, Jos., 241n.
Planning
  and market, 94–7
  and rationality, 88–92
  and socialism, 81, 87–93
Plato, 39
Political economics, xi, 183f., 208
Pool, Ithiel, 261
Population problem, 62, 71, 271–2, 275–6
Postan, M., 19n.
Potts, Malcom, 276
Powell, Raymond, 85n.
Power structure, 247–57
Prediction
  correlational, 194–5
  limits of, 193ff.
  long-run, 205–7
  and science, 267
  short-run, 200–5
  and society, 254, 259–67, 264, 267

Privilege, 122
Production functions, 119,
    200–2, 207
Profit, falling rate of, 134
Property, 215–6

Rand, Ayn, 41
Rationality, 88–90, 91–2
Revolution, 58–60, 72–8 (*see
    also* Development and
    U.S. foreign policy)
Riches, *see* Wealth
Richman, Barry, 85n.
Richta, R., 98, 99, 100
Robbins, L., 170, 193n.
Roper, Elmo, 226n.
Röpke, W., 10, 10n., 219
Rose, Arnold, 247, 255–57
Ruling class, 244–5, 247–57

Sakharov, Academician, 281
Samuelson, Paul, 13n., 120,
    127, 130, 138, 140, 169
Sawers, David, 151n., 152n.
Schmoller, G., 8
Schmookler, J., 151n.
Schonfield, Andrew, 17, 18
Schumpeter, J., 237
Science
    and government, 23f.
    and prediction, 267
    and technology, 163–4
    (*see also* Technology)
Singer, Chas., 27n., 160n.
Smith, Adam, 177, 187, 208
Snow, Sir Chas., 281
Socialism
    defined, 80–83
    and democracy, 110–1, 145

and development, 68f., 85–7
and ecology, 100–2, 248n.
and human nature, 102–11,
    143n.
ideology of, 81–3, 95, 102f.,
    112–3
and market, 94–7
and motivation, 102–9
and planning, 81, 87–93,
    94–7
and rationality, 88–92
and technology, 99–102, 112
and utopian thought, 104, 105,
    113, 141
and work, 98, 142–3
(*see also* Communism)
Sombart, W., 8
Spaak, P. H., 111
Spencer, Herbert, 5n.
Srole, Leo, 240
State, role of in capitalism, 4ff.
    rise of functions, 19ff.
    stationary, 282–3
Steam mill, 147–8, 154
Strachey, John, 14
Stillerman, Richard, 151n.,
    152n.
Summer, William Graham, 5n.
Supply and Demand, law of,
    175f., 184f.
Surplus, 131–2, 135n., 241–3
Sweezy, Paul, 4, 15, 15n., 92,
    96, 109n., 128, 238–
    46

Tawney, R. H., 234–5
Technology
    congruence, 154–5
    constraints, 152–4
    determinism, 147–63
    effect on society, 23–5, 272f.

Technology (*continued*)
  and government, 23f.
  and labor force, 156
  leaps in, 151–2
  and political control, 101–2
  prediction of, 152–4, 200–2,
    207
  and science, 163–4
  sequence of, 149, 151–2
  and socialism, 98–102, 112
  and work, 98, 142–7, 156
Technostructure, 230, 233
Theory, economic, 166ff.
Thomas, Norman, 111n.
Transcendental margin, 218,
  221
Tsuru, S., 14n., 15n.
Tumin, Melvin, 110n.
Twain, Mark, 51, 52, 53, 55

United States foreign policy,
  58–60, 72–8
USSR and development, 66, 68
  and planning, 93
Utopian elements in socialism,
  104, 105, 113, 141

Vietnam, 57–9, 73–4, 75, 76,
  145
Villarejo, Don, 233n.

Walzer, Michael, 110n.
Wealth, 32ff.
  ambivalence toward, 32–6
  and corruption, 143, 143n.,
    147
  drive for, 36f.
  and justice, 42–50
  and morality, 45–50
  and poverty, 42–3
  psychoanalytic view of, 39f.
Weber, Max, 141, 186
Wiener, Anthony, 261–2, 263
Wilbur, Chas., 85n.
Wilde, Oscar, 110–1
Wiles, P., 92n.
Williams, Raymond, 234
Wilson, Jas., 263, 265
Work, problem of, 98, 142–3

Yugoslavia, 96, 97

About the Author

Robert L. Heilbroner is well known
for a series of books that have gone a long way
to transform economics from a dismal science
to an exciting one. *The Worldly Philosophers,*
written while he was still a graduate student,
has sold almost a million copies and has become
standard fare for nearly a generation of
college students. *The Future as History,
The Great Ascent, The Limits of American
Capitalism, The Economic Problem* and other books
and essays have also won a wide audience both
in the universities and among general readers.
A graduate of Harvard, summa cum laude,
Dr. Heilbroner is now Chairman of
the Department of Economics of the Graduate
Faculty of the New School for Social Research,
where he received his doctoral degree.
Professor Heilbroner is a resident of
New York City and of Martha's Vineyard,
where he spends the summers mixing
bird-watching and writing.

VINTAGE POLITICAL SCIENCE
AND SOCIAL CRITICISM

V-428   ABDEL-MALEK, ANOUAR   *Egypt: Military Society*
V-625   ACKLAND, LEN AND SAM BROWN   *Why Are We Still in Vietnam?*
V-196   ADAMS, RICHARD N.   *Social Change in Latin America Today*
V-568   ALINSKY, SAUL D.   *Reveille for Radicals*
V-286   ARIES, PHILIPPE   *Centuries of Childhood*
V-604   BAILYN, BERNARD   *Origins of American Politics*
V-334   BALTZELL, E. DIGBY   *The Protestant Establishment*
V-335   BANFIELD, E. G. AND J. Q. WILSON   *City Politics*
V-674   BARBIANA, SCHOOL OF   *Letter to a Teacher*
V-198   BARDOLPH, RICHARD   *The Negro Vanguard*
V-60   BECKER, CARL L.   *The Declaration of Independence*
V-199   BERMAN, H. J. (ed.)   *Talks on American Law*
V-81   BLAUSTEIN, ARTHUR I. AND ROGER R. WOOCK (eds.)   *Man Against Poverty*
V-513   BOORSTIN, DANIEL J.   *The Americans: The Colonial Experience*
V-358   BOORSTIN, DANIEL J.   *The Americans: The National Experience*
V-621   BOORSTIN, DANIEL J.   *The Decline of Radicalism: Reflections on America Today*
V-414   BOTTOMORE, T. B.   *Classes in Modern Society*
V-44   BRINTON, CRANE   *The Anatomy of Revolution*
V-234   BRUNER, JEROME   *The Process of Education*
V-590   BULLETIN OF ATOMIC SCIENTISTS   *China after the Cultural Revolution*
V-684   CALVERT, GREG AND CAROL   *The New Left and the New Capitalism*
V-30   CAMUS, ALBERT   *The Rebel*
V-33   CARMICHAEL, STOKELY AND CHARLES HAMILTON   *Black Power*
V-664   CARMICHAEL, STOKELY   *Stokely Speaks*
V-98   CASH, W. J.   *The Mind of the South*
V-272   CATER, DOUGLASS   *The Fourth Branch of Government*
V-290   CATER, DOUGLASS   *Power in Washington*
V-555   CHOMSKY, NOAM   *American Power and the New Mandarins*
V-640   CHOMSKY, NOAM   *At War With Asia*
V-538   COX COMMISSION   *Crisis at Columbia*
V-311   CREMIN, LAWRENCE A.   *The Genius of American Education*
V-638   DENNISON, GEORGE   *The Lives of Children*
V-746   DEUTSCHER, ISAAC   *The Prophet Armed*
V-747   DEUTSCHER, ISAAC   *The Prophet Unarmed*
V-748   DEUTSCHER, ISAAC   *The Prophet Outcast*
V-617   DEVLIN, BERNADETTE   *The Price of My Soul*
V-671   DOMHOFF, G. WILLIAM   *The Higher Circles*
V-603   DOUGLAS, WILLIAM O.   *Points of Rebellion*
V-645   DOUGLAS, WILLIAM O.   *International Dissent*
V-390   ELLUL, JACQUES   *The Technological Society*
V-692   EPSTEIN, JASON   *The Great Conspiracy Trial*
V-661   FALK, RICHARD A., GABRIEL KOLKO, AND ROBERT JAY LIFTON   *Crimes of War: After Songmy*
V-442   FALL, BERNARD B.   *Hell in a Very Small Place: The Siege of Dien Bien Phu*
V-667   FINN, JAMES   *Conscience and Command*

V-413   FRANK, JEROME D.   *Sanity and Survival*
V-382   FRANKLIN, JOHN HOPE AND ISIDORE STARR (eds.)   *The Negro in 20th Century America*
V-368   FRIEDENBERG, EDGAR Z.   *Coming of Age in America*
V-662   FRIEDMAN, EDWARD AND MARK SELDEN (eds.)   *America's Asia: Dissenting Essays in Asian Studies*
V-378   FULBRIGHT, J. WILLIAM   *The Arrogance of Power*
V-688   FULBRIGHT, J. WILLIAM   *The Pentagon Propaganda Machine*
V-475   GAY, PETER   *The Enlightenment: The Rise of Modern Paganism*
V-668   GERASSI, JOHN   *Revolutionary Priest: The Complete Writings and Messages of Camillo Torres*
V-657   GETTLEMAN, MARVIN E. AND DAVID MERMELSTEIN (eds.)   *The Failure of American Liberalism*
V-451   GETTLEMAN, MARVIN E. AND SUSAN, AND LAWRENCE AND CAROL KAPLAN   *Conflict in Indochina: A Reader on the Widening War in Laos and Cambodia*
V-174   GOODMAN, PAUL AND PERCIVAL   *Communitas*
V-325   GOODMAN, PAUL   *Compulsory Mis-education and The Community of Scholars*
V-32   GOODMAN, PAUL   *Growing Up Absurd*
V-417   GOODMAN, PAUL   *People or Personnel* and *Like a Conquered Province*
V-606   GORO, HERB   *The Block*
V-633   GREEN, PHILIP AND SANFORD LEVINSON (eds.)   *Power and Community: Dissenting Essays in Political Science*
V-457   GREENE, FELIX   *The Enemy: Some Notes on the Nature of Contemporary Imperialism*
V-618   GREENSTONE, J. DAVID   *Labor in American Politics*
V-430   GUEVERA, CHE   *Guerrilla Warfare*
V-685   HAMSIK, DUSAN   *Writers Against Rulers*
V-427   HAYDEN, TOM   *Rebellion in Newark*
V-453   HEALTH PAC   *The American Health Empire*
V-635   HEILBRONER, ROBERT L.   *Between Capitalism and Socialism*
V-450   HERSH, SEYMOUR M.   *My Lai 4*
V-283   HENRY, JULES   *Culture Against Man*
V-644   HESS, KARL AND THOMAS REEVES   *The End of the Draft*
V-465   HINTON, WILLIAM   *Fanshen: A Documentary of Revolution in a Chinese Village*
V-576   HOFFMAN, ABBIE   *Woodstock Nation*
V-95   HOFSTADTER, RICHARD   *The Age of Reform: From Bryan to F.D.R.*
V-9   HOFSTADTER, RICHARD   *The American Political Tradition*
V-317   HOFSTADTER, RICHARD   *Anti-Intellectualism in American Life*
V-385   HOFSTADTER, RICHARD   *Paranoid Style in American Politics and other Essays*
V-686   HOFSTADTER, RICHARD AND MICHAEL WALLACE (eds.)   *American Violence, A Documentary History*
V-429   HOROWITZ, DE CASTRO, AND GERASSI (eds.)   *Latin American Radicalism*
V-666   HOWE, LOUISE KAPP (ed.)   *The White Majority: Between Poverty and Affluence*
V-630   HOROWITZ, DAVID   *Empire and Revolution*
V-201   HUGHES, H. STUART   *Consciousness and Society*
V-241   JACOBS, JANE   *Death & Life of Great American Cities*
V-584   JACOBS, JANE   *The Economy of Cities*
V-433   JACOBS, PAUL   *Prelude to Riot*

V-332   JACOBS, PAUL AND SAUL LANDAU (eds.)   *The New Radicals*
V-459   JACOBS, PAUL AND SAUL LANDAU, WITH EVE PELL   *To Serve the Devil: Natives & Slaves*, Vol. I
V-460   JACOBS, PAUL AND SAUL LANDAU, WITH EVE PELL   *To Serve the Devil: Colonials & Sojourners*, Volume II
V-456   JONES, ITA   *The Grubbag*
V-369   KAUFMANN, WALTER (trans.)   *The Birth of Tragedy* and *The Case of Wagner*
V-401   KAUFMANN, WALTER (trans.)   *On the Genealogy of Morals* and *Ecce Homo*
V-337   KAUFMANN, WALTER (trans.)   *Beyond Good and Evil*
V-582   KIRSHBAUM, LAURENCE AND ROGER RAPOPORT   *Is the Library Burning?*
V-631   KOLKO, GABRIEL   *Politics of War*
V-361   KOMAROVSKY, MIRRA   *Blue-Collar Marriage*
V-675   KOVEL, JOEL   *White Racism*
V-215   LACOUTURE, JEAN   *Ho Chi Minh*
V-367   LASCH, CHRISTOPHER   *The New Radicalism in America*
V-560   LASCH, CHRISTOPHER   *The Agony of the American Left*
V-280   LEWIS, OSCAR   *The Children of Sánchez*
V-421   LEWIS, OSCAR   *La Vida*
V-634   LEWIS, OSCAR   *A Death in the Sánchez Family*
V-637   LIBARLE, MARC AND TOM SELIGSON (eds.)   *The High School Revolutionaries*
V-474   LIFTON, ROBERT JAY   *Revolutionary Immortality*
V-384   LINDESMITH, ALFRED   *The Addict and The Law*
V-533   LOCKWOOD, LEE   *Castro's Cuba, Cuba's Fidel*
V-469   LOWE, JEANNE R.   *Cities in a Race with Time*
V-659   LURIE, ELLEN   *How to Change the Schools*
V-193   MALRAUX, ANDRE   *Temptation of the West*
V-480   MARCUSE, HERBERT   *Soviet Marxism*
V-502   MATTHEWS, DONALD R.   *U. S. Senators and Their World*
V-577   MAYER, ARNO J.   *Political Origins of the New Diplomacy, 1917-1918*
V-575   McCARTHY, RICHARD D.   *The Ultimate Folly*
V-619   McCONNELL, GRANT   *Private Power and American Democracy*
V-386   McPHERSON, JAMES   *The Negro's Civil War*
V-615   MITFORD, JESSICA   *The Trial of Dr. Spock*
V-539   MORGAN, ROBIN (ed.)   *Sisterhood Is Powerful*
V-274   MYRDAL, GUNNAR   *Challenge to Affluence*
V-573   MYRDAL, GUNNAR   *An Approach to the Asian Drama*
V-687   NEVILE, RICHARD   *Play Power*
V-377   NIETZSCHE, FRIEDRICH   *Beyond Good and Evil*
V-369   NIETZSCHE, FRIEDRICH   *The Birth of Tragedy* and *The Case of Wagner*
V-401   NIETZSCHE, FRIEDRICH   *On the Genealogy of Morals* and *Ecce Homo*
V-642   O'GORMAN, NED   *Prophetic Voices*
V-583   ORTIZ, FERNANDO   *Cuban Counterpoint: Tobacco and Sugar*
V-128   PLATO   *The Republic*
V-648   RADOSH, RONALD   *American Labor and U.S. Foreign Policy*
V-309   RASKIN, MARCUS AND BERNARD FALL (eds.)   *The Viet-nam Reader*
V-719   REED, JOHN   *Ten Days That Shook the World*
V-644   REEVES, THOMAS AND KARL HESS   *The End of the Draft*

92   REISCHAUER, EDWIN O.   *Beyond Vietnam: The United States and Asia*

V-548   RESTON, JAMES   *Sketches in the Sand*

V-622   ROAZEN, PAUL   *Freud: Political and Social Thought*

V-534   ROGERS, DAVID   *110 Livingston Street*

V-559   ROSE, TOM (ed.)   *Violence in America*

V-212   ROSSITER, CLINTON   *Conservatism in America*

V-472   ROSZAK, THEODORE (ed.)   *The Dissenting Academy*

V-431   SCHELL, JONATHAN   *The Village of Ben Suc*

V-375   SCHURMANN, F. AND O. SCHELL (eds.)   *The China Reader: Imperial China, I*

V-376   SCHURMANN, F. AND O. SCHELL (eds.)   *The China Reader: Republican China, II*

V-377   SCHURMANN, F. AND O. SCHELL (eds.)   *The China Reader: Communist China, III*

V-649   SEALE, BOBBY   *Seize the Time*

V-279   SILBERMAN, CHARLES E.   *Crisis in Black and White*

V-681   SNOW, EDGAR   *Red China Today*

V-222   SPENDER, STEPHEN   *The Year of the Young Rebels*

V-388   STAMPP, KENNETH   *The Era of Reconstruction 1865-1877*

V-253   STAMPP, KENNETH   *The Peculiar Institution*

V-613   STERNGLASS, ERNEST J.   *The Stillborn Future*

V-439   STONE, I. F.   *In a Time of Torment*

V-231   TANNENBAUM, FRANK   *Slave & Citizen: The Negro in the Americas*

V-312   TANNENBAUM, FRANK   *Ten Keys to Latin America*

V-686   WALLACE, MICHAEL AND RICHARD HOFSTADTER (eds.)   *American Violence: A Documentary History*

V-206   WALLERSTEIN, IMMANUEL   *Africa: The Politics of Independence*

V-543   WALLERSTEIN, IMMANUEL   *Africa: The Politics of Unity*

V-454   WALLERSTEIN, IMMANUEL AND PAUL STARR (eds.)   *The University Crisis Reader: The Liberal University Under Attack, Vol. I*

V-455   WALLERSTEIN, IMMANUAL AND PAUL STARR (eds.)   *The University Crisis Reader: Confrontation and Counterattack, Vol. II*

V-323   WARREN, ROBERT PENN   *Who Speaks for the Negro?*

V-405   WASSERMAN AND SWITZER   *The Random House Guide to Graduate Study in the Arts and Sciences*

V-249   WIEDNER, DONALD L.   *A History of Africa: South of the Sahara*

V-557   WEINSTEIN, JAMES   *Decline of Socialism in America 1912-1925*

V-585   WEINSTEIN, JAMES AND DAVID EAKINS (eds.)   *For a New America*

V-605   WILLIAMS, JOHN A. AND CHARLES HARRIS (eds.)   *Amistad 1*

V-660   WILLIAMS, JOHN A. AND CHARLES HARRIS (eds.)   *Amistad 2*

V-651   WILLIAMS, WILLIAM APPLEMAN   *The Roots of the Modern American Empire*

V-545   WOOLF, S. J. (ed.)   *The Nature of Fascism*

V-495   YGLESIAS, JOSE   *In the Fist of the Revolution*

V-483   ZINN, HOWARD   *Disobedience and Democracy*